Elements of Quality Online Education:

Engaging Communities

Edited by *John Bourne & Janet C. Moore*

THE SLOAN CONSORTIUM
A Consortium of Institutions and Organizations
Committed to Quality Online Education

Volume 6 in the Sloan-C Series

Cover design by Leighton Ige, Olin College.

Copyright ©2005 by Sloan-C™

All rights reserved. Published 2005

Printed in the United States of America

0 9 8 7 6 5 4 3 2 1

International Standard Book Number 0-9677741-9-5

Elements of Quality Online Education:

Engaging Communities, Volume 6 in the Sloan-C Series

This is the sixth volume in the annual Sloan-C series of case studies on quality education online. In 1999, 2000, 2001, 2002, 2003, and 2004, the Sloan Foundation selected expert contributors to report on work in progress and to collaborate on research of importance to asynchronous learning networks. Each volume publishes contributions in the form of documented, peer-reviewed scholarly studies of learning and cost effectiveness, access, and faculty and student satisfaction.

Other titles available in this series:

Elements of Quality Online Education: Into the Mainstream
Volume 5 ISBN 0-9677741-6-0

Elements of Quality Online Education: Practice and Direction
Volume 4 ISBN 0-9677741-5-2

Elements of Quality Online Education
Volume 3 ISBN 0-9677741-2-8

Online Education: Learning Effectiveness, Faculty Satisfaction, and Cost Effectiveness
Volume 2 ISBN 0-9677741-1-X

Online Education: Learning Effectiveness and Faculty Satisfaction
Volume 1 ISBN 0-9677741-0-1

This book was made possible by a grant from the Alfred P. Sloan Foundation.

SCOLE
Sloan Center for OnLine Education
at Olin and Babson Colleges

Sloan-C has its administrative home at the Sloan Center for OnLine Education (SCOLE) at Olin and Babson Colleges. SCOLE has been established as a center that spans the two campuses of Olin College and Babson College. SCOLE's purpose is to support the activities of the Sloan Consortium, a consortium of higher-education providers sharing the common bonds of understanding, supporting and delivering education via asynchronous learning networks (ALNs). With the mission of providing learning to anyone anywhere, SCOLE seeks to provide new levels of learning capability to people seeking higher and continuing education. For more information about Sloan-C, visit www.sloan-c.org.

For more information about Olin and Babson Colleges, visit www.olin.edu and www.babson.edu.

Elements of Quality Online Education: Engaging Communities

Volume 6 in the Sloan-C Series

INTRODUCTION

Frank Mayadas
President

John Bourne
Executive Director

Janet C. Moore
Chief Learning Officer

In September 2004, the Alfred P. Sloan Foundation convened its sixth annual invitational summer research workshop with researchers and practitioners from forty colleges, universities and organizations. The 2004 workshop was designed to address challenges facing higher education with respect to the potential of asynchronous learning networks (ALN) for achieving the goal of increasing online enrollments tenfold in the next ten years. To produce this volume, *Elements of Quality Online Education: Engaging Communities*, Volume 6 in the Sloan-C quality series, representatives from these groups identified issues and shared solutions:

The Alfred P. Sloan Foundation	The Sloan Consortium
American Distance Education Consortium	Southern Regional Education Board
Babson College	The State University of New York
Brigham Young University	Stevens Institute of Technology
The City University of New York	Thomson Learning
Drexel University	UC Berkeley Extension Online
Empire State College	University of Central Florida
Franklin W. Olin College of Engineering	University of Illinois
Hampton University	University of Illinois at Chicago
Hunter College	University of Illinois at Springfield
IBM	University of Maryland University College
Institute for Healthcare Improvement	University of Massachusetts
Kent State University	University of Massachusetts Lowell
Liberty Mutual	University of Nebraska Lincoln
Maricopa Community Colleges	University of New Brunswick
Massachusetts Institute of Technology	University of Pennsylvania
New Jersey Institute of Technology	The University of Texas System Telecampus
Open University of Israel	University of Wisconsin Extension
Pace University	Virginia Polytechnic Institute and State University
Pennsylvania State University	Washington State University
Rochester Institute of Technology	

In a knowledge society, people demand access to learning as never before. Online education has become the leading modality for distance education. Moreover, academic leadership expects online enrollment growth up to 25% per year; the majority regards online education as critical to long-term strategy; and most believe online education is already equal to or superior to face-to-face education [1]. Thus, the central challenge to the nation is how to engage communities to make education "an ordinary part of everyday life" [2]. To address this central challenge, members of the workshop responded to these related challenges:

- How can online pedagogy improve face-to-face pedagogy?

- How can asynchronous learning networks engage the core of higher education?

- How can the two worlds of academia and industry cooperate to contribute to a tenfold increase in online learning in the next ten years?

- What do we need to learn about the business of education?

A. How can Online Pedagogy Improve on Face-to-face Pedagogy?

Gary Miller of The Pennsylvania State University has pointed out the "The pedagogy inherent in ALN—inquiry-oriented, resource-based learning—is a natural pedagogy for the world in which we live" [3]. Because of ALN's freedom from time and place constraints, its opportunities for reflective thinking and its reach and connectivity, online education engages faculty and students in new interactions with content, with action, with each other, and with the world outside the classroom.

In "A Constructivist Model for Thinking About Learning Online," Karen Swan of Kent State University's Research Center for Educational Technology provides a primer of constructivist learning theory and its "implications for designing online learning environments that are learner centered, knowledge centered, assessment centered, and community centered." Giving an example of this kind of learning environment, Jim Theroux and Clare Kilbane of the University of Massachusetts explain how four universities cooperatively engaged students in "The Real-time Case Method," using ALN and the internet for studying and advising an actual company. In "A Case Study in Blended Learning: Leveraging Technology in Entrepreneurship Education," Barry Bisson of the University of New Brunswick and colleagues describe the engagement of faculty and students at three universities in a resource rich course in entrepreneurship that used synchronous and asynchronous technologies in addition to face-to-face meetings at the campuses. In "Engagement and Learning Communities," Albert Ingram of Kent State University defines engagement as 'the confluence of three important concepts: attention, activation of effective cognitive processes, and, usually, a social context of learning." This sense of engagement is fundamental for understanding and building community.

B. How can Asynchronous Learning Networks Engage the Core of Higher Education?

ALN is changing education as institutions and faculty engage with new technologies and the pedagogies they make possible. New combinations of delivery modes affect faculty and students, so that they can now engage in both face-to-face and online education as a matter of course.

Reporting on a Sloan workshop at the University in Chicago in April, 2004, Mary Niemiec, Interim Associate Provost for External Education at the University of Illinois at Chicago (UIC), and colleagues identified perspectives from institutions, faculty and students on the value of blending ALN and face-to-face education. The 2004 workshop on blending continues its work of developing a framework for best practices in blended education via an online Sloan-C special interest group and plans for future workshops and publications.

In fact, reports George Otte of the City College of New York in "Using Blended Learning to Drive Faculty Development," the virtues of blended learning—heightened interaction, convenience, expanded enrollments, efficiencies of classroom space—are engaging mainstream faculty in building community and knowledge about online instruction, a critical step to full integration.

Chuck Dziuban and colleagues at the University of Central Florida report in "Higher Education, Blended Learning and the Generations: Knowledge is Power—No More" on another kind of blending. Faculty and students from at least four generations—each with distinct learning preferences—engage with each other in the same online and face-to-face classrooms. Learning among various generations means that the time-honored metaphors we use for education are changing, so that we may learn to think of education as teamwork.

In "Adding Clicks to Bricks: Increasing Access to Mainstream Higher Education," Raymond E. Schroeder of the University of Illinois Springfield (UIS) and Burks Oakley II of the University of Illinois demonstrate that providing a wide range of quality online degree programs to individuals who otherwise would not be participating in higher education is truly democratizing higher education.

C. How can the Two Worlds of Academia and Industry Cooperate to Contribute to a Tenfold Increase in Online Learning in the Next Ten Years?

Introducing this challenge to the workshop Frank Mayadas, President of the Sloan Consortium and program officer for the learning anytime anywhere program of the Alfred P. Sloan Foundation and Robert Ubell of the Stevens Institute of Technology explained that:

> Both academic online learning and corporate e-learning rely on the internet and web technologies, and their approaches appear similar at a superficial level. In fact however, the academic and corporate implementations for online learning are quite different. This is not surprising given the motivations, resources and history of the two sectors. In other words, each sector appears to have settled on practices that most suit their particular applications. Nevertheless, we think it is desirable that the "two worlds" be brought closer together, so that each can progress to its goals even more rapidly for the benefit of academe, the corporate community, and society as a whole.

Providing an overview of a global company's e-learning structures, Richard Benner reports in "Implementing Curricula Using a Variety of Learning Modalities at Liberty Mutual Group" that the Sloan-C pillars of quality are effective as metrics for Liberty's learning strategy that "emphasizes training that is relevant to employees, helpful to business, and develops employee abilities via emerging instructional technologies."

Mutual benefits to corporations and to schools evolve come from their engagement with each other. In "Instructional Technology Graduate Programs in Support of Corporate E-learning," Barbara Lockee and Michelle Reece of Virginia Polytechnic Institute and State University assert that "Academia must find ways to weave interactions with business partners into the fabric of their missions and activities," finding that faculty and students appreciate engaging with corporate e-learning to stay current and to apply academic learning to real world opportunities.

D. What do We Need to Learn About the Business of Education?

Understanding the business of education means engaging constituents within and across institutions, according to Stephen Schiffman of the Franklin W. Olin College of Engineering. In "Business Issues in Online Education," Schiffman synthesizes wide-ranging information about business issues in online education drawn from interviews with more than fifty people working in the field of online education at eleven not-for-profit higher education institutions during the winter and spring of 2004. He finds that there is a thirst for knowledge about business models and proposes activities that will discover and disseminate effective business strategies.

In "The Business of Online Education—Are We Cost Competitive?" Rob Robinson of the University of Texas Telecampus points out that "Properly designed and constructed, online courses, when compared to traditional face-to-face courses, can better engage learners, increase retention, improve student outcomes, and greatly increase access to higher education." They can also cost less to develop and to deliver, although consensus about cost effectiveness has not yet emerged.

Doug Lynch, formerly of New York University and now of the University of Pennsylvania, affirms in "Success Versus Value: What Do We Mean by the Business of Education?" that "There is a need, a market, and a moral imperative to be entrepreneurial when it comes to developing and delivering online education." Lynch gives entrepreneurial examples from NYU's cooperative engagement with employers in which competitors find makes sense to cooperate.

Noting that "many in the academy still cling to the notion that a university is not a business," in "Reinventing the University: The Business of Online Education," Tana Bishop of the University of Maryland University College, calls for recognition that the 21st century demands that schools demonstrate quality and efficiency. Bishops says that "Colleges and universities have the unique opportunity to reinvent themselves by leveraging technologies to restructure old processes and breathe new life into the academy."

Indeed, new life comes from engaging communities in improving education for greater access to learning. You are welcome to use this volume as a catalyst in your own communities. Sloan-C invite you to use Sloan-C special interest groups, listserv, online workshops, conferences, effective practices, the *Sloan-C View* newsletter and the *Journal of Asynchronous Learning Networks* as channels for expanding the culture of learning.

1. **Allen, I. E. and J. Seaman.** *Entering the Mainstream: The Quality and Extent of Online Education in the United States, 2003 and 2004.* Needham, MA: Sloan-C, 2004. Online: http://www.sloan-c.org/resources/survey.asp.
2. **Gomory, R.** Sheffield Lecture- Yale University, January 11, 2000, Internet Learning: Is it Real and What Does it Mean for Universities? *Journal of Asynchronous Learning Networks* 5(1): June 2001. Online: http://www.sloan-c.org/publications/jaln/v5n1/v5n1_gomory.asp.
3. **Miller, Gary.** Message to the Sloan-C listserv, August 1, 2004.

How can Online Pedagogy Improve on Face-to-face Pedagogy?

A CONSTRUCTIVIST MODEL FOR THINKING ABOUT LEARNING ONLINE

Karen Swan
Research Center for Educational Technology
Kent State University

- Constructivist learning theory has implications for designing online learning environments that are learner centered, knowledge centered, assessment centered, and community centered.

- Cognitive constructivism is important because it clearly locates learning in the mind of the individual and because it defines it as an active process of mental construction linked to interactions with the environment.

- The Research Center for Educational Technology (RCET) model distinguishes three interacting domains of knowledge construction—conceptualization, representation, and use.

- These domains can guide research to inform practice and advance online learning.

- New and evolving social conventions (of discourse, of interaction, and of netiquette) in online courses in relation to the larger culture of the Internet are an important topic for future research.

I. INTRODUCTION

This paper explores constructivist theory and how it might inform research and practice in online learning. It begins with an overview of constructivist theory and some of its more important instantiations—cognitive constructivism, constructionism, social constructivism, situated learning, and distributed cognition. It then explores some implications constructivism might have for instruction in general and online learning in particular in the development of the four kinds of learning environments advocated by Bransford, Brown, and Cocking in *How People Learn* [1]. Finally, it presents a constructivist model of the effects that online environments may have on learning in terms of the unique external representations of knowledge they afford, their particular effects on student conceptualizations of knowledge, and the social uses made of knowledge and through which knowledge is constructed online.

II. CONSTRUCTIVIST THEORY

Constructivist is the name given to theories of learning grounded in an epistemological alternative to objectivist theories of knowledge. Central to constructivism is the notion that meaning is imposed on the world rather than extant in it. Both objectivism and constructivism agree that there is a real world we experience. However, while objectivists believe that meaning exists in that world to be discovered by us, constructivists believe that we impose meaning on it [2]. They hold that meaning is constructed in our minds as we interact with the physical, social, and mental worlds we inhabit, and that we make sense of our experiences by building and adjusting the internal knowledge structures that collect and organize our perceptions of and reflections on reality.

Hence *constructivism* refers to a set of psychological theories that share common assumptions about knowing and learning. Constructivist theories have implications for both pedagogy and instruction, although they are not theories of either. According to constructivists, all learning involves mental construction, no matter how one is taught. All learning, they argue, occurs in our minds as we create and adjust internal mental structures to accommodate our ever-growing and ever-changing stores of knowledge. Thus, according to constructivists, all learning is an active process and all knowledge is unique to the individual, whether acquired from lecture and text or discovered through experience. All learning is intimately tied to experience and the contexts of experience, no matter how or where that learning takes place [1].

While constructivist theories share common assumptions about the nature of learning and the construction of knowledge, they diverge in focus; particular theories and theorists explore and highlight particular aspects of constructivism. The paragraphs that follow briefly describe some of those aspects. I have chosen these for their importance to the field, for their articulation of significant threads in the constructivist fabric, and for their potential relevance to online learning.

A. Cognitive Constructivism

Jean Piaget, a key figure in educational psychology, originated what is sometimes called *cognitive constructivism* (although all constructivist theories are essentially cognitive) and what he called *genetic epistemology* [3,4]. Piaget focused his attention on what happens in our minds in the course of learning in an era dominated by behaviorism, which held that we can know nothing about what happens in our minds. Piaget is called a cognitive constructivist both because his main concern was the internal development of mental structures and because he thus opened the door for the development of cognitive psychology. Indeed, many cognitive psychologists accept a weak form of cognitive constructivism in that they focus on the internal construction of mental structures while nonetheless maintaining a belief in some sort of meaning existing in the world [5].

A biologist by training, Piaget in his early career observed how organisms, specifically mollusks, reacted to their environment. He applied that approach to studying how children learn, and not surprisingly, he believed that children learn by interacting with the environments in which they find themselves. Learning occurs, he maintained, through the cognitive processing of environmental interactions and the corresponding construction of mental structures to make sense of them. He called these mental structures *schema* and posited two kinds of cognitive processing involved in schema construction. In *assimilation*, new knowledge is incorporated into existing schemas in much the same way that a new wing is added to a building. In *accommodation*, new knowledge conflicts with existing schemas that accordingly must be altered to incorporate it. The analogy here might be the remodel of a building.

Epistemology is the branch of philosophy concerned with the nature of knowledge and knowing. Piaget called himself a genetic epistemologist because he believed that the ways we structure knowledge internally are determined by our genetic make-up, and that these ways change as we mature. Through his observations of children, Piaget identified four distinct developmental stages, each distinguished by specific kinds of mental processing. The *sensorimotor stage*, which is prelinguistic, is characterized by kinesthetic understandings and organizations of experience, while the *preoperational stage* is characterized by egocentrism and the organization of knowledge relative to oneself. In the *concrete operational stage*, knowledge is organized in logical categories but still linked to concrete experience. It is only in the *formal operational stage*, according to Piaget, that knowledge is abstracted from experience and formal reasoning can occur. Although Piaget believed that individuals went through these cognitive stages in order as a natural result of maturation, evidence indicates that in his later years he came to believe that some individuals never reached any formal operational levels, and that no individuals thought formally in all domains. Indeed, most modern Piagetians hold this view.

Why is cognitive constructivism important to us? It is important because it clearly locates learning in the mind of the individual and because it defines it as an active process of mental construction linked to interactions with the environment. Moreover, stage theory reminds us that people in different stages of development construct knowledge in different ways—that, for example, novices in a field construct meaning differently than experts. Cognitive constructivism also posits the interrelated process of assimilation and accommodation (or similar mechanisms; see Rumelhart and Norman [6]) to accomplish mental construction and so links all new learning to learners' pre-existing knowledge, bringing the issue of misconceptions and their nature more clearly in focus. Cognitive constructivism gives us the notion of knowledge organized internally as mental schemas that are in some broad sense peculiarly human. Mental schema have been variously characterized and studied, for example, as frames [7] representing particular scenes, scripts [8] representing complex actions, mental models [9] representing causality, and semantic networks [10] representing relationships among ideas. All of these characterizations tell us something about the ways in which learners naturally organize and construct knowledge, hence suggesting methods of instruction that reflect and support learning.

B. Constructionism

Seymour Papert [11,12] is a mathematician who studied for five years with Piaget before becoming involved with the emerging discipline of computer science at MIT. Papert coined the term *constructionism* to distinguish his particular constructivist focus [12], which "attaches special importance to the role of constructions in the world as a support for those in the head" (p. 142), from cognitive constructivism (although the two are, in fact, clearly related). What makes Papert and other constructionists (see, for example, Resnick [13] and diSessa [14]) of particular interest to us is that they are specifically concerned with the kinds of constructions that are supported by computing technologies. Andy diSessa [14], for example, writes:

> *"Computers can be the technical foundation of a new and dramatically enhanced literacy . . . which will have penetration and depth of influence comparable to what we have already experienced in coming to achieve a mass, text-based literacy."* (p. 4)

Constructionists maintain that computers have the unique capacity to represent abstract ideas in concrete and malleable forms. Papert and his colleagues developed the Logo programming language and variations on it to study these ideas in practice. Their work has demonstrated ways in which computer-based constructions can indeed make abstract concepts more accessible and more readily internalized as mental schema. Constructionists believe that computer-based constructions are personally created, hence more readily linked to existing knowledge (assimilation). They further maintain that computer-based constructions can be used to interrogate existing schema, as in the case of certain simulations, and so lead to changes in knowledge structures and the remediation of misconceptions (accommodation). Constructionism, in short, is important to us because it suggests ways in which computer-based construction activities can be used to support corresponding mental constructions.

C. Social Constructivism

Social constructivism, perhaps the most common version of constructivism currently in favor, is the theoretical framework normally evoked by the term *constructivism*. Learning theories are called *social constructivist* when their main concern is with knowledge construction through social interactions. Social constructivist theories derive primarily from the work of Lev Vygotsky [15, 16], a Russian contemporary of Piaget whose work was suppressed by the Stalinists and rediscovered in the 1960s. Vygotsky maintained that all learning results from social interaction even when it takes place in individual minds and that meaning is socially constructed through communication and interactions with others. He believed that cognitive skills and patterns of thinking are not primarily determined by innate factors (as in genetic epistemology) but rather are the products of the activities practiced in the social institutions of the culture in which the individual lives. Consequently, the history of the society in which one is reared and one's personal history are crucial determinants of the ways in which one will think. Even the solitary scholar alone in a room engages the artifacts and tools of a particular culture, Vygotsky argued, and through those artifacts, their authors and the larger society. Moreover, a history of social and cultural interactions have shaped the scholar's knowledge, attitudes, skills, and behaviors.

Vygotsky viewed the construction of meaning as a two-part, reciprocal process. Meanings are first enacted socially and then internalized individually; internal conceptualizations in turn guide social interactions. Piaget [13] focused on the second part of this process, schema construction, which he viewed, in an important sense, as genetically determined. Vygotsky focused on the first part of the process, the social construction of meaning, which he saw as culturally determined. Interestingly, whereas Piaget viewed the development of cognitive schema as the internalization of environmental interactions, Vygotsky viewed objects in the environment as having a psychological as well as a physical aspect, and so as being in a sense psychologically determined. Objects in the environment, including other people, he maintained, are in important ways what we perceive them to be, and their perceived properties are to a great extent culturally determined.

Vygotsky believed that language and thought were intimately related and was particularly concerned with the role of language in thinking and learning. Although at first a child seems to use language only for superficial social interaction, at some point this language is internalized to structure the child's thinking. Language was to Vygotsky not merely a way of expressing the knowledge one has acquired; the fundamental correspondence between thought and speech means that language becomes essential in forming thought. Language is the crucial tool in the cognitive development process in that advanced modes of thought are transmitted by means of words.

Another important concept in Vygotsky's learning theory is his notion of the *zone of proximal development*, the distance between the actual development level as determined by independent problem solving and the level of potential development as determined through problem solving under adult guidance or in collaboration with more capable peers [16]. Vygotsky claimed that all learning occurs in this zone, which bridges the gap between what is known and what can be known, through either adult/instructor guidance or peer collaboration.

Two other important learning theorists who are sometimes considered social constructivists are Jerome Bruner and John Dewey. A major theme in the theoretical framework of Bruner [17, 18] is that learning is an active process in which learners construct new ideas or concepts based upon their current knowledge. He believed that the individual's cognitive structures allowed learning by giving meaning and organization to such active experiences. Bruner is deemed a social constructivist because of the central role he attributed to language and other people in this process. Similarly, Dewey [19], although he predates the social constructivist movement, is sometimes considered a social constructivist because he understood thought as the product of interaction with the environment, because of the importance he placed on active learning, and because of the central role language and social interaction plays in his notions of teaching and learning.

Why is social constructivism important to us? Social constructivism reminds us that learning is essentially a social activity, that meaning is constructed through communication, collaborative activity, and interactions with others. It highlights the role of social interactions in the making of meaning, especially the support of more knowledgeable others in knowledge construction. Social constructivism encourages us to consider the critical function of language as the vehicle of thought and hence of knowing and learning, and to understand the ways in which knowledge and knowing are culturally and historically determined and realized.

D. Situated Learning/Distributed Cognition

Vygotsky's disciple Alexei Leont'ev [20] took his mentor's ideas one step further. He contended that internal and external constructions of knowledge could not be understood apart from culture and the tools and artifacts that shaped them. He accordingly developed methodologies for examining what he viewed as the seamless and mutually transforming processes of knowledge construction in terms of the activities in which they were embedded. Activities, he maintained, are driven by motives, performed through actions, oriented to goals, and implemented through operations. Learning thus can only be analyzed in terms of the hierarchical activity structures in which it evolves. Many social constructivist theories similarly view thinking and learning as part of and inseparable from whole activity systems composed of culture, community, tools, and symbols.

Situated learning, for example, explores learning as situated in communities of practice. Situative theorists argue that learning as it normally occurs is a function of the activity, context, and culture in which it takes place and hence is inseparable from participation in the communities that support it [21, 22, 23]. An important concept in such theories is the notion of *legitimate peripheral participation*, which argues that mastery of knowledge and skills requires newcomers to gradually move towards full and complex engagement with communities of practice [22, 23]. In school contexts, this occurs as *cognitive apprenticeship* [21], in which students work on authentic problems with the help of more expert adults and peers, and as *knowledge building communities* [24], in which students work collaboratively to co-construct knowledge corpora. The situative perspective encourages us to conceptualize learning as an apprenticeship process in which the individual gradually moves from peripheral to full participation in scholarly activities.

A particularly important modern instantiation of Leont'ev's work can be found in theories of *distributed cognition*. Theories of distributed cognition maintain that thinking, and hence learning, does not take place solely inside the mind of individuals but rather that it is socially distributed among individuals and the tools and artifacts of a culture [25, 26, 27]. Radical versions of distributed learning theories maintain that, although individual cognitions cannot be dismissed, thinking and learning in general should in the main be conceived and studied as distributed, with joint, socially mediated learning activities in cultural contexts as the proper units of analysis [25, 26]. Weaker versions of distributed learning distinguish between individual and distributed thinking and learning but view these as linked through interdependent and dynamic interactions [28, 29]. What the concept of distributed cognition, however conceived, provides us is the idea that thinking and learning are supported by, mediated through, and in some sense reside in, artifacts and tools. This is a particularly compelling and useful notion when considering learning online, where all learning is necessarily mediated through virtual artifacts and tools.

III. IMPLICATIONS FOR INSTRUCTION

As previously noted, constructivism is an epistemological theory and not a theory of instruction. In the field of education, however, our epistemological beliefs dictate, or should at least strongly inform, our pedagogical views. Indeed, the previous section outlined the importance of various versions of constructivism in terms of the ways in which they encourage us to think about learning. Particular conceptualizations of learning in turn suggest corresponding approaches to teaching.

Perhaps the most important implication constructivism holds for instruction is somewhat paradoxical. Constructivism locates meaning and meaning making squarely in the mind of individuals, not in instruction. This distinction is an important one. It suggests, for example, that although it may be possible to standardize instruction, it is not possible to standardize learning, a goal to which some online programs aspire. It also suggests that our concern should be focused more on the design of learning environments and less on instructional design per se [1]. Although such a contrast appears merely semantic, it may be especially important in online learning because it urges us to forgo our traditional focus on the delivery of instruction and the design of instructional materials and instead to approach course development in terms of creating virtual spaces that foster and support active learning, Indeed, the authors of *How People Learn* contend that constructivism suggests we should be concerned with the design of particular kinds of learning environments, namely, learning environments that are learner centered, knowledge centered, assessment centered, and community centered. Each of these characteristics and their application to online learning will be explored in the following paragraphs.

A. Learner-Centered Learning Environments

Environments that are learner-centered acknowledge the constructivist notions that individuals bring unique knowledge, skills, attitudes, and beliefs to the learning experience and that there are many ways to structure experience and many different perspectives or meanings that can be gleaned from any event or concept [1]. Learner-centered teaching thus recognizes the importance of building on the conceptual and cultural knowledge that students bring with them to the learning experience, of linking learning to students' experiences, and of accepting and exploring multiple perspectives and divergent understandings. At the same time, learner-centered teaching must be concerned with diagnosing and remediating students' misconceptions. Constructivism suggests that such remediation requires accommodation—that is, that teachers must help students to make their thinking visible, to test it against experience, and to reconstruct more viable understandings.

Online learning poses many challenges to the development of learner-centered environments, the majority of which stem from the facts that all interactions are necessarily mediated through the online environment and that most online courses must be created before students join them. At the same time, the very characteristics of the online medium that create such challenges offer unique affordances to learner centeredness. For example, computer-based learning in general has long been supportive of individualized instruction. Indeed, when Carol Twigg [30] gathered together a group of innovative virtual educators to discuss paradigm changes in online learning, their overall conclusion was that individualization, which they termed *personalization*, was the key to innovation in distance education. Twigg thus argues that quality online learning should include initial assessments of students' knowledge and skills, individual study plans involving an array of interactive learning materials, and built-in, continuous assessment with instantaneous feedback. Some researchers are even experimenting with adaptive hypermedia that adjusts to individual learning styles [31], but much more research and development needs to be done in the area of individualization.

While such approaches clearly address the conceptual knowledge students bring to their online experiences as well as the diagnosis and remediation of student misconceptions, many would argue that they do little to build on students' unique knowledge and experiences, that they are culturally insensitive, and that they work against the consideration of multiple perspectives. Well-developed asynchronous online discussion, however, can do all of these things. Researchers have found online discussion to be more equitable and democratic [32, 33], more reflective [34, 35, 36], and in surprising ways more personal [37, 38] than traditional classroom discussions. Although many educators thus believe that asynchronous discussion is uniquely suited to support learner-centered knowledge construction, research has yet to support such conclusions [39]. More research is clearly needed.

Similarly, we know very little about the relationship between learner characteristics and learning online. Some evidence suggests that independent learners [40], visual learners [41], and learners who are more motivated and have greater self-regulatory skills [42, 43] fare better in online courses. Some evidence argues for gender [44] and cultural differences [45] in online learning, but we need to learn much, much more in these areas. Finally, we have fairly good evidence that different online learners in fact want quite different things from online courses [46]. If we wish to develop truly learner-centered online learning environments, we clearly have a lot more to learn.

B. Knowledge-Centered Learning Environments

From a constructivist point of view, knowledge-centered learning environments focus on the kinds and structures of information and activities that help students construct robust understandings of particular topics and disciplines [1]. The constructivist approach is concerned with support for the construction of internal knowledge structures through active learning. Constructivism likens knowledge-centered learning to learning a landscape by living in it and exploring it from a variety of perspectives [47, 48] and so argues for the design of learning environments that encourage analogous cognitive activity. Knowledge-centered learning similarly emphasizes sense making and learning with understanding through in-depth explorations of topics. It puts less emphasis on the memorization of unconnected facts and concentrates instead on learning in context, on the development of complex knowledge structures, on authentic problem solving, and on the "doing" of science, mathematics, history, and so forth. The constructivist argument is not that students do not need to learn facts and procedures but rather that these are better learned when they are integrated within the rich corpora of their disciplines.

As with learner-centeredness, the online medium provides unique affordances and constraints to the development of knowledge-centered learning environments. On the one hand, because the Internet is clearly an information environment, online education seems ideally suited for knowledge-centered learning. The manner in which courses are created and placed online not only allows for the design and refinement of well-structured, knowledge-centered materials and activities but also supports a greater variety of ways in which information can be presented [49] than traditional lecture and text environments. Moreover, the Internet itself offers unprecedented access to information and authentic contexts [49] that can be easily incorporated into course materials and activities. At the same time, the nature of the online medium makes it possible for students to visit and revisit diverse course materials and activities in ways and at times of their own choosing [48]. For example, Stanford University has created a set of digital learning objects (DLOs) named *courselets* that are self-contained, integrated tutorials covering a small set of concepts to be used across science and engineering courses [50]. Students can access courselets when they need to acquire or review particular concepts or skills, when they are interested in the cross-curricular applications of those concepts or skills, or when they want to extend their learning for whatever reason.

On the other hand, as Shank [51] reminds us, information is not knowledge. The abundant possibilities for presentation and creation of knowledge, the near-infinite access to information, the freedom learners have to access and navigate course materials—in short, the enormous potential of online learning—challenge knowledge-centered course design because knowledge is constructed in individual minds and does not exist outside them. It is hard to know what information, what kinds of presentations, what sorts of learning activities; in what combinations best support knowledge construction in which learners. It is probably impossible. We can, however, explore the cognitive effects of much smaller intellectual landscapes. Richard Mayer [52], for example, has spent nearly two decades investigating optimum combinations and sequencing of multimedia to support secondary school students' learning of scientific explanations. Similar studies might be made, for example, of characteristic types of DLOs, which are increasingly available to be linked to online courses and programs [53].

In a similar vein, it would be useful to investigate optimal online environments for supporting the construction of particular concepts and skills in specific subject areas. Some research, for example, that suggests online learning in general is more supportive of conceptual learning and less supportive of procedural learning than learning in traditional classrooms [54]. Such findings deserve further investigation in diverse subject domains. Similarly, it might be useful to explore how knowledge is constructed through various online activities (for example, discussion, collaboration, written assignments, simulations) or combinations of activities, again within specific subject areas and among particular populations of learners.

C. Assessment-Centered Learning Environments

Most learning theories recognize the importance of assessment and feedback. Indeed, according to constructivists, learning results from our reflections on feedback from environmental interactions. What is perhaps different about constructivist approaches to assessment is their emphasis on the importance of the individual's processing of environmental feedback and thus on the design of assessment-centered environments [1] that provide ongoing meaningful feedback to learners. Constructivism suggests that self-assessment is integral to learning and implies that opportunities for self-assessment should occur continuously and be embedded within learning activities. Constructivist theory also implies that it is especially important to encourage learners to reconstruct their knowledge—to evolve and change their understandings—in response to feedback. Thus, constructivist approaches contend that good assessment practices are those that value revision and the processes of knowledge construction. Because constructivism views knowledge as complex mental structures, constructivist approaches further contend that good assessment practices emphasize learning with understanding and the application of knowledge, not the memorization of isolated facts and procedures.

In many ways, the online environment offers considerable support for the development of assessment-centered learning. Online course platforms provide complete records of student work, including user logs and discussion transcripts as well as more traditional course assignments, quizzes, and tests, and thus can support multiple and varied forms of assessment. In addition, most course platforms provide tools for embedding assessments within student work and for managing course assignments and grading and making these transparent to students. Moreover, as previously noted, computer-based assessments can be embedded in courses to give automated and instantaneous feedback [30]. For example, the CAPA system, which generates and scores random tests, is being used at Michigan State University to provide science students multiple opportunities to take weekly quizzes, helping them to identify and correct their own misconceptions [55].

On the other hand, assessment and feedback can be particularly taxing for online instructors. The lack of face-to-face meetings makes frequent, periodic feedback critical. Online instructors typically need to develop and assess many more assignments over the course of a semester than face-to-face instructors, who have the opportunity to informally assess and remediate student understandings in the classroom. In addition, online learners expect a much faster turnaround on their assignments than traditional students. Moreover, while automated assessments are easily managed online, some research suggests that students learn better from personal feedback tailored specifically to their needs [56] than from automated feedback, especially when learning involves higher order understanding and the application of knowledge [57]. One solution to this conundrum may be found in Bill Pelz's [58] first principle of effective online pedagogy: "Let the students do (most of) the work." (p 33). Pelz suggests having students lead discussions based on text chapters, locate and discuss Web resources, check and grade their own homework, and provide initial feedback to each other on assignments. The instructor, he argues, can then concentrate on thoughtfully providing structure and direction, supportive and corrective feedback, and final evaluations.

Indeed, the whole area of assessment in online courses and its relationship to learning is perhaps the least researched in the field. For example, we have some indications that the ways in which online discussion is assessed impacts the nature of that discussion [59], but we know little of the relationship between online discussion and learning, and almost nothing of the impact of the assessments on other online activities. Clearly, a great deal more research on assessment in online courses is needed.

D. Community-Centered Learning Environments

Finally, constructivist theory views learning as, to a greater or lesser degree, a social activity. It situates learning in communities and cultures. Thus constructivist approaches emphasize the importance of designing learning environments that are also community centered [1]. Community-centered design is here understood on two levels—the degree to which a learning environment supports the social construction of knowledge and the development of a learning community, and the degree to which it connects to students' larger community and culture. On the first level, constructivism implies that learning is strengthened by environments in which the participation of all students is supported and valued; in which social norms encourage collaboration, the negotiation of meaning, and the search for understanding; and in which multiple perspectives are respected and incorporated into collective meaning making. On the second level, constructivism suggests that learning is enhanced when it is related to students' interests and experiences, when it is situated in authentic real-world problem solving, and when it is linked to and resonates with the larger culture.

It might seem that online learning is particularly ill suited to the development of community-centered learning environments on the first level mentioned above. Indeed, some communication theorists have argued that the lack of the vocal and visual cues available in face-to-face learning diminishes the quality of social interactions online to such an extent as to render the social construction of knowledge all but impossible [60, 61, 62]. Researchers experienced with online teaching and learning, however, contest this view. What is important, they contend, is not media capabilities but rather personal perceptions [35, 36, 63, 64, 65]. Their research demonstrates that participants in online courses often feel less psychological distance between themselves and their classmates in part because they evolve text-based mechanisms to replace vocal and verbal affective indicators. In addition, researchers have documented relationships between learners' perceptions of social presence and their satisfaction in, and perceived learning from, online courses [39, 66] that suggest the development of community-centered environments. Researchers have identified particular teacher behaviors [67, 68] and activity structures [59, 69] that foster perceived social presence and the development of community. Thus, it seems clear that not only can we design for community-centered learning but we have some preliminary ideas of how to go about it. Further research is, of course, indicated.

The second level of development of community-centered learning environments—making connections to students' larger community and culture—is less well documented, perhaps because it seems much more straightforward. The interconnectedness of Internet sites and their frequent updating makes it quite easy, to a greater or lesser degree, to situate learning in authentic, real-world problems and link it to local communities and cultures. Indeed, links to the Internet make it possible to explore a variety of world cultures to an extent that would not otherwise be possible. And as previously noted, one can also design online discussion and learning activities that engage students' interests and experiences. Anecdotal accounts suggest such strategies are effective in supporting learning, but rigorous research in these areas is clearly indicated.

IV. THE RCET MODEL

Constructivism is a theory of learning, not of instruction. However, as we saw in the previous section, constructivist theory can inform pedagogy and instruction. Indeed, constructivism may be especially well-suited for informing teaching and learning online, but a good deal more research along these lines is obviously needed. It is especially noteworthy that, although we have considerable findings supporting and explaining constructivist approaches in face-to-face learning environments, the applicability of these approaches in online environments is not at all clear. Thus, more directed research focusing on explicit features of online learning environments (see Mayer [52]) and conceptualized within specific aspects of a constructivist frame might yield important results.

At the Research Center for Educational Technology (RCET), researchers have been developing a constructivist model to better understand teaching and learning in face-to-face ubiquitous computing environments [70]. The model might also be useful for organizing thinking about learning in virtual ubiquitous computing environments, and thus help guide both the design of constructivist research and the development of related practices in online learning. Specifically, the model distinguishes three interacting domains of knowledge construction within which the unique affordances and constraints of online environments can be isolated and explored.

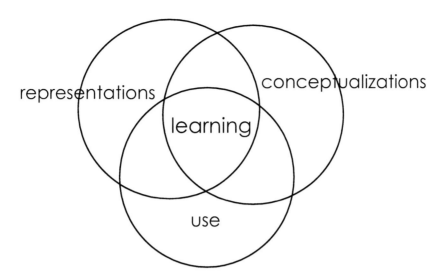

Figure 1: RCET Model of Technology-Supported Learning

Models help us visualize a phenomenon, isolate its significant components, and explore specific interactions among them—in short, they help us make sense of the world. The RCET model is designed to direct study of the effects of ubiquitous computing contexts and particular technologies on learning and thus to inform the practice of technology-mediated teaching and learning. It envisions the effects of educational technologies on learning as determined through their effects on the external representations of knowledge available to and/or created by learners, their effects on learners' internal conceptualizations and organization of knowledge, and their effects on the social interactions through and around which knowledge is negotiated and constructed (Figure 1). Although the model clearly places learning at the intersection of representation, conceptualization, and use, it allows us to investigate separately the mediating effects of technology in each of these domains and to describe how such effects in turn impact learning. In the following paragraphs, each of the components of the model is briefly described and ways in which each might support and focus thinking about learning online are considered.

A. Representation of Knowledge

The description begins with representation or what theories of distributed cognition refer to as the artifacts and tools through which knowledge is constructed. The term *representation* broadly refers to the many ways human beings externally construct and present what they know [70]. The model thus asks us to consider the specific kinds of external representations of knowledge used in online courses, especially those unique to online environments, and to explore their effects on online learning.

Clearly, external knowledge representations enable and shape human learning. In most formal learning (and a large part of informal learning as well), external representations of knowledge precede and shape the construction of internal conceptualizations [20]. In turn, we use external representations of knowledge to communicate our internal conceptualizations and to share them with others. Representations, then, are in one sense a bridge between conceptualization and use, between internal, individual knowledge construction and the external, social construction of knowledge. Because they structure knowledge in particular ways and so afford certain kinds of meaning making while constraining others, representations also make up thinking and learning. Spoken and written language, numbers and mathematical symbol systems, musical notation and music itself, and various types of graphical and visual representations are all tools human beings have invented to construct, represent, manipulate, interrogate, preserve, and communicate different kinds of knowledge in different ways. Indeed, recent psychological research suggests that we employ multiple mental systems to construct differing kinds of meanings [71, 72].

Online learning environments support new kinds of knowledge representations [73, 74] and have the potential to provide access to a much greater variety and a much, much greater quantity of representations of knowledge [49]. The RCET model encourages us to explore such representations and their effects on learning and to pay close attention to the ways in which we represent the concepts we wish to present. Richard Mayer's [52] extensive investigations of combinations and sequences of different media representations, for example, suggest that some of these are more conducive to the learning of scientific explanations than others. Mayer's work is particularly interesting in that he links external representations to internal conceptualizations and the construction of knowledge. More work is clearly needed along similar lines, especially explorations of the uses of video and simulations in online environments and the use of digital learning objects in online courses [50, 53]. The tools for representing and constructing the knowledge provided to learners are subjects of particular interest [11, 12, 13, 14]. Hewitt's [75] research on patterns of interactivity in online discussion, for example, suggest that such patterns are as much a function of features of the interface as they are a result of pedagogical efforts. Similarly, Scardamalia and Bereiter's [24] work on computer-supported collaborative learning suggests that particular representations of knowledge are more supportive of collaboration than others. More investigations into tools for supporting discussion and collaboration online are needed, as are studies of computer-based tools for scaffolding thinking and learning [76]. Finally, initial findings in these areas suggest that studies of online course interfaces in general and their effects on learning might also be important [77].

The RCET model can help guide such research because it focuses our attention on particular online representations of knowledge and asks us to consider specifically what kinds of thinking and learning they afford and constrain [54]. The model thus asks us to explore not only what kinds of representations work and don't work in online courses, but also why they have particular effects on learning. This advantage makes findings more generalizable and so much more useful in informing the practice of online education.

In terms of practice, the RCET model encourages course developers and online instructors to consider seriously the ways in which they represent the concepts and skills they want students to acquire, and perhaps to experiment with different representations that take advantage of the unique capabilities of the online medium. Similarly, the model encourages designers and instructors to think hard about the kinds of activities and tools they ask students to engage in and whether or not these really achieve the purposes for which they are intended. In short, the RCET model can help guide the practice of online education by focusing attention on the ways in which knowledge is represented in online courses. This is particularly important in the online environment because all learning is mediated through such representations.

B. Conceptualization of Knowledge

The conceptualization of knowledge in the RCET model is similar in function to what Piaget [3, 4] identified as the development of mental schemas. The term *conceptualization* is used in the model to refer to the ways in which human beings organize, process, and manipulate knowledge in the mind and so make sense of the world. Conceptualizations unique to each individual develop through our interactions with environments (including social as well as physical environments and cognitive interactions with our own internal conceptual environments themselves) and build up over time into interrelated mental structures. The term *conceptualization* embraces multiple kinds of knowledge and multiple ways of knowing (because meaning making may not be inseparable from language [71, 72]) and includes both cognitive organization and mental processing, (because we believe these two concepts are essentially indivisible [78]). The idea of conceptualization emphasizes technological support for what Bransford,

Brown, and Cocking [1] call *learning with understanding*, or the organization and processing of information in coherent conceptual frameworks that are more meaningful, more accessible, and more useful.

The RCET model thus asks us to consider the ways in which particular technologies and technology environments aid and constrain specific conceptualizations of knowledge. Whereas the domain of representation of knowledge considers external knowledge construction, the domain of conceptualization of knowledge focuses attention on the internal, mental construction of knowledge. In terms of online learning, the model asks us to consider what kinds of mental processing, what kinds of internal organizations of knowledge, and what kinds of cognitive schema are supported by online technologies. For example, we have some evidence that online learning is particularly supportive of the construction of abstract concepts and less supportive than face-to-face environments of the construction of procedural knowledge [54]. It could be very informative to expand on this research and explore precisely the ways in which online learners process conceptual and procedural knowledge. Similarly, some evidence exists that threaded discussion assists the development of knowledge structures that integrate multiple perspectives [39]. Knowing more precisely how such development occurs would inform and improve the design of online courses. Analogous research on the kinds of conceptualizations supported by specific online learning environments could be highly useful, extending in important ways our understanding of both online learning and learning in general.

The notion of conceptualizations in the RCET model also draws our attention to the importance of the knowledge structures and ways of knowing learners bring to their online experiences, and the compatibility between these and learning online. The Dziubans' [40] study of the relationship between reactive behavior patterns and persistence in online courses suggests that independent learning behaviors are more conducive to persistence than dependent ones. Similar explorations of, for example, different ways of conceptualizing factual knowledge and their effects on achievement in online courses might be informative [31]. In addition, research on the effects of gender and culture on the ways in which students conceptualize knowledge in online environments might particularly inform studies of the influences of these characteristics on learning online.

The notion of the unique conceptualizations learners bring to online courses suggests that online instructors need to be especially sensitive to such things as gender [44] and cultural differences [45] in learners' mental models of communication. Indeed, the RCET model suggests that instructors should similarly be sensitive to any learner characteristics that might influence the ways in which students conceptualize knowledge [31, 40, 41, 46]. This aspect is especially important in the online environment because that environment mediates all interactions between instructors and students and so the range of cues to student understandings may be reduced. Thus, the model guides online educators to consider ways in which they can exploit technologies available to them as well as ways in which they might ameliorate any constraints the medium might place on learning.

C. Use of Knowledge

In the RCET model, the term *use* refers to the social activities and interactions through and around which knowledge is negotiated and constructed. This notion of *use* derives from social constructivist theories of learning, although its application in real-world contexts may differ from what the social constructivists had in mind. In particular, the model distinguishes between conceptualizations of knowledge, which are seen as private and internal, and uses of knowledge, which are viewed as public and external, in order to isolate different arenas within which the effects of technology on learning can be considered. Considering use apart from conceptualization and representation directs attention to the ways in which technologies can affect classroom activity [29]—in particular the effects of technology on both social interactions and on the social activities involved in the external constructions of knowledge highlighted by constructionist thinkers [11, 12, 13, 14].

In this vein, a growing body of research examines social contexts created through digital environments. Research on computer-supported collaborative learning has shown that computer-based collaboration can enhance higher order learning [24] and has identified particular program designs and features that support specific external constructions of knowledge [76, 79]. For example, Margaret Reil [80] found that papers written to be shared electronically with peers were more fluent, better organized, and clearer than papers written for a grade alone. Much in these approaches can and probably should be explored for its application to online learning environments. In the online learning domain, research on computer-mediated communication has found asynchronous online class discussions to be more equitable and democratic [32] and more reflective [36] than traditional classroom discussion, and has documented links between online interactions and learning [39, 65, 66, 81]. Interesting research in this area also links specific design features to particular discourse behaviors [75] and particular online teaching behaviors to student learning and course satisfaction [68].

The RCET model can help make sense of findings such as these by suggesting that they reflect characteristic affordances and constraints that, for example, particular kinds of online interfaces, communication tools, and media mixes have on social interactions online and thus on the social construction of knowledge in online courses. The ways in which online communication tools such as games and simulations support the external and collaborative construction of knowledge are particularly interesting [82]. The RCET model's notion of use can also encourage understanding of the changing roles of instructors [68, 83] and students [84] in online learning environments, and of the development of online learning communities [24, 85, 86, 87]. New and evolving social conventions (of discourse, of interaction, and of netiquette) in online courses in relation to the larger culture of the Internet are also an important topic for future research.

The RCET model encourages online developers and course instructors to seriously consider the importance of social supports for knowledge construction and learning, an especially important goal because the online environment may be inherently socially limited [60, 61, 62]. Online instructors should make concerted efforts to project themselves into their courses [68, 83], to facilitate the development of social presence among their students [64], and to encourage the emergence of learning communities in their online classes [85, 86, 87].

V. SUMMARY AND DISCUSSION

Constructivism is the name of a set of epistemological theories that are grounded in a belief that meaning is constructed in the minds of individuals through the cognitive processing of interactions in the world. Significant variations of constructivist theory include the notions that learning is active, social, and situated in particular physical, social, and cognitive contexts; that learning involves the ongoing development of complex and interrelated mental structures; and that the construction of knowledge is to a greater or lesser degree distributed across individuals, tools, and artifacts. Constructivism has numerous implications for instruction, the most significant of which is to shift the focus of pedagogical design away from instruction and toward the design of learning environments that are learner centered, knowledge centered, assessment centered, and community centered. Finally, the Research Center for Educational Technology (RCET) model explores the impact of online learning environments on thinking and learning in terms of effects on external representations, individual conceptualizations, and social uses of knowledge. By narrowing the focus of our thinking about learning online, the model might help guide research to pursue findings that can meaningfully inform practice and advance online education.

VI. REFERENCES

1. **Bransford, J. D., A. L. Brown, and R. R. Cocking.** *How People Learn: Brain, Mind, Experience, and School.* Washington, DC: National Academy Press, 2000.
2. **Duffy, T. M. and D. H. Jonassen.** *Constructivism and the Technology of Instruction: A Conversation.* Hillsdale, NJ: Erlbaum, 1992.
3. **Piaget, J.** *The Origins of Intelligence in Children.* New York: International Universities Press, 1952.
4. **Piaget, J.** *Construction of Reality in the Child.* London: Routledge, 1957.
5. **Mayer, R. E.** *Thinking, Problem Solving, Cognition.* New York: W.H. Freeman, 1983.
6. **Rumelhart, D. E. and D. A. Norman.** Analogical processes in learning. In *Cognitive Skills and Their Acquisition*, ed. J.R. Anderson. Hillsdale, NJ: Erlbaum, 1981.
7. **Minsky, M.** Frame-system theory. In *Thinking: Readings in Cognitive Science*, ed. P.N. Johnson-Laird and P.C. Wason. Cambridge: Cambridge University Press, 1977.
8. **Shank, R. C. and R. P. Abelson.** *Scripts, Plans, Goals, and Understanding: An Inquiry into Human Knowledge Structures.* Hillsdale, NJ: Erlbaum, 1977.
9. **Johnson-Laird, P. N.** *Mental Models.* Cambridge, MA: Harvard University Press, 1983.
10. **Quillian, M. R.** Semantic memory. In *Semantic Information Processing,* ed. M.L. Minsky. Cambridge, MA: MIT Press, 1968.
11. **Papert, S.** *Mindstorms: Children, Computers, and Powerful Ideas.* New York: Basic Books, 1980.
12. **Papert, S.** *The Children's Machine.* New York: Basic Books, 1993.
13. **Resnick, M.** *Turtles, Termites, and Traffic Jams: Explorations in Massively Parallel Microworlds.* Cambridge, MA: MIT Press, 1994.
14. **diSessa, A. A.** *Changing Minds: Computers, Learning, and Literacy.* Cambridge, MA: MIT Press, 2000.
15. **Vygotsky, L. S.** *Thought and Language.* Cambridge, MA: MIT Press, 1962.
16. **Vygotsky, L. S.** *Mind in Society.* Cambridge, MA: Harvard University Press, 1978.
17. **Bruner, J.** *Child's Talk: Learning to Use Language.* New York: Norton, 1983.
18. **Bruner, J.** *Actual Minds, Possible Worlds.* Cambridge, MA: Harvard University Press, 1986.
19. **Dewey, J.** *Experience and Education.* New York: Macmillan, 1938.
20. **Leont'ev, A. N.** *Problems of the Development of Mind.* Moscow: Progress Publishers, 1981.
21. **Brown, J. S., A. Collins, and S. Duguid.** Situated cognition and the culture of learning. *Educational Researcher* 18(1): 32–42, 1989.
22. **Lave, J. and E. Wenger.** *Situated Learning: Legitimate Peripheral Participation.* Cambridge: Cambridge University Press, 1991.
23. **Wenger, E.** *Communities of Practice: Learning, Meaning, and Identity.* New York: Cambridge University Press, 1997.
24. **Scardamalia, M. and C. Bereiter.** Computer support for knowledge-building communities. In *CSCL: Theory and Practice of an Emerging Paradigm,* ed. T. Koschmann. Mahwah, NJ: Lawrence Erlbaum, 1996.
25. **Cole, M. and Y. Engestrom.** A cultural-historical approach to distributed cognition. In *Distributed Cognitions. Psychological and Educational Considerations,* ed. G. Salomon. New York: Cambridge University Press, 1993.
26. **Pea, R. D.** Practices of distributed intelligence and designs for education. In *Distributed Cognitions. Psychological and Educational Considerations,* ed. G. Salomon. New York: Cambridge University Press, 1993.
27. **Hutchins, E.** How a cockpit remembers its speed. *Cognitive Science* 19: 265–288, 1995.

28. **Perkins, D. N.** Person-plus: a distributed view of thinking and learning. In *Distributed Cognitions. Psychological and Educational Considerations,* ed. G. Salomon. New York: Cambridge University Press, 1993.
29. **Salomon, G.** No distribution without individuals' cognition: a dynamic interactional view. In *Distributed Cognitions. Psychological and Educational Considerations,* ed. G. Salomon. New York: Cambridge University Press, 1993.
30. **Twigg, C.** *Innovations in Online Learning: Moving Beyond No Significant Difference.* The Pew Learning and Technology Program, 2000. Online: http://www.center.rpi.edu/PewSym/mono4.html.
31. **Danchak, M. M.** Using adaptive hypermedia to match web presentation to learning styles. In *Elements of Quality Online Education: Into the Mainstream*, ed. J. Bourne and J.C. Moore, 93–108. Needham, MA: Sloan-C, 2004.
32. **Harasim, L.** *On-line Education: Perspectives on a New Environment.* New York: Praeger, 1990.
33. **Eastmond, D. V.** *Alone but Together: Adult Distance Study through Computer Conferencing.* Cresskill, NJ: Hampton Press, 1995.
34. **Hiltz, S. R.** *The Virtual Classroom: Learning without Limits via Computer Networks.* Norwood, NJ: Ablex, 1994.
35. **Poole, D. M.** Student participation in a discussion-oriented online course: A case study. *Journal of Research on Computing in Education* 33(2): 162–177, 2000.
36. **Garrison, D. R.** Cognitive presence for effective asynchronous online learning: the role of reflective inquiry, self-direction and metacognition. In *Elements of Quality Online Education: Practice and Direction,* ed. J. Bourne and J.C. Moore, 47–58. Needham, MA: Sloan-C, 2003.
37. **Walther, J.** Interpersonal effects in computer mediated interaction. *Communication Research* 21(4): 460–487, 1994.
38. **Gunawardena, C. and F. Zittle.** Social presence as a predictor of satisfaction within a computer mediated conferencing environment. *American Journal of Distance Education* 11(3): 8–26, 1997.
39. **Picciano, A. G.** Beyond student perceptions: Issues of interaction, presence and performance in an online course. *Journal of Asynchronous Learning Networks* 6(1): 2002.
40. **Dziuban, J. I., and C. D. Dziuban.** Reactive behavior patterns in the classroom. *Journal of Staff, Program, and Organization Development* 15(2): 85–91, 1997/98.
41. **Meyer, K. A.** The Web's impact on student learning. *THE Journal,* May 2003. Online: http://www.thejournal.com/magazine/vault/A4401.cfm.
42. **Bures, E. M., C. Aundsen, and P. C. Abrami.** Motivation to learn via computer conferencing: exploring how task-specific motivation and CC expectations are related to student acceptance of learning via CC. *Journal of Educational Computing Research* 27(3): 249–264, 2002.
43. **Davies, R. S.** Learner intent and online courses. Paper presented at the annual meeting of the American Educational Research Association, Chicago, 2003.
44. **Gunn, C. and M. McSporran.** Dominant or different? Gender issues in computer supported learning. *Journal of Asynchronous Learning Networks* 7(1): 14–30, 2003.
45. **Morse, K.** Does one size fit all? Exploring asynchronous learning in a multicultural environment. *Journal of Asynchronous Learning Networks* 7(1): 37–55, 2003.
46. **Ehlers, U-D.** Quality in e-learning from a learner's perspective. *European Journal of Open and Distance Learning*, 2004.
    Online: http://www.eurodl.org/materials/contrib./2004/Online_Master_COPs.html.
47. **Wittgenstein, L.** *Philosophical Investigations.* Oxford: Basil Blackwell, 1963.
48. **Spiro, R. J. and J. C. Jheng.** Cognitive flexibility and hypertext: Theory and technology for the nonlinear and multidimensional traversal of complex subject matter. In *Cognition, Education, and Multimedia: Explorations in High Technology*, ed. D. Nix and R.J. Spiro, 163–205. Hillsdale, NJ: Erlbaum, 1990.
49. **McClintock, R. O.** The Educators Manifesto: Renewing the Progressive Bond with Posterity through the Social Construction of Digital Learning Communities. New York: Institute for Learning Technologies, Teachers College, Columbia University, 1999.

50. **The Sloan Consortium.** *Effective Practices: Learning Effectiveness.* 2002. Online: http://www.sloan-c.org/effectivepractices.

51. **Shank, R.** Horses for courses. *Communication of the ACM* 41 (7): 23-25, 1998.

52. **Mayer, R. E.** *Multimedia Learning.* New York: Cambridge University Press, 2001.

53. **McMartin, F.** MERLOT: a model for user involvement in digital library design and implementation. *Journal of Digital Information* 5(3): 2004. Article No. 293. Online: http://jodi.ecs.soton.ac.uk/Articles/v05/i03/McMartin/.

54. **Parker, D. and A. Gemino.** Inside online learning: Comparing conceptual and technique learning performance in place-based and ALN formats. *Journal of Asynchronous Learning Networks* 5(2): 64–74, 2001.

55. **Kashy, E., M. Thoennessen, G. Alberti, and Y. Tsai.** Implementing a large on-campus ALN: Faculty perspective. Online Education, Volume 1. *Journal of Asynchronous Learning Networks* 4(3): 2000.

56. **Kashy, D. A., G. Abertelli, W. Bauer, E. Kashy, and M. Thoennessen.** Influence of non-moderated and moderated discussion sites on student success. *Journal of Asynchronous Learning Networks* 7(1): 31–36, 2003.

57. **Riccomini, P.** The comparative effectiveness of two forms of feedback: Web-based model comparison and instructor delivered feedback. *Journal of Educational Computing Research* 27(3): 213–228, 2002.

58. **Pelz, B.** (My) Three principles of effective online pedagogy. *Journal of Asynchronous Learning Networks* 8(3): 33–46, 2004.

59. **Aviv, R., Z. Erlich, G. Ravid, and A. Geva.** Network analysis of knowledge construction in asynchronous learning networks. *Journal of Asynchronous Learning Networks* 7(3): 1–23, 2003.

60. **Short, J., E. Williams, and B. Christie.** *The Social Psychology of Telecommunications.* Toronto: Wiley, 1976.

61. **Rice, R. E.** Contexts of research in organizational computer-mediated communication. In *Contexts of Computer-Mediated Communication,* ed. M. Lea. New York: Harvester Wheatsheaf, 1992.

62. **Picard, R.W.** *Affective Computing.* Cambridge, MA: MIT Press, 1997.

63. **Rourke, L., T. Anderson, D. R. Garrison, and W. Archer.** Assessing social presence in asynchronous text-based computer conferencing. *Journal of Distance Education* 14(2): 2001.

64. **Swan, K.** Immediacy, social presence, and asynchronous discussion. In *Elements of Quality Online Education, Volume 3,* ed. J. Bourne and J.C. Moore. Needham, MA: Sloan-C, 2002.

65. **Swan, K.** Building communities in online courses: the importance of interaction. *Education, Communication and Information* 2(1): 23–49, 2002.

66. **Richardson, J. C. and K. Swan.** Examining social presence in online courses in relation to students' perceived learning and satisfaction. *Journal of Asynchronous Learning Networks* 7(1): 68–88, 2003.

67. **Anderson, T., and L. Rourke.** Assessing teaching presence in a computer conferencing context. *Journal of Asynchronous Learning Networks* 5(2): 1–17, 2001.

68. **Shea, P. J., A. M. Pickett, and W. E. Pelz.** A follow-up investigation of "teaching presence" in the SUNY Learning Network. *Journal of Asynchronous Learning Networks* 7(2): 61–80, 2003.

69. **Benbunan-Fich, R. and S. R Hiltz.** Impact of asynchronous learning networks on individual and group problem solving: A field experiment. *Group Decision and Negotiation* 8: 409–426, 1999.

70. **Swan, K., D. Cook, S. Diaz, A. Kratcoski, M. Juliana, and M. van 't Hooft.** Representation, conceptualization and use: modeling the effects of technology on learning. Paper presented at the annual meeting of the American Educational Research Association, San Diego, CA, 2004.

71. **Gardner, H.** *Frames of Mind: The Theory of Multiple Intelligences.* New York: Basic Books, 1983.

72. **Paivio, A.** *Mental Representations: A Dual Coding Approach.* New York: Oxford University Press, 1986.

73. **Reinking, D.** Computers, reading, and a new technology of print. In *Reading and Computers: Issues for Theory and Practice,* ed. D. Reinking, 3–23. New York: Teachers College Press, 1987.

74. **Bolter, J. D.** *The Writing Space: The Computer, Hypertext and the History of Writing.* Chapel Hill, NC: University of North Carolina Press, 1991.

75. **Hewitt, J.** How habitual online practices affect the development of asynchronous discussion threads. *Journal of Educational Computing Research* 28(1): 31–45, 2003.

76. **Jonassen, D. H.** *Computers as Mindtools for Schools: Engaging Critical Thinking.* Columbus, OH: Prentice-Hall, 2000.

77. **Swan, K.** Issues of interface. *European Journal of Open and Distance Learning,* 2004. Online: http://www.eurodl.org/materials/contrib/2004/Karen_Swan.html.

78. **Anderson, J. R.** *The Architecture of Cognition.* Cambridge, MA: Harvard University Press, 1983.

79. **Salomon, G., D. N. Perkins, and T. Globerson.** Partners in cognition: Extending human intelligence with intelligent technologies. *Educational Researcher* 20(3): 2–9, 2002.

80. **Riel, M.** Educational change in a technology-rich environment. *Journal of Research on Computing in Education* 26(4): 452–474, 1994.

81. **Jiang, M., and E. Ting.** A study of factors influencing students' perceived learning in a web-based course environment. *International Journal of Educational Telecommunications* 6(4): 317–338, 2000.

82. **Gee, J.** *What Video Games Have to Teach Us about Learning and Literacy.* New York: Palgrave Macmillan, 2003.

83. **Coppola, N. W., S. R. Hiltz, and N. Rotter.** Becoming a virtual professor: pedagogical roles and ALN. *Proceedings of the 34th Hawaii International Conference on System Sciences.* Los Alamitos, CA: IEEE Press, 2001.

84. **Garrison, R. D., M. Cleveland-Innes, and T. Fung.** Student role adjustment in online communities of inquiry: model and instrument validation. *Journal of Asynchronous Learning Networks* 8(2): 61–74, 2004.

85. **Wegerif, R.** The social dimension of asynchronous learning. *Journal of Asynchronous Learning Networks* 2(1): 34–49, 1998.

86. **Rovai, A. P.** A preliminary look at structural differences in sense of classroom community between higher education traditional and ALN courses. *Journal of Asynchronous Learning Networks* 6(1): 2002.

87. **Hawthornthwaite, C.** Building social networks via computer networks: creating and sustaining distributed learning communities. In *Building Virtual Communities: Learning and Change in Cyberspace,* ed. K.A. Renninger and W. Shumar, 159–190. Cambridge: Cambridge University Press, 2002.

VII. ABOUT THE AUTHOR

Karen Swan is Research Professor in the Research Center for Educational Technology at Kent State University and the Learning Effectiveness Editor for the Sloan Consortium. Dr. Swan's research is in the general area of media and learning. She has published and presented nationally and internationally in the specific areas of programming and problem solving, computer-assisted instruction, hypermedia design, technology and literacy, and technology professional development. Her current research focuses on student learning in ubiquitous computing environments and on online learning, in particular, on interactivity, social presence, and interface issues. Dr. Swan has authored several hypermedia programs as well as three online courses and has co-edited a book, *Social Learning From Broadcast Television.* She is the Special Issues Editor for the *Journal of Educational Computing Research* and a member of the national advisory board of the Ubiquitous Computing Evaluation Consortium.

THE REAL-TIME CASE METHOD: THE INTERNET CREATES THE POTENTIAL FOR NEW PEDAGOGY

James Theroux, Ed.D.
Isenberg School of Management
University of Massachusetts

Clare Kilbane, PhD
School of Education University of Massachusetts

- Until the web there was no practical way to distribute cases to students quickly; a real-time case method (RTCM) presents an opportunity for learning that surpasses the traditional method.

- A real-time case (RTC) was launched with 109 students from four universities in the United States and Canada, the University of Massachusetts at Amherst (UMass), the University of New Brunswick, Florida Atlantic University, and Worcester Polytechnic Institute (WPI).

- A semester-long Real Time Case was delivered in weekly, problem-focused installments that covered events at a single company at the same time those events unfolded.

- Students could see and hear the people about whom they read, thus expanding the human element of the case.

- RTCM could deliver high-powered experiential learning more efficiently than field-based courses.

I. INTRODUCTION

The traditional case method of teaching was introduced over one hundred years ago. Today nearly all business schools use the case method to some extent. Harvard Business School views the case method as the best way of training decision-makers and uses it in all courses. The dean of the school, Dr. Kim Clark, states that the purpose of the case method is "to produce graduates who are comfortable making decisions."

Yet despite substantial changes in technology and business practices over the past century, the method of presenting cases has remained virtually unchanged. Might not there be new ways of producing and distributing cases? Could the internet and multimedia technologies responsible for altering the business environment be employed to make the case method more effective?

Until now the production of cases has been conducted at a leisurely pace. Even when new developments in business have prompted case writers to move fast, it normally would take at least 18 months between conception of the case and delivery to students. The average time would be closer to 36 months.

This pace has implications for pedagogy, classroom atmosphere, and teacher-student relations. When a case is historical or "old" and the discussion is essentially a postmortem, chances are that the professor knows "the answer" and the students don't. This has worked fine for professors, who generally like being in a superior position. And students accept it.

Every now and then, students disrupt the arrangement by finding out what happened in the case after it was written. If the students happen to tell the rest of the class what they discovered, much of the discussion and drama go out the window. If students don't know what happened in the real world, their approach to class discussion is often focused on guessing what the professor wants to hear rather than what might benefit the situation being analyzed.

Enter the web. Until the web there was no practical way to distribute cases to students quickly. Even if a case could be written in real time, it couldn't be delivered in real time. The web made us think about what could be done to revamp the case method.

The new method proposed here is the real-time case (RTC) study. RTC is a semester-long case delivered in weekly, problem-focused installments that cover events at a single company at the same time those events unfold.

Whether used in synchronous or asynchronous contexts, this new method creates an opportunity for learning that surpasses the traditional method. As described below, students become more engaged, teachers become partners with students in problem solving, and analysis of cases becomes richer and more complex.

II. PURPOSE

The main purpose of this study was to examine if the real-time case method (RTCM) had the potential to move case-based teaching to a new level of efficacy. Given that it was the initial trial of RTCM, the course developers sought preliminary statistical evidence regarding the way it would be received by students and faculty.

Some were skeptical that a real-time case could ever be produced. It was not obvious that a willing case company could be found, or that high-quality cases could be written on a weekly basis in real time. Accordingly, a secondary objective of the project was to test the feasibility of producing a real-time case and to get a rough gauge of how it would work in the classroom.

III. THE CASE METHOD OF TEACHING

What follows in this section is an overview of the characteristics of both the traditional case method and real-time case method. While the methods are similar, features that distinguish RTCM from the traditional case method are highlighted.

A. Characteristics of the Traditional Case Method

The term *case method* actually refers to a wide range of instructional methods that revolve around the reading and discussion of a descriptive document about a business or business scenario, or case. All cases have three essential elements: they are realistic; they rely on careful research and study; and they provide data for consideration and discussion by users [1].

The traditional case study presents a snapshot of the case company. When used in a typical case-based business course, numerous cases are presented and analyzed during a semester. Each case generally presents a problem based on theoretical and field research and is accompanied by a wide range of supporting information. Case studies have been applied in a variety of professional disciplines, such as marketing, organizational behavior, and finance.

Most cases are presented in written form and range in length from seven to twelve pages excluding exhibits. The creation of a case is a time-consuming and expensive process. According to sources at Harvard Business School, each one costs an average of twenty thousand dollars. Each case often takes a month or more of a researcher's time and a year or more in production [2].

The authors conducted a thorough review of the literature to identify any previous attempts to produce a case similar to the real-time case. Such methods as "active learning," "live cases," and "problem-based learning" have elements in common with the real-time case method, but none presented weekly case installments in real time over the course of a semester. And none produced real-time written case material at the level of quality students are accustomed to seeing in classic case studies.

B. Characteristics of the Real-Time Case Method

The real-time case method (RTCM) builds on the traditional case method and in a similar way asks students to solve a problem presented in a written document. However, its fundamental difference is manifested through technology that alters both learning activities and case materials. The new case becomes transformed through two main avenues that are RTCM's distinguishing features: extended coverage and real-time interactivity.

Extended coverage means that a real-time case reports on a single company for an entire semester or more. The basic building block of the course is a weekly installment of the semester-long case. Assuming that the real-time case is taught over the course of a fourteen-week semester, students receive a volume of information regarding the case company that is equivalent to a book rather than the seven to twelve pages of a traditional case. Weekly case material is organized around a particular problem faced by the case company. RTCM involves not just a chronological story but also a series of case materials and discussions focused on classic business problems that are amenable to analysis.

The extended coverage of real-time cases allows students to see more of the human dimension of business decisions. They get to know the case characters through web-based video that provides well-rounded portraits.

A real-time case also differs from traditional cases in terms of interactivity. Students are able to interact with the case company on a continuous basis over a substantial period of time (a semester). Students interact with the case company about issues and problems as decisions are actually made by the case company. This may involve students asking questions, making recommendations, and gaining feedback from the company's decision makers.

Some interactions between the case company and students are direct and consist of videoconferences, online chat, and regularly scheduled phone conferences with the case company managers. The case writer mediates other interactions, answering questions from his or her own knowledge of the company.

IV. COMPONENTS OF A REAL-TIME CASE

Described above are the main characteristics of the real-time case method; this section presents the components that made up the real-time case actually produced in the fall semester of 2001. These components define for us what a real-time case can be, but modifications should be expected in future cases as the RTCM concept develops.

A case writer was hired to produce most of the weekly case material and was stationed at the case company site full time for the duration of the course. In addition to writing, the case writer also facilitated interaction between the case company and students in a way that avoided putting undue strain on the case company.

The case writer was assigned to report on a company named Optasite Inc, which was and is in the business of maintaining cell phone infrastructure. The company agreed to make its meetings and documents open to the case writer and viewed the case study as a way of getting valuable feedback from the participating students and professors.

A. Background Material

Background material on the case company and its industry were put on the password-protected course website before the beginning of the semester. The background material included both text and video information about the case company's history, industry, market, management, and financials. In the case of Optasite Inc., background writing included descriptions of cell phone technology that could be understood by the typical student. Project staff produced a three-minute video tour of a cell site to help students grasp the technology.

B. Case Installments

The weekly case installments ranged from five to ten pages in length. Each installment described a current problem or issue facing the case company. For example, one week the problem was, "How should the company price its product?" The next week the problem was, "How should the company think about and respond to its competitors?" The case writer produced these weekly installments under the guidance of the academic project director. Source material, including company memos, reports, and transcripts of conversations, supplemented each installment. The case writer also reported on new developments that were related to previous case installments.

C. Video

Students engaged in videoconferencing with executives of the case company. In the first real-time case there were two video conferences, one near the beginning of the semester, and the other near the end. This provided the opportunity to put questions directly to the case company's managers. And it allowed students to see and hear the people about whom they read, thus expanding the human element of the case. Students saw for example, that the chairman of the board was rather traditional and uptight, while the founder was the other extreme. This "data" was referred to throughout the semester.

D. Discussion Boards and Chat

Project staff arranged for one company manager each week to "meet" with students on the course website for live, online chats that lasted about an hour. This provided a regular opportunity to ask questions and receive answers directly from the case company. These sessions were held in the evening, outside of class time, so they were optional. The transcripts were made available on the web for those who weren't able to participate live.

E. Conceptual Articles

Conceptual articles were distributed to the students on a weekly basis to complement the case installments. These articles came primarily from Harvard Business School Publishing, and provided theoretical perspectives on the events occurring in the case company in the relevant case installment. For example, in the case installment on how the company should price its product, there were three HBS articles on the course website dealing with the theory of pricing.

F. Weekly News

Finally, there occasionally was information about the case company and the case characters that did not fit into the weekly case installment. For example, when students were introduced to all the company managers via short video interviews they learned that one manager was commuting three hundred miles to Optasite, and was unwilling to move his family to be closer to the company. When this manager finally did make the move, it was important information, because it showed his increased commitment to the company. This type of information was reported in a separate "news" section of the case website.

V. PARTICIPANTS

The real-time case was launched with 109 students from four universities in the United States and Canada. The participating universities were as follows: University of Massachusetts at Amherst (UMass), University of New Brunswick, Florida Atlantic University, and Worcester Polytechnic Institute (WPI).

The student participants included 63 undergraduate students, 12 on-campus MBA students, and 34 off-campus graduate students, most of whom were taught exclusively online.

Table 1 Student Count at Participating Schools			
	Undergrad	MBA	
School	On-campus	On-campus	Online
UMass	43	12	13
WPI	11	-	-
FAU	9	-	-
UNB	-	-	21

VI.   METHOD

A. Educational Objectives

The case developers created this new type of case study to accomplish several objectives in the classroom. First, the developers wanted to bring students to a new level of energy, engagement, and participation. By doing so, they hoped to create a course that was more appealing than courses to which students were accustomed. Second, with RTC's in-depth, multimedia coverage of the case company, the developers hoped to teach students lessons that were difficult to teach using conventional methods. In particular, the aims were to instill in students a greater appreciation for the complexity of business decision making, to portray a more realistic view of business, to take a more interdisciplinary view of problem-solving, and to teach all these lessons in a way that is more memorable than the conventional case method is.

To determine whether the educational objectives were met, a number of data sources were analyzed. These sources included the following: (1) a student evaluation survey located on the case website, (2) standard course evaluation forms at each university, (3) a focus group interview with the on-campus MBA group at UMass, and (4) phone interviews with UMass online MBA students. Unfortunately, a presentation of findings from the in-depth interviews is beyond the scope of this publication.

The developers plan to conduct more systematic inquiry using experimental design to evaluate the effect of future efforts to use a real-time case. Our main objective in the initial study was to assess whether the benefit to students justified the cost and effort of producing the case.

1. Data Collection

Before presenting the results, it is necessary to explain a few important details about these data. Although standard course evaluation forms were completed at each university, only data from those evaluations taken at UMass were available. These data provided important insights into how the experience of students who used the real-time case compared with the previous experience of students taking the same course with the same instructor but using the traditional case method. Data from the web-based evaluation survey was the primary means for understanding students' experiences of RTCM across all sites.

2. Instrumentation

The UMass evaluation form included student responses to both multiple-choice and open-ended questions. The evaluation form was the same one used in all courses at UMass, excluding online-only course offerings in continuing education. To evaluate the entrepreneurship course in which the real-time case was used, students filled out the same evaluation that had been used in previous years in which traditional cases were used. Thus the courses assessed by the evaluation form were essentially the same except for the type of case material. The response rates for the student evaluations used each year were as follows: in Fall 2000 (when traditional cases were used) 39 of 45 students responded; in Fall 2001 (when RTC was used) 37 of 41 students responded.

The student evaluation survey made available on the case website to all 109 students was completed by 50 percent of the students (N = 55). The survey instrument also consisted of both multiple-choice and open-ended questions. All instruments are available from the authors upon request.

VII. FINDINGS

The following section presents answers questions about the learning experiences of students, relying on data both from the UMass standard course evaluation form and from the standardized online evaluation form.

A. Appeal of RTCM

Data from the UMass course evaluations indicated that students found the real-time case method appealing. On a scale of 1 (lowest) to 5 (highest), students in the on-campus MBA course indicated a mean score of 5.00 on an item rating how much the course "stimulated participation." The rating indicated that every MBA student who responded gave the course the highest possible score in the category. In the category "overall satisfaction" a score 4.90 out of 5.00 was achieved. The 5.00 score and the 4.90 score had not previously been achieved at the School of Management at UMass in the particular categories mentioned.

Of the 37 undergraduates who responded, the real-time case obtained a rating of 4.75 in the "stimulated participation" category (a School of Management record for this category). The undergraduate "overall rating of this course" score was 4.25 compared to 4.00 in the previous year's course.

Table 2		
Traditional Course Evaluation Data at UMass (1-5 scale)		
Survey Criterion	Undergrads	MBAs
Stimulated participation	4.75	5.00
Overall rating	4.25	4.90

In analyzing results for the UMass online-only students, it is important to note that the specific questions on that course evaluation differed somewhat from the on-campus course evaluation questions. It also must be mentioned that the UMass instructor had not previously taught an entrepreneurship course to online-only students. For both these reasons, direct comparisons to previous years are not possible for the online-only students. Satisfaction levels among online-only students were high, but below the level for on-campus students.

The data from the standardized online evaluation completed by 55 of the 109 students indicated that 70 percent of students (x = 39) "enjoyed the RTC course more than a typical business course." In addition, 46 percent (x = 25) indicated that they enjoyed the RTC more than their previous favorite business course (see Table 1). Finally, 22 percent (x = 11) reported that the course using the RTC was equal in appeal to their favorite course.

Table 3 Respondents' Opinions Of RTCM's Desirability Versus Other Courses (%)				
	Enjoyed RTC			
Course for Comparison	More	Same	Less	Uncertain
Typical Business Course	70	14	14	2
Previous Favorite Business Course	46	22	30	2

Additionally, 90 percent of students who responded recommended that their school "provide courses in the future that include a real-time case." Ninety-two percent recommended that RTCM be applied to business subjects other than entrepreneurship.

Other data were collected that may explain the high degree of satisfaction. In answers to an open-ended question on the UMass course evaluation form, undergraduates indicated that the course's use of a case occurring in real time was what they "liked most about this course." In addition, 70 percent (x = 39) of students responding to the standardized evaluation were "very positive" about the real-time nature of the course, while only 4 percent were negative about it. Furthermore, 62 percent indicated that the in-depth nature of the case was "highly valued." Only 2 percent were negative about the focus on one company throughout the entire semester, while 6 percent were neutral.

Table 4: Factors Influencing Satisfaction (%)		
Factor	Positive	Negative
Real-time Coverage	70	4
Semester-long Case	62	2

In addition to the quantitative data from multiple-choice questions and the qualitative data obtained in the form of adjectives, the online evaluation and the standard course evaluation forms at UMass included answers to open-ended questions. All comments were made anonymously. Over 90 percent were characterized as positive.

B. Student Engagement and Motivation

The data reported here regarding engagement and motivation consists of responses to open-ended questions on the online evaluation survey and on the UMass course evaluation form. Additional data were collected from a focus group of MBA students at UMass, but taking into consideration space constraints, those results are not reported.

Comments by students that spoke to the issue of engagement included expressions of an attachment to the case company and the feeling that one was part of the case company. These comments came from the online evaluation form.

Additional information about engagement was available in the comments solicited from the request for course improvement suggestions. Comments included suggestions for visits to the case company, more online chat, and additional phone conferences. A substantial number of comments suggested that the students were engaged and were eager to learn more about the case company.

Although not contained in any of the formal evaluation processes, the UMass instructor observed many behaviors that indicated a high level of engagement. He reported that students in his class were unusually engaged and motivated. The professor at Florida Atlantic University reported that in all his years of teaching he had never witnessed a group of students "so motivated by the material."

C. Student Appreciation of Business Complexity and More Realistic Views of Business

Data from the UMass course evaluation completed by the on-campus MBA students indicated a score of 4.90 out of 5.00 (x = 11) that tied an all-time high at the school for the question "Overall, how much do you feel you have learned?"

On the modified course evaluation completed by the online participants at UMass, students were asked the following: "Now that you have studied a real-time case, how would you assess your view of entrepreneurship?" Eighty percent said it was "more realistic than before." Only 20 percent said "no change."

Students were also asked, "When you leave your business program, how memorable do you think lessons learned in the real-time case will be compared with other learning experiences you have had?" Seventy-six percent (x = 42) said "more memorable"; twenty-four percent (x = 13) said "no difference." Ninety-two percent (x = 50) recommended that RTC be applied to a wide variety of business courses. Positive comments about the learning that occurred outnumbered negative ones by about ten to one

D. Conclusions and Recommendations

The data indicate that the real-time case met the developers' objectives for the initial study. Students were satisfied with their experience and highly engaged with the case material. Students reported gains in their appreciation of the complexity and interdisciplinary nature of business decision-making and also indicated that they believe that the real-time case will be memorable.

The developers must now answer the question of where real-time case method fits into the university curriculum. Because a real-time case offers extended coverage of a case company and can familiarize students with all the functional areas of a company, teachers of capstone courses that attempt to integrate student understanding of the functional areas might well find it valuable. These courses might include strategy, business policy, and entrepreneurship. Other courses to be considered are those that attempt to give students a view of general management such as field studies, consulting courses, independent studies, and practicums. It might be argued that RTCM could deliver high-powered experiential learning more efficiently than field-based courses. In summary, the real-time case method offers a new learning tool either in place of or as a complement to the traditional case method in a variety of business courses.

VIII. REFERENCES

1. **Merseth, K. K.** The early history of case-based instruction: Insights for teacher education today. *Journal of Teacher Education* 42(4): 243–249, 1991.
2. **Learned, E. P.** Reflections of a case method teacher. In *Teaching and the Case Method*, eds. C. R. Christensen and A. J. Hansen, 9–15. Boston: Harvard Business School, 1987.

IX. ABOUT THE AUTHORS

Jim Theroux is the Flavin Professor of Entrepreneurship at UMass-Amherst. Before becoming a professor in 1991, Dr. Theroux had a business career in the cable TV industry that began with a large national company, Time-Warner Cable. After several years at Time-Warner he went out on his own by raising $20 million of venture capital to start a new cable company in the Cleveland Ohio area. At the University of Massachusetts, Dr. Theroux is a specialist in bringing new pedagogical techniques to business education. For his experimental work in teaching inventors he was designated one of the top ten entrepreneurship educators in America by Ernst & Young and the Kauffman Foundation. In the past year he has received three national awards for the innovative nature of the real-time case concept. Theroux received his MBA at Harvard University and his doctorate in educational technology at the University of Massachusetts.

Clare Kilbane is an assistant professor of Educational Technology at the University of Massachusetts Amherst. She teaches courses in the graduate program for the School of Education's Department of Teacher Education and Curriculum Studies. She studies how new technologies combine with existing instructional methods to promote student learning. She is particularly interested in researching the case method and web-based technologies.

A CASE STUDY IN BLENDED LEARNING: LEVERAGING TECHNOLOGY IN ENTREPRENEURSHIP EDUCATION

Barry Bisson
Dr. J. Herbert Smith Centre
University of New Brunswick

Edward Leach
Faculty of Management
Dalhousie University

Timothy Little
Department of Electrical and Computer Engineering
Dalhousie University

Robert Richards
Faculty of Business Administration
Memorial University of Newfoundland

Brian Veitch
Faculty of Engineering and Applied Science
Memorial University of Newfoundland

Karin Zundel
Dr. J. Herbert Smith Centre
University of New Brunswick

- To combine the flexibility of asynchronous learning with the ability for real-time interactions, five faculty and administrators from three universities used a blended approach in the delivery of a new entrepreneurship course, Business Planning and Strategy in an Entrepreneurial Environment.

- Blended learning is "a learning program where more than one delivery mode is being used with the objective of optimizing the learning outcome and cost of program delivery."

- Faculty members were highly motivated to enhance collaborative entrepreneurship education; they were encouraged by institutional initiatives to share intellectual assets by using emerging technologies.

- The course employed a variety of activities—reading assignments, workshops and lectures, case studies, guest speakers, a business simulation game, and an entrepreneur's toolkit.

- The learning technologies created a synergy and net gains in the educational experience that could not have been achieved in the physical classroom.

I. INTRODUCTION

This paper describes a pilot project in online entrepreneurship education that was undertaken in January 2004 by faculty and students at three universities in eastern Canada: Dalhousie University in Nova Scotia (DAL), Memorial University in Newfoundland and Labrador (MUN) and the University of New Brunswick in New Brunswick (UNB).

Two driving forces spearheaded this project. First, the faculty members at each of the three universities were highly motivated to explore new ways of enhancing entrepreneurship education through collaboration. Second, the academic vice presidents of the universities had announced an initiative designed to encourage faculty to use emerging learning technologies as a means of enhancing the sharing of intellectual assets among universities.

The Dr. J. Herbert Smith Centre, housed within the Faculty of Engineering at the University of New Brunswick, has been offering a selection of courses in Technology Management and Entrepreneurship (TME) online for several years. Students work on their own, at their own pace, and complete the same course requirements as students taking the course in the classroom. Although this option has allowed students to earn the centre's diploma when they cannot attend classroom courses, the traditional face-to-face environment still offers a much richer experience. Swan [1] suggests that there are three contributing factors in the success of online courses: interaction with the course content, interaction with the instructor(s), and peer-to-peer interaction. Students in the regular classroom courses can work in groups on projects; they can interact with the instructors, their peers, and invited guest speakers from industry; and ask questions and get feedback in real time. To combine the flexibility of asynchronous learning with the ability for real-time interactions, faculty and administrators decided to use a blended approach in the delivery of a new entrepreneurship course.

Blended learning can be described as "a learning program where more than one delivery mode is being used with the objective of optimizing the learning outcome and cost of program delivery" [2]. The pilot project delivered one of the centre's courses (Business Planning and Strategy in an Entrepreneurial Environment) to engineering students from all three schools using a variety of e-learning mechanisms. The blend itself had several dimensions: self-paced courseware as well as live workshops and lectures, structured learning in a classroom setting as well as unstructured learning in a simulation game, and independent reflective readings as well as instructor-led case study discussions. In addition, faculty members at each school were available for face-to-face meetings with students. Through this blended approach, the primary objectives of the pilot were to

- stimulate the entrepreneurial behavior of engineering students,
- enhance their business literacy,
- develop a holistic learning model in which students are highly motivated to learn the course concepts,
- use technology to leverage the intellectual assets of the participating universities,
- enhance networking of faculty and students between and within schools,
- provide faculty and student enrichment through the development of an innovative educational delivery model, and
- provide leadership and a role model for collaboration among universities and across disciplines.

The three-credit-hour course commenced in January 2004 with a six-member instructional team and twenty-three students representing three universities (nine from UNB, seven from DAL, and seven from

MUN). The course finished in April with nineteen students successfully completing (ten from UNB, five from DAL, and four from MUN).

The purpose of this paper is to describe the virtual classroom technology, the course design, and the results of the pilot project evaluations, and to discuss positive aspects of the experience as well as lessons learned along the way.

II.   THE COURSE

The primary objective of the course was to introduce students to business planning and analysis concepts with an emphasis on entrepreneurship in the small business environment. Studies have shown [1, 3, 4] that one of the strongest factors in student success and satisfaction with online courses is the opportunity for interaction. It is especially important to design activities that will lead to rich and meaningful discussions [4]. Through class lectures and discussions, group projects, and interaction with guest speakers, students had a variety of opportunities for meaningful communication at various levels. When designing the course, instructors wanted to incorporate pedagogy that fostered active learning through exposure to real-life examples and situations. The course used pertinent case studies, and with the provision of an entrepreneur's toolkit, students were able to apply their knowledge by participating in an online business simulation game and creating actual business plans. In addition, students were given the opportunity for self-paced study of online courseware, the completion of review exercises, and independent readings. Consequently, students were exposed to the entire spectrum of corporate activities in an entrepreneurial environment. Each of these pedagogical modes is described below.

A. Workshops/Lectures

Each week the class met online in vClass (vClass is now renamed Elluminate *Live!*) for a three-hour session. The sessions were typically broken down into three one-hour sessions with a workshop or lecture pertaining to the topic of the week in the first hour The remaining time was spent in small group meetings, case study discussion, or with an invited guest speaker, as indicated below.

B. Assigned Readings

Readings were assigned for each session, and students were expected to complete them prior to class. For the most part, these readings consisted of articles from the Harvard Business School or *Harvard Business Review* and were intended to supplement information presented in the sessions. The collection of these resources constituted an excellent contribution to the students' personal library.

C. Case Studies

Students were usually expected to read a pertinent Harvard Business School case study in preparation for an online discussion led by one of the faculty. Often the discussion of the case served as the teaching component for the session topic. The cases were chosen to excite students about entrepreneurship while at the same time exposing them to the difficult challenges associated with launching a business.

D. Guest Speakers

Several guest speakers made online appearances throughout the course. Speakers were selected based on their experiences related to the weekly session topics, and their geographic locations varied from local to international (one speaker addressed the class from Jerusalem). In one instance, the subject of the week's case study sat in anonymously on the discussion and was later introduced to the class. Students were then able to ask specific questions about the case, and the guest offered the students additional information and advice.

E. Courseware and Review Exercises

Students were required to complete several units of online business courseware asynchronously in the second half of the course. The courseware modules provided basics in business management and were used as background information for corresponding vClass sessions. Review exercises and online quizzes were included in the courseware.

F. Business Game

To add an action-learning element to the course, students played Capsim's Capstone Business Simulation Game throughout. The online game allowed them to learn through application of various areas of business, including strategy, finance, marketing, human resources, and production planning. Students competed in virtual teams with representation from all three schools on each team. Instructors emphasized the competitive aspect of the game to develop student understanding of how competing companies have an impact on each other.

G. Entrepreneur's Toolkit and Other Resources

The students were engaged in online workshops that provided them with hands-on experience in the use of a variety of analytical tools for the purpose of planning and evaluating business ventures. In these sessions the virtual classroom was effectively converted into a virtual computer lab.

III.   THE CLASSROOM

To capture the richness of the traditional classroom experience, the course would need a synchronous component that would allow real-time interaction between students and faculty. The Dr. J. Herbert Smith Centre licensed vClass by Elluminate *Live!* to provide two-way audio, a whiteboard, and a variety of additional tools for this purpose. To enter the classroom, participants performed a one-time download of Java Web Start and then logged in with a supplied user name and password. Figure 1 shows the vClass screen that participants would typically view during a session. Online lectures, workshops, seminars, and discussions were enhanced through the use of the vClass components described below.

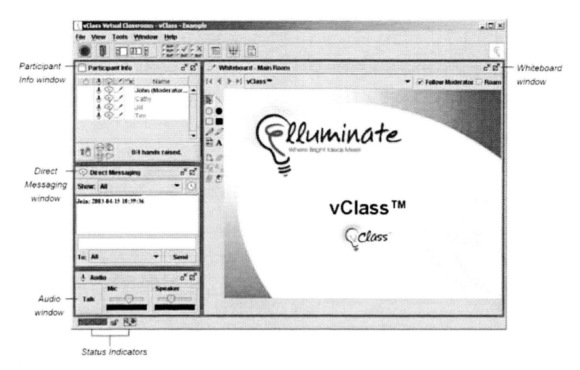

Figure 1. Typical screen view in the virtual classroom

A. Voice over IP (VoIP) Technology

With vClass, the instructors could permit students to speak by assigning them microphone privileges. Students simply had to press the talk button or a hot-key configuration and speak into their computer's microphone. The VoIP technology allowed for two-way audio regardless of the users' connection speeds. In most cases, the instructor would assign a student a microphone when he or she indicated a raised hand; however, all students could be given microphone privileges at the outset if a less formal discussion was desired.

B. Hand Raising

When students had a question or wanted to make a comment, they could click on the Hand Up button. When several students raised their hands, the instructor's view indicated the order in which hands were raised, and questions could be addressed in that (or any) order.

C. Emotion Indicators

Students were able to provide visual feedback to instructors by selecting one of four emotion indicators: laughter ( ), applause ( ), confusion ( ), or disapproval ( ). When a student selected an indicator, instructors saw the icon flash next to the student's name for a short duration. This function gave instructors a general sense of the students' reactions to various situations or questions.

D. Direct Messaging

Students were also able to communicate via the Direct Messaging (chat) function in vClass. Public or private messaging was available, and students could save the contents of a discussion to a text file to review at a later time. If students had problems with their audio components, they would post an alert in the direct messaging window that would draw the attention of the instructor or another student, and the problem could be addressed.

E. Whiteboard

All participants in the virtual classroom were able to view presentations and collaborate on the whiteboard screens. The instructor could make available to students a number of tools (selection, text, rectangle, pen, import image, highlighter, text, and more). In addition, PowerPoint presentations could quickly be converted for display on the whiteboard and loaded in prior to class.

F. Step Away

Participants in a vClass session could excuse themselves from class simply by clicking the Step Away button. They were still connected and could hear the class; however, their name became grayed out on screen, thus indicating that they were away from their computer and unable to respond. This was a useful feature to enable students or instructors to deal with the inevitable distractions that occur at their individual sites.

G. Polling

At any time during a session, the instructor could poll the class using a selection of formats (Yes/No, Multiple-Choice, Class Pace). Students were able to respond to questions by clicking on the response buttons made available on their toolbars by the instructor. The responses became visible to the instructor but were hidden from the student unless revealed (by the instructor).

H. Quizzes

Instructors created multiple choice and short answer quizzes either prior to or during a class session. The quizzes consisted of any number of questions, and results were immediately tabulated as students responded. The instructor had the option to share the quiz results with the class or to keep them hidden.

I. Breakout Rooms

To facilitate small group activities or private team meetings, instructors made use of the Breakout Room feature. These rooms were either created ad hoc or set up formally (for regular team meetings) and had the same features as the main room. Instructors could easily move in and out of breakout rooms or could simply view the content of the whiteboard screens of individual rooms to gauge progress. The whiteboard screens could also be copied and pasted back into the main room for large group discussion.

J. Application Sharing and Web Push

By enabling the Application Sharing feature, instructors could share application(s) that were running on their desktops, allow another participant to control their desktop (e.g., entering information into a spreadsheet), give hosting privileges to other participants thus allowing them to share their applications, and view or control another participant's desktop. Instructors could also launch every participant's browser to a selected website using the Web Push feature.

In addition to the virtual classroom, the course also made use of WebCT to provide course management functions and to act as a homeroom for the class. Links to the courseware, resources, quizzes, and the student directory were accessed through this portal.

IV.   RESULTS OF STUDENT FEEDBACK

As active participants in a pilot project, the students were encouraged to provide both formal and informal feedback to the instructional team throughout the course. Partway through the semester, students submitted a formative evaluation survey that gave them the opportunity to rate various aspects of the course, to provide qualitative feedback about areas that they particularly liked and disliked, and to suggest ways in which their experiences could be improved. Toward the end of the semester, a summative evaluation of the course was conducted in two parts. The students were asked to complete a formal evaluation instrument during the last week of class, and then they participated in a group evaluation workshop during their final vClass session (this was affectionately termed the Bearpit session).

A. Formative Evaluation

It was apparent from this initial survey that the students were enjoying the virtual classroom and the course itself. All of the students who submitted the evaluation survey agreed that they were comfortable using the technology and that the format of the class was engaging their interest. They all agreed that learning through case studies was effective and that the online discussions on the cases and the readings were helpful to them in understanding the concepts. The variety of expertise both within the instructional team and among guest speakers added significantly to the value of the course. Most of the students (76 percent) agreed or strongly agreed that the business game was an effective way to learn the course concepts; the remaining students were neutral on whether it was effective. They also had a number of suggestions for the instructors, their peers, and themselves to help improve learning in the course. Some students expressed concern about the length of the class with respect to attention span, and in the same vein, some requested that the class be made more interactive. Some students felt that one or two people were dominating the online discussions. With this feedback the instructors were able to make adjustments (where feasible) to subsequent sessions and to encourage more participation from certain students and less from others.

B. Informative Feedback

Students were also encouraged to contact the instructors or the course coordinator with concerns. Some students raised questions about the method of assessment for class participation, which was based on the quantity and quality of questions or comments made during online discussions. The instructional team met to discuss the issue and eventually agreed that, although this method was perhaps a tried and true one in a traditional classroom, providing alternative participation mechanisms made good sense in a virtual classroom. Instructors decided to permit students to submit additional comments or questions via email and considered the possibility of creating an asynchronous discussion board. With increasing familiarity and practice in the virtual classroom, however, the students began to participate more, and the other mechanisms were rarely employed.

C. Summative Evaluation

The final evaluation survey looked at the following specific areas: course content and instruction, the vClass technology, specific design elements, a comparison with the traditional classroom, and the achievement of the course objectives. The students were eager to provide this feedback, and the evaluation generated valuable data on the successes and shortcomings of the course.

1. Course Content and Instruction

Students used a Likert scale to rate specific elements of the course from a low (1) to a high (5) rating. The modal values of the responses were used to classify elements into five categories: poor, below average, average, above average, and excellent. Table 1 shows the frequency of the students' ratings for each category. The areas that were highly rated included the relevance and usefulness of the course, the amount learned, the case study approach, and instructor feedback. The effectiveness of the instructional design, the relevance of the course to students' learning goals, and how well the course met expectations were rated as above average. No elements were rated poorly (mode 1 or 2), but the areas rated as average included components of the course that were not necessarily related to the distance aspect (difficulty level and grading schemes, for example). The courseware and accompanying review exercises and quizzes were also rated as average and are consequently under review for improvement. As with any course, some areas require improvement, but overall the students were satisfied with course content.

	Frequency of Response					
	Poor (1)	-Av (2)	Av (3)	+Av (4)	Excell (5)	Mode
Clarity and organization	0	1	7	5	4	3
Relevance and usefulness	0	1	5	4	7	5
Effectiveness of instructional design	1	3	2	6	5	4
Amount you have learned	1	1	5	3	7	5
Fairness of evaluation and grading	2	0	7	3	3	3
Usefulness of assigned readings	1	0	6	8	2	4
Usefulness of case studies	0	0	1	6	10	5
Usefulness of online courseware	3	0	5	5	4	3
Usefulness of review exercises and self-tests	1	0	10	2	2	3
Usefulness of quizzes	1	2	8	4	2	3
Difficulty level of course	0	3	10	3	0	3
Workload in course	0	1	6	7	3	4
Quality and reliability of online support	1	2	6	5	2	3
Instructor feedback	1	1	2	1	12	5
Relevance to learning goals	0	2	2	8	4	4
Content	2	3	2	7	3	4
Quality	1	1	1	8	6	4
Overall rating of course	1	1	3	8	4	4

Table 1. Frequency of ratings for course content and instruction

2. vClass Technology

The students liked the vClass technology and felt that it was an essential component of distance learning in that it added a classroom atmosphere. Table 2 shows the frequency of students' ratings indicating on a scale from 1 to 5 how much they disliked or liked (1=disliked to 5=liked) specific elements of vClass. The participant tools (emotion indicators, hand raising, and polling) were popular features, as was the direct messaging chat tool. Students often used these to add opinions or comments without interrupting the instructor and to chat among themselves prior to class or during breaks. Application sharing was considered a useful tool; however, it was slow to load on some computers. Students generally agreed that the breakout room feature was essential for team meetings and small group interactions. In some instances a perceived lack of leadership prevailed in the rooms; however, with experience and training this problem can easily be reduced. The whiteboard was generally felt to be a helpful feature, although a few students complained about not being able to read the instructor's handwriting (the use of the text tool—a feature not available with a traditional classroom whiteboard—could eliminate this issue). Some students said that it would be beneficial to see a photo of the speaker in order to add a visual aspect that is currently missing. This element could easily be incorporated on the whiteboard, especially for the first few classes, but with large numbers of students it could become too time-consuming and therefore distracting. Although one student commented that the online classroom was impersonal and uncomfortable, most students believed it to be a vital component of distance learning.

	Frequency of Response				
	Disliked...................Liked				
Participant Tools (hand up, emoticons)	-	-	2	7	7
Application Sharing	-	1	8	3	4
Breakout Rooms	1	1	4	3	7
Direct Messaging (Chat Tool)	-	-	2	5	9
Whiteboard	-	-	4	5	7

Table 2. Frequency of ratings for vClass elements

3. Specific Design Elements

Students gave valuable qualitative feedback regarding specific elements of the course design. For example, teams were intentionally formed with a mixture of schools represented on each, and for the most part the students believed this to be a wise decision. The diversity of perspectives from students in different schools and the avoidance of school-on-school competition were indicated as positives to this approach. However, a few students said that they were not able to get to know their teammates as well in this way and that the lone student from one school (i.e., when the other group members were from the same school) was at a disadvantage. The involvement of faculty from each school in the instructional team was also positively received. Students cited the variety of experience represented by the instructors ("the whole being better than the sum of its parts") and the availability of an instructor on each campus for face-to-face consultation as important benefits. Incorporating the business game to reinforce concepts and to motivate through competition was considered effective, although it increased the workload in the course significantly. The game added excitement to the course and incentive for improving between rounds. A couple of students disliked the competitive nature of the game, and some believed that having virtual teams was a drawback (see above). When asked to comment on the blend of asynchronous components (courseware and readings) and the online sessions, students indicated that the blended learning aspect allowed them to expand on a topic at their own pace and to the extent desired. Some thought that it was difficult to keep up with the readings and that the organization of the various components of the course could be improved through the use of a course calendar within WebCT.

4. Comparison to Traditional Classroom

Students were asked to rate and comment on various aspects of the learning experience in comparison to those in a traditional classroom setting. They marked their preferences on a scale from 1 to 5 (1=preference for traditional classroom, 5=preference for vClass) as shown in Table 3. The results indicated that for none of the items included in the question did more students prefer the traditional classroom. Areas in which the vClass option was clearly preferred included the quality and diversity of guest speakers and, interestingly, case study discussions. In an online class, no geographic limitations (other than the limitations of Internet service) restrict the options for selection of guest speakers. Students commented that they felt more confident in their preparation for class because the materials were easily accessible. They felt less inhibited about contributing because they were not seen during the discussions, and they gave more attention to asking relevant questions. Also interesting were the elements that appeared to be unaffected by the delivery venue: participation, interaction with instructors, and attentiveness. Students who participated regularly in traditional classrooms also participated regularly in the online classroom, and students who were hesitant to raise their hand in person were hesitant to click the Hand Up button online. Students were able to get up and move around without interfering with instruction, which was believed to increase overall attentiveness in class as long as other distractions (e.g., telephone, email) were intentionally kept to a minimum. With respect to group dynamics, appeal to learning styles, spontaneity in class, feedback from instructors, and teamwork/team building, group preferences for traditional or virtual classrooms split about equally.

	Frequency of Response Traditional..........vClass				
	(1)	**(2)**	**(3)**	**(4)**	**(5)**
Group dynamics	4	3	3	5	2
Spontaneity in class	3	4	3	4	3
Degree of attentiveness	2	3	6	3	3
Appeal to learning style	2	5	2	6	2
Interaction with instructors	-	4	7	5	1
Feedback from instructors	-	5	5	5	2
Teamwork/team building	3	3	3	5	3
Diversity of guest speakers	-	-	-	2	15
Quality of guest speakers	-	-	-	3	14
Case study discussions	-	-	4	10	3
Participation in class	1	2	9	4	1

Table 3. Frequency of ratings for traditional versus virtual classroom preferences

When asked if there was a net gain or loss in offering the course in this format, the majority (12 of the 17 respondents, or 71 percent) of the students polled indicated that there was a net gain. The online format allowed tapping into more resources, thus creating an overall richer experience. The convenience and flexibility of the course appealed to many of the students and will allow more people to take it in the future. Three students did not respond to this question, indicating that it was difficult to answer without having taken the same course in a regular classroom. Two of the students in the pilot project clearly preferred learning in a traditional environment, indicating that it was difficult to sit and listen to the computer for extended periods of time without any face-to-face contact, and that no group dynamics were developed in this venue.

5. Achievement of Objectives

Students were asked to indicate whether they felt that specific primary objectives of the course were achieved and to add comments or recommendations. Table 4 shows for each objective the number of students who indicated that the objective was achieved, partially achieved, or not achieved. Fifteen students believed that the objective to stimulate entrepreneurial behavior in students was achieved or partially achieved. They commented that the case studies and the selection of guest speakers sparked their interest and that the Capstone game provided valuable experience. Some students thought that, although they learned a lot about business and entrepreneurship, they were not interested in being or ready to be entrepreneurs. One student indicated that not much was learned about actually starting a business. Fifteen students thought that the business literacy of engineering students was achieved or partially achieved, indicating that the course was very effective in teaching and demonstrating the main components of business management and the "language of business." The Capstone game especially helped in understanding the business spreadsheets that were introduced in the course. Students indicated that the tools used throughout the course for this objective were appropriate and relevant. Fifteen students indicated at least partial achievement of the objective to develop a holistic model in which students are motivated to learn the course concepts. They felt that the course concepts, the case studies, and the game tied together well and that the competition in the game especially added incentive and motivation. Sixteen believed that the technology was used successfully to leverage the intellectual assets of the three universities. They indicated that the synergy of the combined teaching resources was immensely beneficial to the course. The same sixteen students also thought that networking of faculty and students was enhanced to some extent by offering the course in this blended format across campuses. They had the opportunity to work with people from a variety of backgrounds and learning environments that they otherwise never would have known.

Objective	Frequency of Responses		
	Achieved	Partially Achieved	Not Achieved
To stimulate entrepreneurial behavior of students	6	9	2
To enhance business literacy of engineering students	12	3	2
To develop a holistic model where students are highly motivated to learn course concepts	8	7	2
To use technology to leverage intellectual assets of participating universities	12	4	1
To enhance networking of faculty and students	9	7	1

Table 4. Student Opinions on Achievement of Course Objectives

D. The Bearpit Session

To give participants the opportunity to reflect and offer feedback on their experiences and to identify the most important positive and negative elements of the program, students and instructors were asked to come to the last online session having given thought to the following three questions:

- When this program is offered again, what elements should remain essentially the same because they worked so well?
- What elements should be dropped or altered?
- What elements should be added?

Students were divided into groups and sent to breakout rooms to discuss individual responses to the three questions and to arrive at a consensus of the three most important elements for each. This nominal group activity generated a number of recommendations.

The elements of the course that the students agreed should be kept the same were the diversity of guest speakers and instructors, the Capstone Game, the use of case studies, and the group activities in vClass.

Students agreed that the quizzes and review exercises in the courseware required some editing to achieve congruence with the course content. The length of the online class sessions was another area of common concern. It was suggested that the online environment would be more conducive to two shorter classes per week and that longer lecture topics could be broken up into several components. The construction of the teams was debated throughout the course, and in this session the students recommended that in the future either teams should consist of students all from one school or the schools should be equally represented on each team.

The students had several noteworthy suggestions as to what elements could be added to the course. As indicated previously, some students thought that a visual component would be helpful in the online sessions (e.g., video, photos). They also agreed that the course would benefit from having a smaller, specialized project associated with it. A product concept or idea generation component, for example, could be incorporated. Alternatively, it was suggested that a second course could be created that would take the concepts learned and allow students to apply them in an entrepreneurial venture. Ideas for additional topics or speakers included more emphasis on entrepreneurship over management and some practical topics such as accounting, tax planning, bookkeeping, and so forth. Adding a stock market component to the business game was suggested, as was the idea of incorporating an individual assignment of writing the Capstone stockholder's debrief/report.

V. DISCUSSION

The learning technologies employed in this pilot project facilitated the blending of a variety of learning resources and pedagogies. The engagement of five faculty from three different universities, each bringing a particular expertise to the virtual classroom discussions, created a synergy that undoubtedly enhanced the educational experience for the students. The opportunity to bring world-class guest speakers to the classroom in a convenient and affordable way was certainly one of the greatest benefits of delivering a course in this fashion.

Student satisfaction in the course is evident in the feedback results. This may in part be because the design of the course included strategies consistent with Keller's [5] motivational ARCS model. In this model, four conditions have to be met (attention, relevance, confidence, and satisfaction) for people to become and remain motivated in a course. Attention strategies such as variety in the instructional team and format of instruction, shifts between student-instructor and student-student interaction, content-related case studies, problem-solving activities, and the online business simulation game produced high levels of motivation among most students to learn critical course concepts. The use of polling to get students to take a position on issues discussed in class was effective in enhancing the interactivity of sessions. The use of case studies and guest speakers was an effective relevance strategy. Providing self-evaluation options and regular feedback fostered the development of confidence in the students as they progressed through the course. Finally, putting their knowledge to work in the business simulation game and the business plan was an effective satisfaction strategy.

As expected, the pilot project also produced some challenges and opportunities for improvement. Four students decided to drop the course, each giving course workload as their reason for not continuing. Although discomfort with the learning environment was not expressed, the students may have experienced dissatisfaction that could have contributed to their decision. In addition, the concept of establishing virtual teams of students across the three universities worked successfully in some cases and was not effective in others. Faculty concluded that this element should be used again; however, greater attention should be given to coaching students on techniques for developing high-performance teams in a virtual environment. The pace of verbal communications is somewhat slower and less fluid in the virtual classroom. As a consequence, it took longer than in the physical classroom to complete certain types of learning activities, such as case study discussions. In many sessions, planned instruction had to be eliminated because of insufficient time to cover all material.

Notwithstanding the above observations, the participating faculty strongly agreed that the project broke new ground in the delivery of entrepreneurship education. As expected, certain benefits arising from face-to-face engagement between faculty and students in a physical classroom simply cannot be replicated in the virtual environment. The lack of measurement of student performance and success limits the applications of this study, although the general consensus is that the learning technologies used created net gains in the educational experience that could not have been achieved in the physical classroom. Because this particular course is offered in three delivery formats—traditional classroom, asynchronous online, and the new blended approach—the potential for future research in measuring and comparing the results of student achievement in the three environments is great.

VI.   REFERENCES

1. **Swan, K.** Building communities in online courses: The importance of interaction. *Education, Communication and Information* 2 (1): 2002.
2. **Singh, H. and C. Reed**. A white paper: Achieving success with blended learning. Lexington, MA: Centra Software, 2001.
3. **Shea, P., M. Pickett, and W. Pelz**. A follow-up investigation of "teaching presence" in the SUNY Learning Network. *Journal of Asynchronous Learning Networks* 7 (2): July 2003.
4. **Jiang, M. and E. Ting**. A study of factors influencing students' perceived learning in a Web-based course environment. *International Journal of Educational Telecommunications* 6 (4): 317–228, 2000.
5. **Keller, J. M.** Development and use of the ARCS model of instructional design. *Journal of Instructional Development* 10 (3): 2–10, 1987.

VII.   ABOUT THE AUTHORS

Barry G. Bisson is a professor in the Faculty of Engineering at the University of New Brunswick. He holds the Dr. J. Herbert Smith/ACOA Chair in Technology Management and Entrepreneurship (TME), a business and entrepreneurship program for engineers and others with an interest and/or background in technology. In addition to administering the Dr. J. Herbert Smith Centre, Barry teaches four courses in the TME Program: Technological Creativity and Innovation, Technological Risk and Opportunity, Business Planning and Strategy in an Entrepreneurial Environment, and Entrepreneurial Finance. Barry is also the Program Director of the UNB Shad Valley Program (a program focused on science, technology and entrepreneurship for gifted high school students) and is a member of the Board of Directors of Shad International; the New Brunswick Training Group, Inc.; and the Board of Governors of the University of New Brunswick. He serves as a mentor to a number of young entrepreneurs. He has also been a Big Brother since 1993. Email bisson@unb.ca.

Edward Leach is a pracademic and lecturer in the Faculty of Management at Dalhousie University and is currently ABD in the Computing Technology in Education doctoral program. His entrepreneurial experience includes being president and owner of a significant industrial distribution business service; president of Independent Specialists, Inc. (ISI), a national buying group; and chapter chairman of the Atlantic Canada Chapter of the Young Presidents Organization. Consulting projects have included curriculum development for a national anti-poverty demonstration project; subject matter expert for an online course in small business; development of a business plan for a telemedicine business, and mentoring of the lead entrepreneur for a quick capture system for navigable images. Email eleach@mgmt.dal.ca.

Timothy Little is an associate professor in the Faculty of Electrical and Computer Engineering at Dalhousie University in Halifax, Nova Scotia. He teaches both graduate and undergraduate students in a wide variety of courses covering topics including electric machines, power systems, instrumentation, controls and design. Tim conducts research in alternative energy systems including wind, solar, wave, and fuel cell energy systems. He has also conducted creativity enhancement seminars for the Department of Electrical and Computer Engineering, the School of Business, the School of Management, and the Young Entrepreneurs Conference held in Halifax in 1999. Email tlittle@dal.ca.

Robert Richards was appointed Chair in Youth-Focused Technological Entrepreneurship at Memorial University of Newfoundland in September 1999. He is president, director, and co-founder of Richards and Pinsent Associates, an education consulting firm. He is also president, CEO, and co-founder of Genesis Organic, Inc., an innovative company that recycles wood bark and fish waste into organic compost. Dr. Richards has an international reputation as a presenter and motivational speaker specializing in education, entrepreneurship, and the human issues arising from technology and change. He has served on a variety of boards and committees. Currently, he is a member of the Board of Governors for the Atlantic Provinces Economic Council. He is a member of the Admissions Board for the Genesis Center at Memorial University and a Steering Committee member of the Strategic Plan for Marine Biotechnology in Newfoundland and Labrador. Email rrichards@mun.ca.

Brian Veitch is a graduate of Memorial's undergraduate co-op engineering program (1988) and has a Masters of Engineering degree (1990). He obtained both a Licentiate of Science in Technology degree (1993) and a Doctor of Science in Technology degree (1995) from Helsinki University of Technology. He joined the Faculty of Engineering and Applied Science in 1998 and is currently an Associate Professor in the Ocean and Naval Architectural Engineering discipline, holds the Terra Nova Project Junior Research Chair in Ocean Environmental Risk Engineering, and is the present Director of the Ocean Engineering Research Centre. Brian is an active researcher and works on a range of applied research projects including offshore and marine safety, marine propellers, and ocean environmental risk. He is also involved in several professional associations, including the Royal Institution of Naval Architects and the Society of Naval Architects and Marine Engineers. Email bveitch@mun.ca.

Karin E. Zundel is the Program/Quality Coordinator at the Dr. J. Herbert Smith Centre, Faculty of Engineering, University of New Brunswick. Karin oversees all aspects of the centre's Quality Management System and diploma program administration. Prior to joining the centre, Karin developed expertise in the areas of adult education and instructional design in both the public and private sectors. She first worked in conjunction with the centre in 1996 to develop and pilot an entrepreneurial program for youth with a background in environmental studies. Karin received her B.Ed. in 1986 and her B.Sc. in 1983 from the University of Toronto, and is currently working toward her M.Ed. in Instructional Design at the University of New Brunswick. Email kzundel@unb.ca

ENGAGEMENT IN ONLINE LEARNING COMMUNITIES

Albert L. Ingram, Ph. D.
Kent State University

- We need common understanding of the terms *engagement* and *learning communities.*

- Engagement includes:

    o Deep *attention* to the learning tasks and activities at hand.

    o *Activation of effective cognitive processes* that improve both performance in the tasks and learning.

    o Usually, a *social context*, especially in collaboration and collaborative learning activities.

- True collaboration is probably a fundamental part of building an effective community of practice or learning community.

I. INTRODUCTION

Two terms are becoming widespread in discussions of online learning: engagement and learning communities. The terms are used in many other contexts as well but seem to be especially prevalent in the current environment for developing and improving online courses. What is lacking are common and precise understandings of what these terms mean, how we can measure and study them, what their effects are on things such as learning, and what the relationship is between them. This paper takes a look at those issues.

A. Engagement

Engagement is thought to be a key variable for enabling and encouraging learners to interact with the material, with the instructor, and with one another, as well as for learning [1]. What does engagement mean? Does it refer to attention to an activity, time on task, motivation (especially intrinsic motivation), or some combination of these concepts? Is it related to Csikszentmihalyi's [2] idea of flow? Is engagement just a trendy word to refer to longer-standing ideas, or is it an important concept on its own? We can create a more focused concept.

In some formulations, engagement appears to mean simply that students pay close attention to and are engrossed in a task. This meaning is clearly an important part of the construct, but it can be argued that we already have concepts to describe the state of deep attention and that adding the term "engagement" does not help. Other usages include attention but also discuss the use of "active" cognitive processes [3]. Other authors suggest that engagement occurs only in a social context, and they therefore stress service learning, collaborative learning, and other social learning situations.

Is engagement important to and effective in promoting learning? Certainly we know that some of the proposed elements of engagement are vital for learning. In most cases what we pay attention to determines what we learn, and the kinds of cognitive processes we use while encoding information certainly determine what we learn and can later retrieve. However, the descriptions we have from many writers on the efficacy of engagement for learning suggest that they believe that the concept goes far beyond such mundane processes as simply paying attention to the material, processing it, and being motivated to learn. Engaged learners are, according to some, doing more than those basic processes, as they become deeply involved in the subject matter and their learning. What do learners do when they are engaged? How do we know? These questions are not well researched. Instead, we find that the answers are usually assumed, and researchers discuss the implications of those assumptions.

Some authors appear to have a very simplistic definition of engagement which has little to do with the deep learning that engagement suggests. One paper measured engagement in an online discussion as simply the self-reported frequency with which participants logged into the course website [4]. Another merely tracked the amount of time students spent on the web pages available for the course in question [5]. These simplistic views present problems because participation in a discussion or looking at a page of instructional materials (if indeed the students spends that time even reading the page) is not sufficient to tell us much of anything about the discussion, whether the student is engaged in learning, or whether he or she is learning anything. For example, Hathorn and Ingram [6, 7] show that participation alone cannot tell us whether learners are collaborating. The same is likely true of other specific learning situations, whether online or not.

More complex definitions and measurements of engagement are needed. One approach is suggested by Ormrod [8], when she talks of cognitive engagement, which she defines as the activation of effective learning strategies and cognitive processes while doing a task. Such activation is a consequence of high motivation, according to Ormrod. Thus, in this view, motivation may lead to engagement but is not part of it. This approach is more helpful but not easily measured. There is little doubt that when people use a variety of effective cognitive processes, they are more likely to learn well. This would appear to be related to Laurel's definition of engagement in her discussion of theater as a useful metaphor [9]. In her view, engagement occurs when we completely immerse ourselves in some new representation of reality. In a variety of settings, such complete immersion is frequently a goal of personal and educational activities.

B. Multi-faceted Concept

The definition proposed here assumes that engagement is a multi-faceted concept. It requires several elements and will consequently be difficult to measure, but it seems to capture what many writers mean by the concept, and it may have important consequences. Finally, it may be possible to measure it, leading to the further possibility of useful research. I define engagement as consisting of three important things:

- Deep *attention* to the learning tasks and activities at hand.

- *Activation of effective cognitive processes* that improve both performance in the tasks and learning.

- Usually, a *social context*, especially in collaboration and collaborative learning activities. There may be exceptions to this last component, but it is most common. It may be that the social aspects of engagement help define a subset of engagement, called *interactive engagement* (http://serc.carleton.edu/introgeo/models/IntEng.html).

1. Attention

Attention clearly must be a part of engagement. Attention is the limited capacity we all have to devote cognitive resources to particular tasks. The more attention we devote to a learning task, the more likely we are to learn the material [8]. Without paying deep attention to the situation, a student cannot be said to be engaged. At the same time, most writers who mention engagement appear to mean more than just that students are paying attention. Attention has always been important for learning, but engagement seems to imply something more. The concept of flow [2], which implies a deep attention to an activity almost to the exclusion of other concerns, does not seem synonymous with engagement either. It should probably be reserved for those more extreme situations where people lose themselves in the activity.

2. Effective Cognitive Processes

The second component of the present definition of engagement has to do with using effective cognitive processes. Cognitive processing, by its nature, is active. The important distinction is between effective processes and ineffective ones. Effective processes are those which help the individual solve problems, learn the material, and accomplish other cognitive goals. These processes can be entirely internal or involve overt actions and interactions with other people.

The definition of engagement proposed here includes such processes. It is possible for students to pay attention and yet use such basic processes as maintenance rehearsal (repeating something over and over). Repetition is certainly active, but it is unlikely to be very effective. Computer games are often spoken of as engaging the players, but the low-level "twitch" games may not activate the kinds of cognitive processing that are being discussed here. Hence, they are not engaging in our sense.

Instructors can critically affect student engagement by providing the learners with tasks that encourage or even require more effective processing. It is also possible that learning communities provide a way to promote better processing among students.

Some specific effective cognitive processes include:

Activating prior knowledge: As the influential educational psychologist David Ausubel [10] noted, the most important factor that determines how much we can learn is how much (and what) we already know. It is important, however, that the prior knowledge be activated and in working memory in order for it to help us learn the new material. By this definition, engaged students may connect what they are learning now to things that they already know. They also may compare, question, and evaluate.

Elaboration: Rote memory, or memorization, is an ineffective way to learn new material, although it is a widely used strategy among students. A good alternative is to *elaborate* on the material being learned. This process involves such things as making new examples, drawing conclusions, and various other methods for making the new material one's own. This qualifies as an effective strategy as part of engagement.

Monitoring comprehension: Good learners use a variety of self-regulation strategies to control, guide, and improve their own learning. One important strategy is monitoring their own comprehension. They can do this in a variety of ways, such as self-questioning, taking practice tests, and trying out ideas with other people. Students who use such strategies regularly are more engaged than those who do not.

Organization: Random, unconnected facts are very difficult for most people to remember. A better strategy is to organize information. Organization is the rationale behind such learning techniques as concept mapping, timelines, outlining, and a variety of others. Learners who seek out and use their own organization of new material are displaying a higher level of engagement, according to this definition.

Visual imagery: People are remarkably good at remembering visuals of all kinds. By using visual imagery as a learning strategy, engaged learners may actively create and use images to help remember.

Enactment: Enactment is a learning strategy whereby students perform actions that are analogous to what is being learned. Instances of enactment include a geometry student drawing triangles while proving theorems, a computer scientist drawing a flowchart of a process, or a cross-country runner going over her strategy on a map of the course [8].

There are two key points about the cognitive processes and strategies listed here. First, the ones discussed are only a sample of those that are used frequently by learners at all levels. Second, the definition of engagement proposed here does not require that individuals use any specific cognitive processes or strategies, just that they use some effective ones.

3. Social Process

Social process is the third component of engagement. Many writers treat engagement as primarily a social process, as in community engagement projects and other activities. Many emphasize the importance of collaborative and cooperative learning in engagement. Conrad and Donaldson [11] define engagement as an interaction between student and instructor; others emphasize student to student interactions. Others make it clear that they believe that engagement can occur in an individual learning situation. Here I posit that engagement is commonly found in collaborative and cooperative learning situations more often than in individual ones. As noted, it may also be possible to define a subset of engagement specifically as *interactive engagement*, based on whether this social context is present.

Therefore, a reasonable view of engagement defines the concept in terms of the extent to which learners pay attention to the tasks, use effective cognitive processes, and interact with other people. In this view, engagement is almost synonymous with good learning. This definition does not yet guarantee that engagement is different from other constructs, but it is a step in that direction. This definition allows us to test some of the myriad assumptions made about engagement and its effects. Still missing from this formulation is the question of how to measure the extent to which students are engaged in any particular learning task. With so many different kinds of cognitive processes contributing to engagement, it may be difficult to find ways to define engagement operationally.

II.   LEARNING COMMUNITIES

The other widely used term examined here is *learning community*. With the current emphasis by many theorists on social constructivism, it comes as no surprise that more and more emphasis is being placed on group learning as found in cooperative learning, collaboration and collaborative learning, and, now, learning communities. Learning communities are frequently seen as the apotheosis of learning, where all members are involved in mutual explorations of deep and important content.

A. Definitions of Learning Communities

Many writers discuss learning communities without spending much time defining exactly what they mean by the term. Does it refer to any group of people working and, perhaps, learning together? Can it only be defined subjectively, as a feeling of "community" connecting the members? Are there more objective ways of defining what a community is and whether they have been successfully created? Most teachers know that classes do not always gel into learning communities, even when that is an explicit goal. Even when they believe that such a community has developed, they may be hard-pressed to say why they think so or how they attained that state. They also know that they cannot always count on every participant being a full member of the community.

Often when they start an inquiry such as this, they begin by citing a dictionary definition. Dictionary.com shows a few related definitions at http://dictionary.reference.com/search?q=community:

- A group of people living in the same locality and under the same government.

- A group of people having common interests: the scientific community; the international business community.

- Similarity or identity: a community of interests.

- Sharing, participation, and fellowship.

Students in a class often have common interests, and, in higher education, are often seeking to become a member of a larger community. A starting point is that a learning community would have people with a set of common interests (often evidenced by the fact that they are taking a common course or program of study) who participate and share their knowledge.

Various disciplines have tried to define communities with a view toward doing research on them. With the advent of online communications, this effort has taken on new meaning, since there is no longer a geographic component to the definitions. For example, Cherny [12] reviews some of the definitions of community given by sociologists and anthropologists in her discussion of communities in MUDs (Multi-User Dungeons) noting, "There has been an astounding lack of consensus in the social science literature about just what is meant by the word 'community'" [12]. Various definitions do find a little common ground in the notion of interactions among people, in the importance of communications, and in shared language properties, while others talk about common goals and cooperation and setting boundaries.

Going beyond the basic dictionary definitions, some writers delineate important features of learning communities more specifically. Currently many educators seem to be looking to Wenger's [13, 14] ideas about "communities of practice" as a model for learning communities. In his initial book on communities of practice [13] Wenger lists three key elements: joint enterprise, shared repertoire, and mutual engagement. These, he says constitute the "practice" part of the community of practice and in doing so enable the community to cohere.

In a more recent book, Wenger, McDermott, and Snyder maintain that communities of practice "are groups of people who share a concern, a set of problems, or a passion about a topic, and who deepen their knowledge and expertise in this area by interacting on an ongoing basis" [14]. According to these authors, communities of practice share a structure that is a domain of knowledge to define the issues, a community of people who care about the domain, and the shared practice within the domain that they are developing together. The community portion of this formulation refers to the social aspects of the group: "It is a group of people who interact, learn together, build relationships, and in the process develop a sense of belonging and mutual commitment." [14]. It is important to recognize that members no longer have to be located in the same place for a community to develop. It is also clear that these communities of practice are learning communities, as well, since learning is a key part of the definition for Wenger. The relationship between these communities in organizations and learning communities that may (or may not) come together in a classroom or online for a semester is not clear. Does the time-limited nature of such educational communities change their character in significant ways? Or is an implication that the idea of communities of practice should be to restructure education to take advantage of the deeper and longer-term nature of this kind of community?

Ormrod [8] identifies key concepts when she lists the following as features of learning communities in educational settings:

- All students are active participants

- Discussion and collaboration are common and key

- Diversity in student interests and progress is expected and respected

- Students and teachers coordinate in helping one another learn; no one has exclusive responsibility for teaching others

- Everyone is potential resource for others; different individuals serve as resources for different topics and tasks

- The teacher provides guidance and direction for activities, but students contribute, too.
- Constructive questioning and critiquing of one another's work is practiced
- Process is emphasized as much as product [8].

So we have a variety of formulations of the concept of *community* in general and of *learning community* in particular. Although social scientists have had a great deal of difficulty reaching consensus on it, we have several specific definitions that appear highly relevant. These include the idea of communities of practice as, in part, learning communities. One point that more and more people are agreeing on is that communities can exist online as well in person.

B. What Makes an Online Learning Community?

If we know what learning communities are, we still have the questions of what makes an online learning community and what is similar and different between face-to-face communities and online ones. A key question would seem to be whether the social aspects of communities are the same in both cases. This is not the same as asking whether online communities are "as good as" face-to-face ones. Instead, it is likely that each venue has its own strengths and weaknesses.

Palloff and Pratt [15] discuss communities as dynamic wholes in which a variety of shared experiences and activities may take place. A learning community, for them, comes about at the intersection of teamwork, collaborative learning, mutual commitment, and the active construction of meaning and knowledge.

We can provide ways for students to work together online by sharing files, for example. Students can also question one another and discuss issues from the material readily in asynchronous discussion boards or synchronous chat rooms. In fact, all of Ormrod's [8] criteria are at least theoretically possible online. The question is whether learning communities are more difficult to establish and maintain online than they are face-to-face. Can online technologies provide the same immediacy of experience and interpersonal interactions?

Online interactions also have many advantages over face-to-face discussions that can actually be more facilitative of the development of community. These include that it is easier to base the status of participants on the level and quality of their participation and interaction than on more superficial characteristics such as race, gender, and others. Asynchronous discussions are also independent of time and space, so that people can participate when, where, and how they prefer.

III.   MEASUREMENT

One way to ensure that we have good definitions of concepts is to find ways of measuring them. This can be done either as a way of establishing the presence or absence of the construct or, more likely, of quantifying the extent to which the construct exists in a specific situation. Either way, the goal of establishing an operational definition of key constructs is a worthy one too often neglected in educational research. I do not denigrate the value of qualitative research in identifying good research questions and establishing the basic outlines of the answers. But it is also important and useful to harness the power and precision of quantitative research in studying specific questions, especially if we can get more detailed and reliable answers before the field has moved on to the next "latest thing." In the case of the two most important concepts here—engagement and learning communities—it is clear that both are multidimensional. This means that measuring them will require a variety of means.

A. Measuring Engagement

In exploring how we might measure engagement, we need to look for how we might know the extent to which a variety of the learners' cognitive processes have been activated. Such measures might include subjective measures where students report the extent to which they felt engaged. Objective measures are more difficult. Harris, Bolander, Lebrun, Docq, and Bouvy [16] point out that indicators of academic engagement might include cognitive, affective, conative, and relational factors. These are similar to the suggested definition here, which would require us to look for attention, activation of cognition, and social processes. The National Survey of Student Engagement (http://www.indiana.edu/~nsse/) takes a very different tack, concentrating on overall institutional characteristics and the actions of students within them.

In general, I would like to see an instrument and/or a procedure that would help us capture some of the essence of engagement. This would include a measurement of attention, preferably as a continuum, not just an on-or-off measure as well as the length of time the attention has been sustained. In addition, there would be some measurement of what learners were doing cognitively during that time. In social situations, transcripts of discussions may show us that. For other settings, perhaps self-reports, taken after or even during a task, might work.

B. Measuring Learning Communities

Measuring the extent to which a learning community has been developed can be equally tricky. Is the community defined primarily by the feeling of community that members have? This is the approach taken by Rovai [17, 18] in his Sense of Classroom Community Index (SCCI). He has validated his instrument as a useful way to measure the subjective elements of a community. Alternatively, one can measure the types of variables mentioned in some of the definitions of community, such as active participation by all the members, extensive discussion and interaction among group members, and shared responsibility for learning. In examining online learning communities, researchers may have some distinct advantages, given that so much of the communications take place through text, which can be archived and analyzed.

IV. BUILDING ENGAGEMENT IN A LEARNING COMMUNITY

Assuming that we can define and identify both engagement and learning communities, how then do we proceed? Two key issues are how to engage learners and build a sense of community. If I am right about the importance of effective cognitive processing in engagement, then a key issue is how to make that happen within a group context. Today, a key means for this is to stress collaborative learning.

Hathorn and Ingram [6] distinguish between cooperation and collaboration, stating that cooperation is more a "divide-and-conquer" strategy in which individuals work separately on different parts of a project. As such, it appears less well-suited to community building than does truly collaborative work, in which the group is interdependent and works to create a product that is a synthesis of diverse views and contributions. True collaboration is probably a fundamental part of building an effective community of practice or learning community. Hathorn and Ingram [19] discuss a variety of ways to encourage online collaboration.

In his book *Design for Community*, Powazek [20] provides a wealth of suggestions for creating online environments that are conducive to good communities of all types. These include the very basic dictum that "content is king." Clearly in learning communities, good learning will take place only when the focus is on the content and process of the learning, not on superficial aspects of the layout or interface. Beyond that, he notes the importance of choosing technologies, setting policies, and specific procedures for keeping things going.

V. NEEDED RESEARCH

If online learning communities are as important as many theorists maintain, then they deserve serious research. We have a variety of case studies of different learning communities, but the detailed research that is needed has only just begun. If we can find and create good ways of measuring engagement and learning communities, then we are in a better position to do the research needed to understand how both of them work and interact.

A. Characteristics and Correlates of Learning Communities

What are learning communities really all about? In online learning situations we can potentially measure a variety of variables. What we don't know yet is which of them are related to the development of a learning community. For example, we can use web server logs to get very precise information about how students use an educational website, such as which pages they visit, how long they stay there, what paths they pursue through a site, when they access the site (days of the week, times, and other information) [21]. Turning to the information available from online asynchronous discussions, we can easily find out how many postings each student makes, how long they are, and other overall measurements. We can also do content analyses of the discussions, which are likely a more valid and accurate indication of actual levels of collaboration [6, 7] and community behaviors. The web makes it easy to gather small and frequent surveys of student attitudes or larger and infrequent (but more information-rich) questionnaires.

The point is that almost any of these variables could be related to the development of effective learning communities. They may also be related to engagement in such communities. If we develop ways of identifying and measuring the key variables of engagement and community, then such research becomes possible. The follow-up research will be to identify the locus and direction of causation in the relationships.

B. Factors Affecting the Development of Learning Communities

How do learning communities develop? Does the process work differently face-to-face and online? As we aim to establish online learning communities and reap their benefits, we need to know what works and what doesn't. We do know that not every attempt to develop a functioning learning community in a course is successful. We also know that just proclaiming a community's existence does not ensure that it occurs. So what can an instructor do to increase the likelihood that a class will develop the feelings, the behaviors, and whatever else it takes to make the community a success?

C. Effects of Engagement in Learning Communities on Learning and Achievement

If learning communities are as effective as their proponents claim, then we should be able to see improved learning as a result. One potential barrier, after we understand how to define the initial concepts, is how to measure learning. This is something we might have once taken for granted, but the rise of constructivist philosophies of learning and education has led to central questions about how to assess what students have learned. Constructivists are likely to distrust the use of standardized tests. More traditional approaches to educational measurement usually stress assessments that are both valid and reliable, which are likely to be difficult to apply to newer constructivist assessments. At the same time, it can be difficult to document the learning of individuals if all the projects are cooperative or collaborative.

D. Effects of Learning Communities on Social and Affective Variables

Many of the claimed benefits of learning communities go beyond the cognitive learning that is the target of most educational systems. Traditional cognitive learning gains are not the only benefits claimed for learning communities. Various writers suggest that students also learn social skills and interactive skills, and improve their attitudes toward the instruction and the institutions. We need research that addresses what those gains are, what factors affect them, and how they can be produced reliably. Thus the basic question becomes joining a learning community results in greater engagement in learning tasks.

VI. SOFTWARE TO SUPPORT AND ENCOURAGE ONLINE LEARNING COMMUNITIES

Successful learning communities have been reported to use all sorts of software, from simple threaded asynchronous discussion boards to complex systems designed specifically to encourage community, feeling, and collaboration. Even so, it seems clear that some software will be better at encouraging the development of good communities than others. What are the characteristics of such software? They include:

- Multiple communications media (text, graphics, animation, audio, video, etc.).

- Synchronous communications (instant messaging, chat, voice, video).

- Asynchronous communications (email, listservs, discussion boards).

- Presence awareness. The knowledge of who else is online and capable of communicating at any specific time.

- File sharing. The ability to transfer files among group members.

- Co-editing. The ability to work simultaneously on a document, probably while communicating synchronously.

- Tools to support ways that people like to work (and that support engaged learning). These could be such things as outliners or drawing tools that allow people to work on more than just textual materials. Some tools may be specialized to specific professions. One useful tool in education may be one that encourages collaborative concept mapping or pre-writing strategies.

- Subjective feelings of being in an exclusive "space" with other community members.

An endless line of companies offer various systems to enable and encourage collaboration that are sometimes also sold as ways to encourage community. Here I discuss a few of the basic approaches to the problem of providing Internet software to support the development of online learning communities. I assume that most people are now familiar with basic threaded asynchronous discussion boards, so I look at a few ways to go beyond that technology.

1. Blogs and Wikis

Blogs (Weblogs) create a personalized communications channel to a group of people interested in the same topics. Sometimes the groups are very small; sometimes they may be quite large, as with a political or technology-related blog. Frequently, the blogging software provides ways that others can reply to the messages from the original blogger. At this point, the blog can become the focus of the community.

Wikis enable groups of people to work collaboratively on online documents. Many proponents of Wikis extol the communities that can develop as individuals, perhaps distributed around the country or the world, collaborate on creating the content stored in the software.

2. Sharepoint and Other Web-based Systems

The most common way to create spaces for learning communities uses the World Wide Web. In theory these sites could be as simple as some static pages with a simple discussion board, but in the last few years a variety of companies have developed complex systems that provide a variety of tools for collaboration and community building.

One such system is Microsoft's SharePoint Team Services. This system provides such basic tools as a threaded discussion board, a place to store and share files, a calendar, and others. As a web-based service, SharePoint is available through an up-to-date version of Internet Explorer anywhere that the user can access the Internet. But it can seem sluggish, and by itself it offers no synchronous communications or presence awareness features. Other systems may use Java applets or other means to add these features.

3. Groove

Groove (www.groove.net) exemplifies a peer-to-peer approach to the problem of collaboration and community. In Groove an instructor can set up a class space, with a variety of tools for the students to use. There are synchronous communications (text and audio) facilities, a threaded discussion board, easy file sharing that displays the date, time, and originator of the most recent changes in files, co-editing capabilities (wherein two or more people work on a document together while discussing it), and a variety of more specialized tools. Groove has excellent presence awareness and a more realistic feeling of both immediacy and common space than most systems. The peer-to-peer nature of the communications avoids some of the drawbacks of having a server mediating all the interactions.

VII. SUMMARY AND CONCLUSIONS

This paper is a preliminary attempt to affect the direction of research on engagement and learning communities by looking primarily at the terms themselves and the lack of common definitions, especially operational definitions of them. Frequently, our discussions of these concepts and their effects on learning appear to be almost circular. Engagement may both define a learning community and explain it, for example. Right now, we have growing literatures on both engagement and learning communities without much consensus on what those key concepts mean. Hence, we may have research studies as well as practical guidelines that appear related but that actually refer to very different concepts and constructs.

Common problems in educational research and practice are the lack of standard operational definitions of key concepts so that research can build reliably over time, instead of jumping from one movement to another without fully understanding them and their effects. Online learning is developing into an important trend, especially in higher education, but we have only about a decade of experience with it.

The technologies available to support it are changing rapidly, so what we can do with students online has evolved faster than we can get good research done. One function of academic research should be to stand back and take a closer look before we accept things uncritically.

Engagement can be defined as the confluence of three important concepts: attention, activation of effective cognitive processes, and, usually, a social context of learning. Such a definition may help us distinguish engagement from other similar constructs. I also suggest that we define learning communities not by a single variable, but by several, perhaps building on the concept of communities of practice that has become popular in organizations and on some existing literature on learning communities. An important issue will be generalizing these definitions to online learning communities. As we refine and operationalize these definitions, we have the opportunity to research the relationships among them and learning. Doing so will give us a much more coherent view of both the theory and practice of online learning communities.

VIII. REFERENCES

1. **Lim, C. P.** Engaging learners in online learning environments. *TechTrends* 48(4): 16–23, July/August 2004.

2. **Csikszentmihalyi, M.** *Flow: The Psychology of Optimal Experience.* New York: Harper and Row, 1990.

3. **Kearsley, G. and B. Shneiderman.** Engagement theory: A framework for technology-based teaching and learning. *Educational Technology*, 20–23: September/October 1998.

4. **Shin, N. and J. K. Y Chan.** Direct and indirect effects of online learning on distance education. *British Journal of Educational Technology* 35(3): 275–288, 2004.

5. **Miller, M. D., R. K. Rainer, and J. K. Corley.** Predictors of Engagement and Participation in an On-Line Course. *Online Journal of Distance Learning Administration* 6(1): 2003. Online: http://www.westga.edu/~distance/ojdla/spring61/miller61.htm.

6. **Hathorn, L. G. and A. I. Ingram.** Cooperation and collaboration using computer-mediated communication. *Journal of Educational Computing Research* 26(3): 325–347, 2002.

7. **Ingram, A. L. and L. G. Hathorn**. *Methods for Analyzing Collaboration in Online Communications. Online Collaborative Learning: Theory and Practice.* Ed. T. S. Roberts. Hershey, PA: Idea Group, Inc., 2004.

8. **Ormrod, J. E.** *Human Learning* (4th Ed.). Upper Saddle River, NJ: Pearson, 2004.

9. **Laurel, B.** *Computers as Theatre.* Reading, MA: Addison-Wesley, 1993.

10. **Ausubel, David P.** *Educational Psychology, A Cognitive View.* New York: Holt, Rinehart and Winston, Inc., 1968.

11. **Conrad, R. and J. A. Donaldson.** *Engaging the Online Learner: Activities and Resources for Creative Instruction.* San Francisco: Jossey-Bass, 2004.

12. **Cherny, L.** *Conversation and Community: Chat in a Virtual World.* Stanford, CA: CSLI Publications, 1999.

13. **Wenger, E.** *Communities of Practice: Learning, Meaning, and Identity.* New York: Cambridge, 1998.

14. **Wenger, E., R. McDermott, and W. M. Snyder.** *Cultivating Communities of Practice: A Guide to Managing Knowledge.* Boston: Harvard Business School Press, 2002.

15. **Palloff, R. M. and K. Pratt.** *Building Learning Communities in Cyberspace: Effective Strategies for the Online Classroom.* San Francisco: Jossey Bass, 1999.

16. **Harris, R., K. Bolander, M. Lebrun, F. Docq, and M. Bouvy.** *Linking Perceptions of Control and Signs of Engagement in the Process and Content of Collaborative E-Learning.* Networked Learning Conference, 2004.

    Online: http://www.shef.ac.uk/nlc2004/Proceedings/Symposia/Symposium10 /Harris_et_al.htm.

17. **Rovai, A. P.** Building Sense of Community at a Distance. *International Review of Research in Open and Distance Learning* 3(1): 2002. Online: http://www.irrodl.org/content/v3.1/rovai.html.

18. **Rovai, A. P.** A preliminary look at the structural differences of higher education classroom communities in traditional and ALN courses. *Journal of Asynchronous Learning Networks* 6(1): 2002. Online: http://www.sloan-c.org/publications/jaln/v6n1/v6n1_rovai.asp.

19. **Hathorn, L. G. and A. L. Ingram.** Online collaboration: Making it work. *Educational Technology* 42(1): 33–40, January-February 2002.

20. **Powazek, D. M.** *Design for Community: The Art of Connecting Real People in Virtual Places.* Indianapolis: New Riders, 2002.

21. **Ingram, A. L.** Using web server logs in evaluating instructional web sites. *Journal of Educational Technology Systems* 28(2): 137–157, 1999–2000.

IX. ABOUT THE AUTHOR

Albert L. Ingram, Ph.D. is Associate Professor of Instructional Technology at Kent State University, where he teaches a variety of courses in instructional design and technology. He received his Ph.D in Educational Technology from Arizona State University in 1984. Along the way, Dr. Ingram has taught at Governors State University and Kent State University and worked at a variety of other organizations including Digital Equipment Corporation, The American College, the Software Engineering Institute, and the University of Medicine and Dentistry of New Jersey. Dr. Ingram is co-author of Exploring Current Issues in Educational Technology with Drew Tiene and of FrontPage 2002: An introduction to Web design for educators and trainers with Ruth Watson. He has published papers in a variety of journals, including Educational Technology, the Journal of Educational Technology Systems, Educational Technology Research and Development, the Journal of Educational Computing Research, and Computers in the Schools. Email aingram@kent.edu.

X. ACKNOWLEDGEMENTS

Thanks to Lesley G. Hathorn of Kent State University for her invaluable comments on early drafts of this article.

How can Asynchronous Learning Networks Engage the Core of Higher Education?

USING BLENDED LEARNING TO DRIVE FACULTY DEVELOPMENT (AND VICE VERSA)

George Otte
The City University of New York

- The virtues of blended learning include convenience for students, expanded enrollments, physical plant efficiencies and community building.

- Blending has a special virtue in involving mainstream faculty in online instruction, a critical step on the way to full integration of ALN in the academy.

- Students registered higher levels of interaction and perceived learning in blended courses than in either classroom-based or fully online courses.

- Faculty are being asked to change from modes of delivery that have proved successful for them to modes they see as new and untried, and they are understandably reluctant.

- Collaborative models for engaging faculty will work.

I. INTRODUCTION

A. What's Up with Blended Learning?

A Sloan-sponsored workshop on Blended Learning [1] produced a fascinating and complex picture of what is being done with blended learning and why. Despite examination, however, no clear picture, no easy consensus, no standard definition emerged. We are still feeling our way with blended learning. But our experience in CUNY, now stretching over half a decade and hundreds of courses, points us in a direction some may find surprising and by no means wholly institution-specific. Though we do see the standard virtues that cause many to pursue blended learning elsewhere—convenience (prized both by students and faculty), heightened interaction, even the possibility of conserving classroom space—CUNY's chief interest is actually faculty and course development, and above all the community-building and idea-dissemination that blended learning ideally entails.

B. Blended Learning and Faculty Development

Why would blended learning be a driver for faculty development? Well, for one thing, it has a special appeal to mainstream faculty, the still largely untapped mass of the professoriate who have not yet taught online or who are just beginning to work with online instruction. And the reasons have to do with much more than meeting faculty halfway (promising them they can keep one foot in the classroom as they venture online). The most important reasons have to do with what is emerging as the special nature of blended learning. Blending tends to deal in pedagogical units which are more digestible and importable than whole courses, yet far less atomistic and fragmentary than course documents or learning objects. Its currency, or stock-in-trade, comprises the sort of teaching resources faculty are especially likely to see as important, mutually enriching assets.

C. Blended Learning as Via Media

Originally viewed as a kind of via media between in-class and online instruction, blending has emerged as a different kind of middle path: it allows the development of course materials that are generative without being template-like, that are evocative of a pedagogical philosophy and not just an assignment or learning exercise. Blended learning bridges different teaching styles, even different student constituencies, while remaining tied to specific disciplinary and institutional contexts. It allows those doing faculty and course development work to navigate between the all-too-generic and the thoroughly individualized, and even the downright idiosyncratic.

At CUNY, blending has evolved to create special opportunities for growing online instruction, not least of all from a pedagogical perspective.

II. HISTORY AND BACKGROUND

A. The CUNY Experience

A union-imposed moratorium on distance education, in effect well into 1999, had taken work in online learning off the agenda at the City University of New York. Once it was lifted, however, a grant from the Sloan Foundation supported the piloting of online course development in CUNY. Based on that 1999–2000 pilot, a proposal for 2000–2003 was made and funded. Over the four years of grant support, CUNY Online, the University-wide online course development program, sustained by the grant from Sloan, made online courses available at every campus and every level of instruction. For the grant period, CUNY Online delivered 750 courses (with 16,000 enrollments) and trained 380 faculty—outcomes very nearly double the projections and grant targets.

B. The Emergence of Hybrids

Even an apparent setback contributed to success: exhausting its small stock of early adopters (faculty already avid about teaching online), CUNY Online found mainstream faculty almost as eager to work with online instruction but much less eager to develop fully online courses. Expecting such cases, but also expecting them to be rare exceptions to the rule, plans included provisions for hybrid courses (courses that had to be at least one-third online) at a lower level of support. Given the way applications were tending (most faculty were opting to develop hybrids), permission was obtained to facilitate and even foster hybrid or blended courses. Beyond mandating a significant tradeoff between in-class and online time, the requirement was that those faculty proposing to develop hybrid courses had to provide a rationale for doing so and a fairly detailed description of the "online component." Such descriptions ultimately became key elements in an online catalog. Here, for example, is how the "online component" is described for an introductory course in "Computer Fundamentals" at one of the community colleges in the system:

> Though we are using the computer lab as a home base, 60% to 70% of the course will be conducted online. We will use Blackboard, our on-line course software, for interacting with each other outside of class. You will complete and submit application assignments online, use the Internet as a communication and research tool, and create your own home page. Expect to spend a minimum of three hours each week in contact with class members and the instructor via e-mail, discussion board forums, virtual classroom sessions, and ongoing-guided application and Internet projects. There will be over 65 assignments, including quizzes, and exams to complete. You will be required to log onto Blackboard at least three times a week. Quizzes and exams will be administered online. In order to succeed in an online course setting, you must be especially self-motivated. You must be able to work independently without a tutor, and to actively participate in your own learning experiences!

C. The Virtues of Hybrids

Instructors want to take advantage of an opportunity that simply hadn't been there before online instruction. Hybrid courses proved very popular with students as well as faculty, extending experience with online instruction to students who might otherwise have been excluded (students in larger courses, for instance, and freshman or remedial students). Since more than half the courses developed were hybrids, blended learning effectively doubled course development and faculty participation. CUNY was able to take an early lead in blended learning.

Of the significant outcomes, perhaps the most important was that students registered higher levels of interaction and perceived learning in these courses than in either classroom-based or fully online courses. What's more, it turned out that one kind of interaction was especially heightened: interaction with other students was 30%–50% higher than in traditional courses (and higher, though by a lesser margin, than in fully online courses).

It would be nice to say the correlation between heightened perceived learning and heightened student-to-student interaction was cemented; nice, too, to claim that both were ultimately due to significant increases in experiential or inquiry-based learning and collaborative learning. The basis for such inferences is there, but it will take further evaluation to give those claims a truly solid basis. In any case, the hybrids did prove to be successful, partly due to the urban setting and the need of both students and faculty to commute (and the ability of blended learning to obviate that need). Another assumption, supported by student responses on evaluations, was that some students, like many faculty, wanted to experience online learning without committing to a fully online experience.

D. Online Instruction Changes the Landscape

Success with blended learning was actually one of a number of profound effects of CUNY Online not fully anticipated at the outset. These began with the initial adoption of Blackboard as a shared course management system during the 1999–2000 pilot, at a time when campuses were pursuing half a dozen such systems. Having a "shared landscape" proved critical to a developing a shared vision of online instruction, as did the creation, the next academic year, of an entirely new position: a Director of Instructional Technology to coordinate faculty development in online learning for the whole University. Currently, that position has its counterpart at each campus in CUNY—proof that a signal sent by the central administration registered with that of every college. Work with online instruction has become the most significant focus of faculty development throughout the University, with the University-wide program, CUNY Online, sparking complementary faculty development programs at each campus in the system. The CUNY Online Distributed Learning Network (or DLN), an online compilation of information on online offerings University-wide, was created for students, but has also become a resource for faculty development, as faculty are able to view current or archived online offerings in their disciplines. An annual University-wide conference (now in its third year) showcases best practices in online teaching. Clinching the University's commitment to online instruction is the new contract for an enterprise version of Blackboard 6, implemented University-wide and maintained centrally, creating new opportunities for coordinated resource management as well as faculty development for online instruction.

E. Funding Follows Innovation

Such activity does not happen of its own accord, of course. In fact, a major question may well be how the University could afford to accommodate such changes. The surprising truth is that hard times— recessionary circumstances and their impact on a university system reliant on tax-levied funding— actually helped to create conditions that made expenditures on academic technology feasible as well as desirable. Recessions tend to drive up college enrollments, especially at public institutions; that's part of a well-established pattern. Those enrollments brought funding with them, of course, but they also helped to focus a need for development in instructional technology, not least of all because increased use of technology was something the culture seemed to be shifting towards. Reports from the Pew Internet and American Life Project—"The Digital Disconnect: The Widening Gap between Internet-savvy Students and Their Schools" [2] and "The Internet Goes to College: How Students are Living in the Future with Today's Technology" [3]—were making the front page of the *New York Times* in 2002.

Changes seemed called for, and changes were made—changes that actually stand to benefit CUNY financially in the long term, and so help to sustain the spread of online instruction. The early success of CUNY Online both provoked and allowed the imposition of a student technology fee: provoked because of the demands on technological resources, and allowed because the heightened visibility of academic technology justified levying such a fee. The fee itself, $75 per student per term, amounts to more than a million dollars in annual revenue for each of the campuses. Independent of the vagaries of public funding, this steady revenue stream in turn encourages and even mandates strategic planning around academic technology: support for faculty development, adequate support personnel, regular upgrades, and so on.

F. Student Growth Means Administrative Interest

Growth in enrollment has aided this growth in academic technology; enrollment has increased 13% over the last three years. In public systems, still more than in private, every additional student amounts to revenue. What's more, being public, CUNY has little revenue from other sources (endowments and the like). Now that CUNY has experienced significant enrollment growth and has, in consequence, substantially increased its faculty over the past three years, the only thing standing in the way of accommodating more students (and the revenue they bring with them) is classroom space. To the extent that online instruction frees up classroom space, it more than pays for itself, and we have reached a point where the University and college administrators are eager to see that happen.

Administrative interest has much to do with the fact that online instruction is so broadly targeted in CUNY. From the beginning, the plan has been to permeate the curriculum. Which student constituencies are served? The answer is all of them. There is no campus, no discipline that does not offer online instruction. From a student perspective, the only problem with online instruction is that there is not more of it currently available. (Online and hybrid sections are always the first to close out during registration). From an administrative perspective, the one unmet challenge is that hybrid courses are not offered in such numbers and in such programmatic ways that they can free up enough classroom space and so accommodate expanded enrollments in the land of expensive real estate. The one thing needed to satisfy the interests of both the administration and the students is faculty readiness and willingness to engage in online instruction.

III. THE CHALLENGE OF FOSTERING FACULTY READINESS

A. Are the Faculty Interested?

Everything about the situation in CUNY now, from motivations to resources, seems to suggest the University is poised for exponential growth in online instruction. Technically, for instance, the new enterprise version of Blackboard is capable of creating a course site for every course offered in CUNY. And the prospects for saturation look almost as good from a user's standpoint: recent surveys done by CUNY's Office of Institutional Research show that students at most campuses (even freshmen—indeed, especially freshmen) have at-home access at rates of 90% or more. They are already online, waiting for the faculty to show up.

Will they? That *is* the question. Because let's face it: faculty need to show up in droves. Those same surveys showing most students' have Internet access also show most are eager to participate in online learning. Is that eagerness shared by their teachers? Here's a better question: Why should faculty be eager to teach online? Why should they trade in established practices and proven methods for new-fangled approaches? There is still a vast reservoir of doubt and resistance, as documented by 2003 Sloan Survey of Online Learning. While that survey finds that trends among students and academic institutions point to significant growth for online learning, "The findings for faculty are less clear than for either students or institutions. Some, but by no means all, faculty have embraced online education..." Indeed, the last of item in the survey's Summary of Findings acknowledges faculty attitudes "remain more conservative with regard to the quality of online education and its ability to equal face-to-face learning." Clearly, as the survey itself states, persuading faculty of the effectiveness of what seems to many of them "a new and unproven delivery method is a formidable challenge" [4].

B. Reasons for Faculty Resistance

Since change is not always easily embraced, what will prompt faculty to engage in the work it takes to make the move to online instruction? And since doing this work is not (or at least should not be) a mere shift or dump—online instruction is a transformative medium that alters as well as facilitates forms of interaction—how do faculty get support in the many little changes this big change entails? The questions become all the more important when we consider how little training in pedagogy academics usually have.

Typically, a professor learns to teach primarily on the basis of models (teachers that teacher had as a student), rounding these out with a makeshift but increasingly settled repertoire of self-made lesson plans and teaching moves. The relevance this product of extensive trial and error and emulation has to online instruction is unclear at best; at worst, the uncertainty this might give rise to can make an experienced teacher feel like an utter newbie when it comes time to move instruction into an online environment.

This intimidating prospect is made more so by the fact that most faculty offering online instruction have never been on the receiving end of it. If teaching for them has been like parenting—something they had been subjected to extensively when younger even if they had no formal training in it—online instruction may make them feel like orphans in a strange land, performing in a medium they have little acquaintance with even (especially?) on the audience end of things. They may be so unfamiliar with customs and procedures of the new medium that they feel their authority and competence undercut. Support in the form of instructional design teams, besides being expensive, can often actually exacerbate this sense of not being up to the challenge. For those institutions able to afford it, there can be too much of a good thing: extensive work done by others besides the instructor can lack integration with the actual instruction, while chipping away at the instructor's sense of ownership.

Even if the problems are largely problems of perception, they cannot be waved away. And they are serious problems. Anyone acquainted with online instruction knows what the Sloan survey [4] has recently confirmed: the great bottleneck is no longer a matter of technology or access, and there has never been a problem with the will and interest of students to engage in learning online, but the issue of motivating faculty remains a problem. Faculty—especially established faculty—are being asked to change from modes of delivery that have proved successful for them to modes they see as new and untried, and they are understandably reluctant.

IV. RISING TO THE CHALLENGE (I): THE SILVER LINING

A. What Won't Work

There is a positive dimension to this picture of reluctance and resistance. For one thing, it's good to know what won't work. And I respectfully suggest that, especially as we try to ratchet up the scale and capture the core, mandates and directives and even incentive packages won't work. As for what will--where mandates fall on deaf ears, models will open closed eyes and minds.

B. Neither Carrot nor Stick

Let me say that I think we have to abjure the carrot as well as the stick. Among the things that won't work is incentivizing everyone who does or develops online instruction with released time or some form of compensation; that's really no more realistic than ordering faculty to teach online by administrative fiat. Release time also presents insuperable barriers to scalability and sustainability; it's too expensive. It works as a way of getting things started, but it simply won't scale to full integration. To get the great mass of faculty to work in online instruction, you can't pay them or order them to do it: you have to make them *want* to do it, and want to do it well.

C. Neither Faculty Champions nor "Shock and Awe" Models

Some kinds of models won't work, including any that are too generic, too easily dismissed with a reaction on the order of "That's all very nice, but it won't work in my discipline (or for my students or with my content or whatever)." Models also won't work even and especially if they are quite specific, wonderfully realized models developed by extraordinary faculty. "Faculty champions," critical as they may be during the proof-of-concept stages, are not enough. There will always be faculty admired for their teaching or research by their colleagues. The object is to make successful online instruction not the exception but the norm of a changed teaching culture. A colleague said of an especially wonderful set of high-end, media-rich models developed at one of the CUNY campuses that they achieve a "shock and awe" effect, as in "I'm shocked that you ever found the time to do all that, and I'm truly in awe of it." "Shock and awe" models inspire admiration, but not emulation. The onlooker only marvels—doing more would be like playing in the sand next to the winner of the sand castle competition. Inspiring change and not awe is the goal, and it's not easy. It takes community-building and not just individual faculty and course development, however admirable.

D. Blended Learning: The Right Step

The need for community-building is one reason for embracing blended learning: in terms of going online, blended learning is all some faculty will be able to commit to, at least initially. And those faculty are needed: community-building means the kind of outreach that brings in those who resist being involved, ideally so their resistance can be part of what they testify to later as initial reluctance, gradually overcome. As a recent report in the *Chronicle of Higher Education* put it, "Even some professors who have been skeptical of online-education projects say that hybrid models could work—as long as faculty members are left in control of the courses." And that embrace of blended learning is even reported of one faculty member "who helped organize a letter-writing campaign in 1998 protesting what the writer said was a 'frightening' and potentially 'disastrous' drift toward replacing instructors with computerized teaching tools" [5].

E. Web-Enhanced Learning: Not Stepping Up

On the other hand, you can make it too easy for resisters: another danger to avoid is mere dabbling. Fully realized models done by faculty champions are not the ticket, not if the faculty can be dismissively labeled as exceptional (and so beyond emulation); but fully realized models *are* key. In other words, you can't have "faculty control" leading you down the path of least resistance: mere dabbling with online instruction in the form of web-enhanced courses. One of the things that community needs to be built around is real commitment to online learning.

Blended learning or hybrid instruction—as something quite distinct from web-enhanced instruction— should prove vital both for eliciting "real" commitment and for showing what it amounts to. But for that to happen, you have to be willing to draw lines. In CUNY, we have defined hybrid instruction as minimally one-third online: a third of what had formerly been taught in the classroom must, in a hybrid course, be accomplished by online means. And we are preparing to make that third a full half (since drawing the line there greatly improves the recuperation of classroom space). Draw the line where you will: there must be a trade-off between in-class and online instruction to forge a real commitment to online teaching. As long as online teaching is a matter of getting to know the tools and supplementing the "regular" instruction, it will be at best ancillary (and the question will be whether the added value is counterbalanced by the added work). A commitment to online instruction means planning to break with the status quo (the two or three class meetings a week) and trying to teach in a new way.

F. Blended Learning as Via Media (Again)

The role blended learning has to play in defining that commitment is another way it serves as the via media. Web-enhanced instruction makes online instruction a mere add-on. Fully asynchronous courses have no choice—everything must be and happen online. Hybrid courses function in that in-between realm where choices must be made and are critical, where you have to acknowledge that online will displace some but not all of the face-to-face interaction. What's more, you have to acknowledge that instruction occurring online occurs in a transformative medium, where it's not just old wine in new bottles, but the very nature of the game is changed. Because hybrid courses consistently offer the juxtaposition of both kinds of instruction and necessitate choices about which to use for what, they heighten a sense of the possibilities as well as the limits of online instruction; they accentuate its special nature, its contrast of the unfamiliar with the familiar, the new with the old, the tried and true with the experimental and innovative.

G. The Goal: Not Comparable, But Better

The last and possibly the most controversial of the things to get beyond: online instruction as comparable instruction. I think we are reaching a point where comparability in accomplished goals (if not instructional means) is established, even for the laity. It's time to accentuate the difference, to hold out a different kind of goal: not to meet in-class instruction but to beat it. The venture has to be billed as an adventure in enhancing teaching and learning for everyone, not just pursuing it by other, newer means or for specific student constituencies.

V. RISING TO THE CHALLENGE (II): THE END OF THE RAINBOW

A. The Challenge to Teachers: To *Improve* Instruction

The challenge is to realize blended instruction's virtues in facilitating depth of commitment (not web-enhanced instruction), instructional specificity (not the generic approach), collaborative or community-based work (not isolated individual work), and most importantly, enhanced teaching and learning as the goal (not comparable instruction but *better* instruction). We are talking about reaching out to experienced teachers, asking them to extend their capacity to teach. If the goal is mere conversion of in-class instruction to online instruction, the faculty can (and will) assume a fairly passive role. They are presumably being treated to some how-to-teach-with-tech training. But if the idea is not to tell them how to do a new kind of instruction but instead to *ask* them how instruction might be improved—and the question is not answered for them but put to them—then they have a challenge to rise to, an invitation to take their expertise with pedagogy and re-invent it in a new context, with new tools.

B. Example 1: In-Class Discussion Meets Online Discussion

Let me start with an early case in point. In 1999, before becoming Director of Instructional Technology at CUNY, I was a director of a communication institute at one of the campuses. A wealthy alumnus had funded the institute to facilitate communication-focused instruction (not just written but also oral or verbal). I used some of the funding to buy an extra weekly hour for a college-wide requirement called the Great Works sequence. Every student had to take two semesters of classics, one from the ancient epic to the Renaissance, one from the Enlightenment to the present. Though section sizes were kept small (30 students max) to facilitate discussion, concern was growing that there was not enough discussion. (This was partly because instructors felt the burden of so much to cover—particularly in what some called the "Homer to Hamlet" term—that discussion was seen as an inefficient use of class time.) I provided the extra hour with the catch that it had to occur online. Instructors' workloads were adjusted, but not classroom scheduling. The additional hour would have to occur in Blackboard sites.

At the end of the first term of the experiment (now an institutionalized change), there was a debriefing. One instructor got up and said that she had found just how to mix online and in-class discussion: before each discussion, the key question about a work was posted (e.g., why does Hamlet delay?). When she met with the students, they had already responded to that central question online, and in-class discussion hit the ground running, giving her the best discussions she'd had in a quarter century as a lit professor. Another person got up and said, no, he'd found that the best way to mix online and in-class was to have students start the discussion in class (where eye contact and the like cued him to how clear they were on the key questions), then continue it online. Yet another got up and said the virtue of online was the opportunity, prior to the class meeting, for the students to ask *him* questions, sounding him out on key issues. Still another said she had the students wrestle with questions online in groups, reporting out in-class, giving the in-class discussions a lively competitive flavor. And so it went. What I sensed amidst all the disagreement about just how to use online discussion was the underlying consensus: no one said online discussion didn't work or seemed redundant; everyone saw it as contributing to better learning; and all agreed it added something in-class discussion alone could not. What leapt out as the most valuable thing in this exchange was not one person's idea of how to use online discussion but this smorgasbord of ideas, this range of possibilities to pick from depending on one's teaching style and proclivities. I resolved, the next time I did something like this, to make sure the discussion on how to handle discussions was also online.

C. Example 2: Writing-Intensive Instruction Goes Online

I soon had the opportunity. Right after being named Director of Instructional Technology at the beginning of 2001, I set up the Online Writing-Intensive Initiative, which quickly became OWI. It was an attempt to tie online instruction to the major University initiative of the time, writing across the curriculum, which had taken the form of urging the development of writing-intensive courses without being prescriptive about how they would be constituted. If you know about writing-intensive courses, you know the prospect of teaching them makes faculty uptight in the same way online courses do: anxieties spike about time drain, interference with coverage, the burden of more work.

OWI might seem to be a bid to double the problem, but it was cast as a two-birds proposition; faculty were asked to imagine writing doing what it could not in regular courses, serving the powerful purpose of functioning as the means of communication and especially as a major way of conveying course content. That being the case (and with reference to Peter Elbow's distinction between high stakes and low stakes writing—the latter being more about writing to learn than writing to be evaluated [6]), issues of writing (from errors to overall coherence) became matters of a students' reading (as well as writing) experience, not causes for police actions by the instructor. Students noticed that some peers seemed to write awfully well, others just, well, awfully—and seeing this taught lessons about writing for an audience more powerfully than any exhortations from the instructor every could. Again, online instruction was doing what the classroom-based instruction could not: solving a problem a group of instructors had, one they could talk through amongst themselves and ultimately see online tools allowing them to solve.

D. Example 3: Learning History Becomes "Doing" History

The biggest success, and also the most recent, was something that began as the United States History Initiative (spawning another acronym, USHI). Like the others, it began with a problem: pressure from trustees to develop a single "core" course in American history. This had the faculty up in arms, but some among them were encouraged and supported by the administration, not simply to resist, but to offer a counter-proposition: to collaborate on a set of shared resources for American history courses. That way, faculty wouldn't have to submit to an externally imposed mandate or give up ownership of their own courses, but they could still seem to be responding to the trustees' concerns, and in a proactive rather than merely reactive way.

This is where CUNY Online came in. Each professor had to commit, not just to a hybrid, but to a sustained, multi-stage assignment that could be put up online and shared with other instructors. The initial meeting showed the typical concerns over time, coverage, etc. But the invitation was to wrestle with a what was less a problem than an opportunity: the web now makes available amazing materials for historical investigation and archive work, perhaps most notably the Library of Congress's American Memory project [7]. Nor were the faculty invited simply to swim in such oceans. They were exposed to structured web assignments like those available on San Diego State University's WebQuests page [8]. Throughout the term, the faculty (representing almost every campus in CUNY) shared syllabi, suggestions, and sources. At the end, with the display of astonishingly rich assignments designed to play out over a number of days and even weeks, the faculty revealed they had effectively changed pedagogies; from seeing their primary goal as getting the students to learn history, they had decided the goal was to get the students to *do* history: to function as historians would, interpreting events and evidence, making use of past documents, making sense of what had happened and why. The modules the faculty created, on things as general as the Reconstruction and as specific as the Triangle Shirtwaist Fire, were leveraged into an NEH grant to expand the project. What's more, even without filing a proposal, CUNY was given considerably more funding from the NEH to extend such work (and access to it) to the high schools.

E. The New Project: Developing Discipline-Based Communities

On the basis of these experiences, we proposed, and have been fortunate enough to have Sloan endorse and fund, doing the sort of work prototyped by the OWI and USHI projects across a dozen disciplines. The project, just now getting underway, will run over the next several years, concentrating on high-enrollment disciplines (particularly because courses in them function as requirements in the core curriculum or the popular majors). Here's a brief outline of how it will work:

- Each academic year, four fields will mount faculty/course development projects. For each of these, every campus will be invited to nominate at least one representative. Project cohorts in each case will include a faculty coordinator or lead developer and a Technology Fellow, both from that discipline. (Technology Fellows are advanced doctoral candidates working on instructional technology projects; for the last several years, almost all of them have worked with the CUNY Honors College and have been funded out of donor support for the CHC.)

- Under the direction of the group coordinator (culled from among particularly successful past participants in CUNY Online), the Tech Fellow will maintain both the online "course" site for the project participants and develop and maintain the long-term "community" site for general access (once it is released, which will be the term after the course development phase).

- Faculty will get released time (or equivalent stipends) to develop online courses, work that will also contribute to a website housing shared resources for instruction in the focused field: online instructional materials, linked collections, research activities, critical thinking exercises, and writing/research assignments. The term of development will be spent working collaboratively online, sharing ideas and concerns, especially about the implications and dispensations of online instruction in that particular disciplinary area.

- After the term of course development, ongoing support (the equivalent of release from one course for an academic year) will be provided to these faculty by their campuses; this will support their mentoring work in the community site and on their campuses.

- The faculty coordinator and Tech Fellow will maintain the community site, providing access to discussions and mentoring for faculty interested in online instruction in that field. It will be a place to raise questions, join conversations, find mentors, and access resources.

To my mind, I confess, the resources are not really the point. The collaboration that produces them is. We've done enough building of resources sites like WebCT's Exemplary Course Project [9] or MERLOT [10] or EdNA [11] to have learned one of the great post-boom lessons: if you build it, they may come, but don't count on it. Anything that relies on overworked people taking their own initiative to teach themselves more and extend their reach is going to have mixed results at best. It won't change the teaching culture of an institution.

F. Making Pedagogy Visible

Why will collaborative communities change the culture? One reason, probably my best reason at present, is that I've seen it work several times, in unrelated fields. But a still better reason may lie in one more model, the Visible Knowledge Project [12], a grant funded project co-directed by Randy Bass of Georgetown University and Bret Eynon of CUNY's LaGuardia Community College. The Visible Knowledge Project (VKP) focuses on technology-enhanced teaching and learning, taking things further down the road than the collection *Engines of Inquiry: Teaching, Technology, and Learner-Centered Approaches to Culture and History*, now in its second edition [13]. Faculty design projects that they share extensively with faculty at their own and other campuses—presenting full narratives, questions and answers, results and assignments.

The project is about "visible knowledge"-- the pedagogy is shared, opening out to collective collaboration and critique. Too often, teaching, despite its aspect as public performance, is intensely private work: faculty can be remarkably ignorant of the teaching methods of colleagues in the same department, to say nothing of the members of the same discipline situated at other schools. The VKP seeks a new spirit of openness and inquiry about "what works" and what effect technology has on teaching and learning, for good or ill. Technology has of course actually facilitated this openness, making it possible to "look into" the teaching of others as never before. Seeing and using technology in this way, the VKP becomes a prominent and powerful metaphor for how we can use technology to enhance teaching, above all on a "meta" level where teachers pursue collaborative inquiry into pedagogy together. It is this experience that matters most, not the resources (which, really, are more about baiting the hook than reeling in the catch).

VI. CONCLUSION: GOING FOR REAL CHANGE

What is really being modeled is an experience, and the question becomes, simply (or not so simply), why is that experience so important? Is the experience the key to getting faculty online? Is the goal to develop repositories of resources? Is the expectation that there will be teaching secrets uncovered, if not for all instruction in higher education, at least for some disciplines? I have to say no, even though I think these are all worthy and achievable goals. What really matters, what's been behind everything I've said, is one more thing online teaching and learning will get us that the status quo and the traditional ways of proceeding never could: we can open up our teaching to each other. I just finished writing a history of instruction going back in one field over a hundred years, and it's amazing how little has changed fundamentally, including a number of things teaching practitioners regard as chronic and serious problems with the field. One reason, certainly, is that solutions finally have to be forged by individuals confronting less than ideal working and teaching conditions, one class at a time. They can hear about new methods and procedures in an offhand way or in journals, but what they can't do is get the kind of close look that lets them see what makes a course tick. Online instruction changes all that, opening up instruction to colleagues as never before. To believe that this should matter, that teachers talking collaboratively about teaching will really change the very culture of teaching, you have to have faith in collaboration. But there is more to justify this faith than ever before: an outstanding and very recent example is *The Wisdom of Crowds* by James Surowiecki [14], which demonstrates that groups are better than individuals in fostering innovation.

It's not the online means we need to urge, nor even the adoption of online means. That will happen. In half a decade, the one thing those of us in higher education probably won't have a choice about is whether we will be using technology in our teaching. In the *Chronicle of Higher Education* [5], John Bourne is quoted as saying, "Within five years, you'll see a very significant number of classes that are available in a hybrid fashion." He adds this prediction: "I would guess that somewhere in the 80- to 90-percent range of classes could sometime become hybrid." I'm confident that's right. What I'm a good deal less certain about is whether teaching will be better in consequence.

The tools, in and of themselves, do not transform teaching. They can, in fact, become mere means of content management for faculty who continue teaching in much the same way that they have for decades. Course management systems like Blackboard can become document repositories, not very different from electronic reserve systems established by many libraries. This can save photocopying costs (but by rather expensive means), but it will not automatically raise levels of interaction or learning. If we play through this scenario—we could call it the path of least resistance—we could have a world where everyone uses technology and yet nothing, really, has changed.

Now consider the alternative, where faculty receive the support and engage in the collaboration that allows them to re-envision teaching and learning, to plan strategically and organize to optimize time-on-task and learning effectiveness. The tools are constantly considered as means, with pedagogical ends paramount. Once faculty are satisfied in creating exemplary instruction in their discipline, they become mentors of other faculty, teachers teaching teachers, spreading new ways of configuring instruction designed with the goals of their disciplines as well as the assets of new technologies in mind. Their colleagues are exposed to models, not mandates, and learn from experience, not templates. All the while, no one is asked to jump ship, to abandon the classroom for the online environment. An interesting consequence is that the limits of the classroom become even more the issue than the challenges posed by teaching online. Above all, in this scenario, faculty themselves are the primary drivers behind a change in their methods; and they negotiate this change by the same means that they are using to revolutionize instruction: they interact and collaborate online, inhabiting the kind of teaching and learning environment they will model for others. A change in the degree of use of such environments, coupled with changes in the kinds of use and the kinds of instruction, will result in institutional transformation and cultural change in teaching and learning that will be impossible to stop.

VII. REFERENCES

1. **Sloan-C Invitational Workshop on Blended Learning**, conference, University of Illinois at Chicago, April 26–28, 2004. Online: http://www.blended.uic.edu.
2. **Levin, D., S. Arafeh, A. Lenhart, and L. Rainie.** The Digital Disconnect: The Widening Gap between Internet-savvy Students and Their Schools. Pew Internet and American Life Project: August 14, 2002. Online: http://www.pewinternet.org/pdfs/PIP_Schools_Internet_Report.pdf.
3. **Jones, S. and M. Madden**, The Internet Goes to College: How Students Are Living in the Future with Today's Technology. Pew Internet and American Life Project: September 15, 2002. Online: http://www.pewinternet.org/pdfs/PIP_College_Report.pdf.
4. **Allen, I. E., and J. Seaman**, *Sizing the Opportunity: The Quality and Extent of Online Education in the United States, 2002 and 2003.* Needham, MA: Sloan-C, 2003. Online: http://www.sloan-c.org/resources/sizing_opportunity.pdf
5. **Young, J. R.** 'Hybrid' Teaching Seeks to End the Divide Between Traditional and Online Instruction. *Chronicle of Higher Education*: March 22, 2002.

6. **Elbow, P.** High Stakes and Low Stakes in Assigning and Responding to Writing. *Assigning and Responding to Writing in the Disciplines.* Ed. M. D. Sorcinelli and P. Elbow. San Francisco: Jossey-Bass, 1997.

7. **The Library of Congress.** American Memory: Historical Collections from the National Digital Library. Online: http://memory.loc.gov/.

8. **The WebQuest Page.** Online: http://webquest.sdsu.edu/.

9. **The WebCT Exemplary Course Project.** Online: http://www.webct.com/exemplary.

10. **MERLOT (Multimedia Educational Resource for Learning and Online Teaching.** Online: http://www.merlot.org/Home.po.

11. **EdNA (Education Network Australia).** Online: http://www.edna.edu.au/edna/go/pid/.

12. **The Visible Knowledge Project.** Online: http://crossroads.georgetown.edu/vkp/.

13. **Bass, R.** Engines of Inquiry: Teaching, Technology, and Learner-Centered Approaches to Culture and History. *Crossroads.* Georgetown University: September 2003.
    Online: http://www.georgetown.edu/crossroads/guide/engines.html.

14. **Surowiecki**, J. *The Wisdom of Crowds: Why the Many Are Smarter Than the Few and How Collective Wisdom Shapes Business, Economies, Societies and Nations.* New York: Doubleday, 2004.

VIII. ABOUT THE AUTHOR

A professor for over two decades, **George Otte** is on the doctoral faculties of the CUNY Graduate Center programs in English, Urban Education, and Technology and Pedagogy. Since March 2001, when he was named Director of Instructional Technology for CUNY, he has been supervising CUNY Online, the City University's faculty/course development program for online instruction, supported by the Sloan Foundation. Email: George.Otte@mail.cuny.edu

HIGHER EDUCATION, BLENDED LEARNING AND THE GENERATIONS: KNOWLEDGE IS POWER—NO MORE

Charles Dziuban, Patsy Moskal, and Joel Hartman
Research Initiative for Teaching Effectiveness
University of Central Florida

- Metaphorical and generational perspectives suggest that the language of higher education is evolving.

- Generational markers for Mature, Baby-Boomer, Generation X, and Millennial learners impact satisfaction with blended learning.

- Millennials responded least positively to their blended learning experiences.

- The generations that populate our campuses now suggest how we might transform or rebuild higher education for the next generations.

- Millenials' metaphor is "knowledge is teamwork."

I. INTRODUCTION

Blended learning is transforming higher education and altering the metaphors we use to define our profession. Sir Francis Bacon's famous proclamation that "knowledge is power" has been the foundation of the academy for hundreds of years [1]. His claim implies that knowledge is a commodity and access is the key. However, even a casual review of the ALN and blended learning literature indicates changes in higher education.

The structure of metaphors provides us with a device for understanding the world and our actions in it. Lakoff and Johnson, for instance, contend that, "Our ordinary conceptual system, in terms of which we think and act, is fundamentally metaphorical in nature" [2]. Cytowic agrees, affirming that metaphors explain how we think and act [3]. By describing an object or idea in terms of something else, we provide ourselves with a concept map and a universal language of understanding. For instance, the common metaphor in our society, "good is up; bad is down," is found in language such as, "She went to a top university, but he bottomed out." Another example, "argument is war," is described by phrases such as, "He attacked my main point."

Over time metaphors have evolved for higher education other than "knowledge is power." A good example is that the university is an ivory tower intimated in words such as, "That program is a bastion of excellence," or "At the university, he isolated himself from the real world." Another illustration might be that the university is a ship: The president is charting a wonderful course for us." Additionally, metaphors surface for the roles of groups at the university. We characterize students as consumers, empty vessels, clients, disciples, raw material, budding flowers, and blank slates among many others [4, 5]. Metaphors describe faculty as storytellers, performers, task masters, facilitators, counselors, coaches, directors, oracles, mentors, and cheerleaders, just to name a few [4, 5, 6].

Given these metaphorical habits, it is no surprise that metaphors are developing for blended learning [7, 8, 9]. For instance, blended courses are a hybrid species—"From the way he teaches now, you wouldn't recognize the class," or a confluence—"Her face-to-face and online teaching are really coming together." Undoubtedly, the metaphors we use impact the language for conducting business in higher education. The student as consumer leads to a particular model aligned with the university as a community and the faculty as facilitators. In a sense, reconciling our metaphors defines the linguistic strategic plan for the university. Undoubtedly, however, generational time periods give rise to quite different metaphors for students, faculty, and higher education. With that in mind, we explore some recent developments about today's students and their satisfaction with blended learning.

II. THE NEW LEARNER

Recently, scholars have turned their attention to a phenomenon named the new or next generation learner [10, 11, 7], using sociological, cultural, economic, and political perspectives rather than individual preference or psychological constructs one might incorporate when studying learning styles. Defining today's students as new learners suggests a fundamental difference in the way they approach knowledge acquisition, problem solving, and moving into the workforce [12]. The paramount questions become: is higher education meeting the needs of the present generation learner and, possibly more important, who is generation-next? These questions cause speculation about how we might transform or rebuild higher education. Let's briefly consider the generations that populate our campuses now.

III. THE GENERATIONS

When investigators consider the generations they generally reference four groups: Matures (born prior to 1946), Baby Boomers (1946–1964), Generation X (1965–1980), and Millennials (1981–1994) [13]. Undeniably, these classification dates are arbitrary: for instance, someone born in 1945 is labeled a Mature while another person born in 1946 is a Baby Boomer, although their life-shaping political, social, and economic milestones are nearly identical. However, these categories do provide useful referents for contextualizing behavior.

A. Matures

World War II, the Korean Conflict, The Depression, and the New Deal were some of the major markers of this generation. Even though people born later in the cohort didn't directly experience these events, the events shaped their lives, because this generation lived in extended families (same house, same block, same town) and told stories. Later Matures remember well their parents recounting (over and over) the impact of World War II and the Great Depression. These narratives had a profound impact. Furthermore, there were consistent messages in conversations, on the radio, in the movies, and in newspapers and magazines: "hard work is the key to success," "the common good above all," "be thrifty and save your money for a rainy day—there are hard times ahead," "there are good people and there are bad people," "authority deserves respect," and above all, "one should be loyal to one's family, friends, job, country, and community." These events and themes played a powerful role in shaping the mindset of the Mature generation. Technology markers for this group included such things as trans-Atlantic radio signals, stereo phonographs, and the development of electronic computers These citizens, who believed in an honest day's work for an honest day's pay, saw the university as an ivory tower: "Go to college, I want better for you "[13, 14, 15].

B. Baby Boomers

Baby Boomers, through their sheer weight of numbers, have had a monumental impact on the country—politically, economically, socially, and culturally. The beginning period of the generation saw rapid and sustained economic expansion, giving rise to a strong sense of financial security. Life was good. However, other events impacted this generation: divorce, consumer debt, the Cuban missile crisis, the Kennedy and Martin Luther King assassinations, and Vietnam. Even in the face of these events, Boomers remain optimistic, are willing to go into debt, remain process-oriented, and strive for convenience. They occupy high positions in government, commerce, and industry, and they are becoming legendary for their potential impact on the social security system. Some of the major technology markers for this generation include PLATO, the fax machine, the BASIC computer language, and the minicomputer. For the Boomers, the university was a great expectation: "Buy it now, pay later. Everything is going to work out once I get my degree" [13, 14, 16].

C. Generation X

Generation X experienced a significantly different set of markers from the Baby Boomers and was the first generation to feel the profound impact of technological developments. They encountered events such as Watergate, anti-war protests, excessive inflation, massive layoffs, the Challenger tragedy, the energy crisis, Three Mile Island, AIDS, and the Exxon Valdez. After school they became resourceful, since both parents were working, forming the first "Latch Key Generation." As a result, Gen-Xers grew up skeptical and mistrustful of established organizations, institutions, and traditions. Viewed as disrespectful, they speak up and look out for themselves because they feel societal expectations such as employment and security are ephemeral. Because they see job security as a myth, they work to live, putting very little stock in future stability. For Generation X, versatility provides security. There were many important technology markers for this generation: Windows keyboard mouse, the UNIX operating system, Intel's introduction of the 4004, 8008, and 8080 microprocessor chips, the C programming language, the foundation of Microsoft, and Apple Computer. For Gen Xers, the university experience was an uncertain mediation: "I have no idea what's happening after graduation" [13, 17, 18].

D. Millennials

The Millennial generation is described by many as the new learner, the Net Generation, Generation Y, Nexters, the Internet Generation, and Generation Why? Media exposure has taught these young people to challenge any tradition, institution, value, or person they choose, and in many respects they are confused by media-highlighted scandal and dishonesty in industry and the government. They have seen meteoric rises in stock prices, and they grew up in a world of cell phones, pagers, the Internet, and the Web. Millennials take class notes on personal digital assistants, get their information from blogs and wikis, and are asked by their professors to turn off their cell phones in their face-to-face courses. They have access to worldwide events that are unprecedented in history. However, they view these sometimes gruesome situations through the aloof templates of television and unfiltered websites that are repositories of pornography and extreme violence. At the same time these influences tell them what to think. They see political campaigns as media spin, and they see job expansion at the minimum wage level. Millennials are the most diverse generation in the history of our nation and can navigate complicated software with such ease that they intimidate members of previous generations. They can complete a task, listen to the portable CD player, and talk on the cell phone simultaneously, but employers report that their basic skill levels, critical thinking ability, and initiative are developmentally lacking. Millennials bring a mindset and approach to the workplace and the world community that many simply cannot comprehend. Their technology markers are impressive indeed: the PC is introduced, the Internet is established, CD sound systems marketed, Microsoft introduces the initial version of Windows OS, Apple introduces the Macintosh, the development of HTML, and the first e-commerce sites appear in the Web. The technologies of the decades after their boundary year (1994) have been even more impressive: the first Internet search engines, DVDs, MP3 audio format, more than 172 million Internet hosts, and a Google database claiming 4.28 billion Web pages. The Millennial generation experiences the university through bricolage: "I'm piecing together a program from four departments" [13, 19, 20].

IV. LITERATURE REVIEW ON BLENDED LEARNING

A. Today's Students

Today's students are increasingly more diverse than ever before. Incoming undergraduates are in many cases more technologically proficient than their faculty with 80% reporting that they have a computer by the time they reach college. With the majority of these students having already surfed the Internet for homework purposes (78%) and two-thirds having used e-mail, they are approaching college courses already experienced in Web technologies [21].

Undergraduates also appear to be more non-traditional than in years past with 43% being 24 or older. The majority of these older undergraduates also report being employed (82%). and as a result, are approaching college with responsibilities above and beyond what they encounter in their classrooms [22].

B. What's the Perfect Blend?

Many faculty and universities are experimenting with courses that use both fully online and face-to-face instruction. Faculty, students, and administrators are realizing a number of advantages in these blended courses, and many see them as offering the best of both instructional worlds. *Webster's Revised Unabridged Dictionary* defines "blend" as "to mix or mingle together; esp. to mingle, combine, or associate so that the separate things mixed, or the line of demarcation, cannot be distinguished" [23]. Within the context of blended courses, this definition can be related to the combination of web and face-to-face that is necessary to produce a course using the best of both instructional worlds. Some educators define blended learning approaches as "finding a harmonious balance between online access to knowledge and face-to-face human interaction" [24] or the "thoughtful integration of classroom face-to-face learning experiences with online experiences" [25].

Courses that replace a portion of face-to-face instruction with Web components allow for using Web resources flexibly to reduce on-campus time, yet also to allow face-to-face interaction. Just how many of the face-to-face components are replaced with online instruction varies widely by universities and instructors. The mix is influenced by many factors including the course instructional goals, student characteristics, instructor experience and teaching style, discipline, developmental level, and online resources [24]. In fact, there is no defined standard as to how much or what part of courses go online widely [25, 26]. Many replace 25–50% of in-class time with Web components [7, 27, 28].

Programs are beginning to see the usefulness of using blended learning, particularly when they serve students whose lifestyles preclude them from attending full face-to-face courses, such as graduate nursing programs [28]. Through blended learning, accreditation and high standards can be maintained while providing the additional flexibility that students require.

The number of universities utilizing blended courses is growing rapidly. Some estimates are that between 80 and 90% of courses will someday be hybrid [29].

C. Why Blend?

A number of potential advantages to blended learning are emerging. Some of these revolve around accessibility, pedagogical effectiveness, and course interaction. Many of today's college students are non-traditional, attempting to balance family, jobs, and university life. Coming to campus is often difficult for many of them and reducing the number of required face-to-face hours can help students manage. Universities and faculty are looking for ways to reach and retain these students. Students can access the material on the Web at any time of day and review it as needed, gaining increased flexibility [28, 30, 31]. Busy students don't have to spend time commuting and parking, so blended courses can add up to significant time savings [26, 29]. Students like the ability to access course materials any time, any place, and appreciate convenience and flexibility [7]. Because many students are older and working, blended courses help provide them with the flexibility they need to juggle jobs, school, and family [32, 33, 34]. By reducing time and space commitment, access is easier and thus many students have come to prefer the blended courses to fully face-to-face courses.

D. Increased Interaction

An additional benefit often reported in blended classes is an increase in interaction over what students and faculty typically perceive in face-to-face courses [35, 33, 7]. Web resources, and course management systems offer easier access to both students and faculty through discussion groups and e-mail, and they also allow access to material and experts who might not be available otherwise. The end result is a learning environment in which students can be actively engaged, and potentially learning more than in a traditional on-campus classroom.

Faculty at Mercy College find an increased sense of community and collaboration in the blended format because their pedagogical strategy has been to "address varying learning styles, increase interactivity, promote community, and meet the special needs of online students" [36]. Researchers from Brigham Young University also use the blended format to compensate for student differences in experience with content, realizing that some students had prior experience with the material and, thus, might not have to review the material as much as other novices [37]. Providing online material for review as often or as much as needed can be a strategy by which faculty address students' varying styles and skills [28].

Through available Web resources, faculty change the organization of the course and add enhancements to accommodate students' unique needs or learning styles. Students who need more repetition and exercises can have that opportunity without taking face-to-face class time away from those who might not need the extra reinforcement [33].

Blended courses have the potential to facilitate a community of inquiry. By forcing students to be independent and have control over their learning, blended formats can help foster critical thinking and facilitate collaborative learning [25]. To maximize the benefit of individualizing instruction through blending, Schwartzman and Tuttle [38] provided redundancy to students in the form of audio, video, and textual versions of modules and increased the variety of ways students could engage the material. Without the bounds of in-class time, students can spend as much time as necessary to master the material.

An increase in student engagement in blended courses also occurs as students and faculty experience a level of comfort facilitated by student-to-student and faculty-to-student interactions [38]. When students become comfortable with the instructor and their peers, they become more involved with the course material.

E. Student and Faculty Perceptions

While there is much variation in blended courses (and in face-to-face courses as well), one apparently consistent finding is student and faculty satisfaction with this modality. Both students and faculty are positive regarding the flexibility and convenience and the perceived increase in interaction they have with blended courses [39, 40, 7, 37].

Students rate the quality of their blended experience as high as or higher than their face-to-face courses. They also report high satisfaction with instructor interaction. Weaknesses often refer to problems with technology, including difficulty with course management systems [35]. Researchers at Ohio State University surveyed 201 students from three universities about their experience in courses spanning the distance education continuum from completely face-to-face to completely online. Students indicated that the intuitive structure of the course—clearly defined objectives, assignments, deadlines, and encouraging dialogue and interaction—was most important to their satisfaction with the course [41].

Rovai and Jordan [42] compared three education graduate courses—traditional, blended, and fully online—and found that students in the blended course measured highest in a sense of community, similar to those students in the face-to-face section, but higher than those in fully online section: "since students in the blended course exhibited similar sense of community and variability as students in the traditional course, offering the convenience of fully online courses without the complete loss of face-to-face contact may be adequate to nurture a strong sense of community in students who would feel isolated in a fully online course." Students in the blended courses praised the benefits of the online portion of the course which allowed them the freedom to perform some of the course activity at their own discretion, flexibility important for these students, many of whom needed to work. However, many of them also mentioned the value of the face-to-face component which they felt helped them both academically and in building professional relationships and a strong sense of community. In addition, some students in the fully online course misread the instructor's comments as being "sharp and frank," while students in the blended and fully online courses did not convey such impressions, possibly because of the opportunity for face-to-face discussions which allowed everyone to become acquainted.

For the most part, faculty report that student performance in blended courses is as good as, or in some cases better than, face-to-face [35]. The Pew Grant Program in Course Redesign found improved student learning in 19 out of 30 projects with 11 having no significant difference from face-to-face sections [43]. Comparing face-to-face and blended introductory statistics courses, Utts et al. [44] found performance was equal, although hybrid students were slightly less positive.

O'Toole and Absalom [45] found students in the blended format, accessing both online resources and attending lectures performed better than students who attempted to perform without attending lectures. They posit that the lecture provides high motivation for students to maintain progress, thus equating to higher student achievement.

V. A STUDY OF GENERATIONAL SATISFACTION WITH BLENDED LEARNING

A. Methods

The University of Central Florida conducted a satisfaction survey of its blended learning student population. Eleven five-point Likert scale questions formed the basis of this study, asking students to index their blended learning experience with respect to overall satisfaction, ability to integrate technology into their learning, ability to control their own learning, study efficiency, ability to meet their educational objectives, willingness to take another blended course, ease of interaction, amount of interaction with students, quality of interaction with students, amount of interaction with the instructor, and quality of interaction with the instructor.

These items were inter-correlated and the (11x11) matrix was subjected to a principal components analysis [46]. Components were extracted according to the number of eigenvalues of the correlation matrix greater than one. The components were transformed using the promax [47] procedure. Coefficients in the transformed pattern matrix absolutely greater than .3 were considered salient. Prior to any "factoring" procedures the domain sampling properties of the data were indexed with the measure of sampling adequacy (MSA) [48]. Component scores for each responding student were computed using the regression method. Subsequently, a one-way analysis of variance was completed for the component scores by the generations (Boomer, Gen X, and Millennial). Finally, decision trees were derived for each set of scores using generational membership, gender and ethnicity as predictors. Chi-square Automatic Interaction Detection (CHAID) [49] derived the tree structure on the sample that was validated with a ten partition fold. The objective of these procedures was to gain a better perspective of the generational perceptions (metaphors) of blended learning. Of the 2000 survey instruments distributed, 491 were returned.

B. Results

Table 1 presents the percentage distribution, with no Matures responding to the survey, and showing the majority of student respondents (80%) representing Generation X and Millennials. The majority of

Millennials (92%) represent undergraduate education while the majority of Boomers (78%) come from graduate classes. Generation X is split between the upper undergraduate level (42%) and graduate classes (51%).

Table 1. Percentage of Students Responding to the Survey Instrument and Registrations

Questionnaire Responses (n=487)			Student Registrations		
	N	%	Low Und %	High Und %	Graduate %
Boomer	99	20	2	20	78
Gen X	206	42	7	42	51
Millennial	182	38	55	37	10

Table 2 gives the promax transformed pattern matrix for the principal component analysis with a measure of sampling adequacy (.87) indicating excellent domain sampling. The eigenvalue selection criterion (>1) retained two components. The pattern coefficients for component one show substantial values for overall satisfaction, integrating technology, more learning control, study efficiency, willingness to take another blended course, and meeting educational objectives. The construct associated with these coefficients is probably best described as **learning engagement.** The second dimension is entirely related to **interaction value:** ease, quantity, and quality with students and instructors. The correlation between the two components is .47.

Table 2. Promax transformed Pattern Matrix
Principal Components Solution for Students' Rating of Blended Learning (n = 491)

	I	II	H²**
Overall Satisfaction	83	00	68
Better Integrate Tech.	75	01	57
More Learning Control	73	05	57
Study Efficiency	80	.04	67
Take Another Blended Course	80	-07	60
Met Educational Objectives	74	02	57
Easier Interaction	08	70	54
Amount of Student Interaction	-19	95	77
Quality of Student Interaction	-02	87	75
Amount of Instructor Interaction	.10	75	64
Quality of Instructor Interaction	.19	70	66
Eigenvalues	5.2	1.8	
% Variance	48	16	

Measure of Sampling adequacy = .87

Component Correlation = .47

Decimals Omitted for Pattern Coefficients

**Communality

Table 3 presents the results of the one-way analysis of variance of the component scores for learning engagement and interaction value scores. The reader should be cognizant that component scores are not a simple sum of the items with high "loadings" but rather a function of the transformed pattern values used as regression coefficients. One advantage of component scores is that, because of their scaling, they produce values in a unit normal metric, thus presenting differences in standard deviation units. The learning engagement scores produced a significant difference (p=.00) showing Boomers most positive (.404) and Millennials least favorable toward their blended learning experience (-.204). Those values place Boomers and Millennials over one half a standard deviation apart. The interaction value component scores produced a similar result (p=.00) with Boomers showing an average component score of .246 and Millennials producing an average score of -.273, again locating those two groups over one-half standard deviation apart. Note from Table 3 that the correlation between the learning engagement and interaction scores was .71 – supporting the supposition that student satisfaction is positively related to interaction.

Table 3. Average Learning Engagement and Interaction Component Scores by Generation in Blended Course

Learning Engagement	n	Mean	SD	p
Boomer	90	.404	.823	.00*
Gen X	199	.000	1.024	
Millennial	179	-.204	1.003	
Interaction	n	Mean	SD	p
Boomer	96	.246	1.055	.00*
Gen X	199	.134	1.004	
Millennial	179	-.273	.903	

*Probabilities based on one way analysis of variance

Learning engagement/interaction component score correlation = .71

Figure 1 presents the decision tree for learning engagement using generational membership, gender and ethnicity as predictors. One conclusion from Figure 1 is that of the predictors, only generation and gender were selected by the decision rules. Three noteworthy outcomes appear in Figure 1—male Millennial students can be expected to score over one-half of a standard deviation below the mean on learning engagement with the distance between Boomers and Millennial males being almost one complete standard deviation. Also, male Millennials (-.545) scored considerably lower than female Millennials (-.061) who have an average value close to the group mean. Figure 1 indicates that the correlation between age and learning engagement is quite low, r =.172.

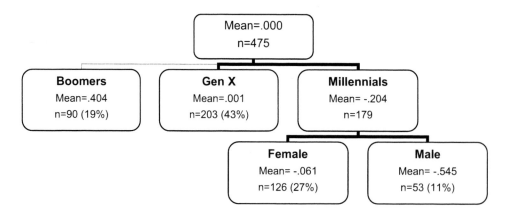

Chi Square Automatic Interaction Detector

Predictors = generation, gender, ethnicity, engagement

r (age x learning engagement) = .172

Figure 1. CHAID* Based Decision Tree for Learning Rngagement Component Scores

Figure 2 presents the decision tree for interaction value with generation, gender, and ethnicity, once again, used as predictors. For this structure, the lowest interaction score for male millenials is more than one half a standard deviation below the group mean (-.549). The greatest distance in the tree may be found between male Millennials (-.549) and females in the combined Boomer and Generation X group (.273). In this diagram, males score below the mean of their parent node while the females score above the average. Figure 2 indicates that the correlation between age and interaction component scores is .173.

.

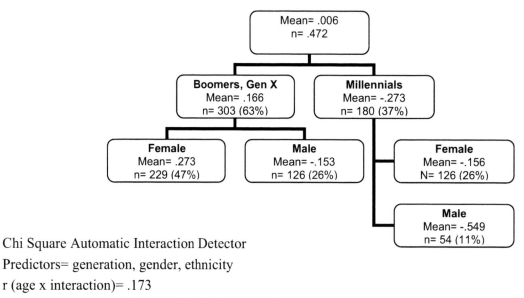

Chi Square Automatic Interaction Detector

Predictors= generation, gender, ethnicity

r (age x interaction)= .173

Figure 2. CHAID* based decision tree for interaction component scores

Table 4 shows the percentage of each generation responding to the questionnaire indicating that they changed their approach to learning as a result of blended learning. The familiar pattern of these data continues. Fifty percent of the Boomers indicate a change while only 20% of the Millennials claimed to have transformed their approach to classes.

Table 4. Percentage of Generations That Changed Their Approach to Learning in Blended Learning Courses

	n	%	p
Boomer	47	50%	.00*
Gen X	76	38%	
Millennial	36	20%	

*Probability based on a chi square contingency test

VI. CONCLUSION

A. Knowledge is Power

In our introduction, we suggest that the blended format modifies the commonly held metaphor for higher education: "knowledge is power." Historically, the university sequestered knowledge in its library, laboratories, in professors' notes, correspondence, experience, and in their communication with colleagues across universities. Faculty members controlled access to that knowledge, especially at the graduate level where Matures and Boomers served their "Ph.D. serfdom." To further reinforce the concept that he (or she) who controls the knowledge has the power, we now inform the reader that Francis Bacon's actual quote is "For knowledge itself is power." Under this organizing metaphor, faculty can be oracles, students can be blank slates, and universities can be ivory towers.

We believe the new metaphor for higher education is **"The ability to use knowledge effectively is power."** The immediate availability of data, information, and knowledge to university students is astounding. The Millennial generation has much more access to information than its professors did. Hindman and Cukier [50] assert that Google and Yahoo (or entities using their technologies) handle 95% of all Web searches in the United States. Google, with more than four billion Web content pages, handles hundreds of millions of searches each day.

We should not be surprised, therefore, that when Millennial generation students evaluate their blended courses for learning engagement, interaction value, and changed learning habits, they report that they are the least positive (or satisfied). Possibly, the new technologies that universities offer these students do not relate to their view of technology-based learning, and surely, only the most engaging face-to-face presentation will hold their attention. Millennials declare:

I spend more time reading and reviewing without the professor telling me everything there is to know.

I respect myself more as a self-teacher.

Learning that takes place in the classroom isn't as important as time studying on your own.

Online gives me something to do when I'm bored with the professor.

Wendover [13] states that when students view general education course requirements that do not translate into usable job skills as irrelevant, their metaphor for university is an *"unresponsive object."* For students who are obliged to obtain a degree to become eligible for promotion in certain industries, the metaphor for university is *"right of passage"*. Overall, therefore, the ability to use knowledge as a *structure* becomes the dominant metaphor for these students, and to some degree, blended learning contributes to this ability. Millennials have access to the world and they bring it into the classroom. They visit an expert's blog on the topic being taught, discuss the class assignment with several students around the world, and question the inconsistencies about the instructor's requirements. Who has the power?

B. Generational Satisfaction with Blended Learning

We identify two major components for student satisfaction with blended learning: learning engagement and perceived ability to communicate effectively. Within the limitations of our instrument, these two components hold for Baby Boomers, Generation X, and Millennials. However, the generational cohorts do not reveal the same levels of satisfaction for blended learning on these two dimensions. Are the explanations for this phenomenon different than generational markers? An insight might be the metaphor, "perception is reality," even if perception is not accurate. Laing, Phillipson, and Lee [51] offer one hypothesis about interpersonal perception. They present a three-level model of perception, in which the final stage is called meta-meta perspective. In a husband and wife dyad, meta-meta perspective asks the husband to convey how his wife would describe him (and vice-versa). Laing and colleagues indicate problems if one or both spouses cannot accurately portray the other's point of view [51]. We suggest, therefore, that Millennial students' decreased satisfaction rates in blended courses (and probably others) affirm that instructors do not accurately understand how their students perceive them.

Our professors are shocked when student subgroups assign them low values on items such as "The instructor was interested in your learning," or "Expression of expectations for the course." The professors are dismayed when students write statements such as "If only she taught as well as she dressed." Here, we have mixed metaphors or inaccurate meta-meta perspectives. Instructors perceive themselves in a particular pedagogical style, but their students see them differently—a discrepancy of which the instructor is unaware. This discrepancy is greatest for the Millennial generation. Is it a question for future research?

C. Another Explanation

Richard Clark's work on motivation in the workplace offers an alternate hypothesis for declining satisfaction across the generations [52]. His CANE model (commitment and necessary effort) bases itself on three multiplicative components for determining commitment: personal agency ("Can I do this and what are the barriers?"), emotion ("Do I feel like doing this?"), and task value ("Will this do me any good? Am I interested? Is this important to me?"). The second two components are particularly important for understanding Millennial students in blended learning. Certainly, as we have discussed, technological personal agency is not a problem for them. However, emotion and task value also interact with blended learning satisfaction. If the task is something that students just don't feel like doing or they see very little value in its completion, then the CANE model predicts low commitment. The multiplicative nature of the model dictates that only one component needs to approach zero or be negative for commitment to diminish. The CANE model features an additional dimension that predicts the effort one is likely to expend on a task depending on his or her perceived personal agency. Interestingly, Clark demonstrates that when personal agency is excessively high or low, effort diminishes. Accordingly, Millennials with high facility for technology but negative affect and low task value are likely to express lower satisfaction. On the other hand, Baby Boomers with moderate technology capability (in general) but positive affect and high task value are likely to expend more effort, evidence more commitment, and express higher satisfaction.

D. Blended Learning and the Millennial Generation: A Final Metaphor?

Designing a blended learning course that maximizes the potential of both the face-to-face and online components raises questions: What is the best definition of blended learning? How much of each modality should comprise a course? We argue that students and faculty should not view the face-to-face aspect of a blended course and the online element as separate components [53]. The instructional design perspective, therefore, requires a reevaluation of teaching and learning to blend or harmonize the distinction between the two—a challenging task, made even more formidable by the presence of the new learners [11].

Some characterize the Millennials by their technological empowerment as stimulus junkies and gamers, who multitask, demand response immediacy, and communicate by text messaging; Millenials are characterized as generally facile with rapidly emerging technologies. Others [13], however, suggest that Millennials are not proficient in higher order thinking, and are unwilling to take intellectual risks and view problem-solving as a series of choices on the monitor. If older generation faculty confuse the Millennials' extensive technological sophistication with maturity, the faculty may forget that many of these new learners are still adolescents. Howe and Strauss [19], however, describe Millennials differently: conventional, confident, special, sheltered, pressured, achieving, and team-oriented. Despite their technological savvy, these students face more stress than prior generations, especially when their need for team orientation pressures them to persist in a milieu of higher education that emphasizes individual accomplishment.

Millennials' diminished satisfaction with blended learning reflects their cooperative approach to problem solving. Their metaphor is **knowledge is teamwork**. Because of this viewpoint, Strauss believes that this generation ultimately will be defined as possibly the next greatest generation, just as the GI generation defined the twentieth century. Our challenge, then, is to develop teaching and learning strategies for the blended learning environment that will capitalize on the Millennial students' strengths while accommodating their immaturity and helping new metaphors develop.

VII. REFERENCES

1. **Spedding, J., R. L. Ellis, and D.D. Heath, eds.** *The Works of Francis Bacon.* St. Clair Shores, MI: Scholarly Press, 1969.
2. **Lakoff G. and M. Johnson.** *Metaphors We Live By.* Chicago and London: University of Chicago Press, 1980.
3. **Cytowic, R. E.** *The Man Who Tasted Shapes.* New York, NY: G. P. Putnam's Sons, 1993.
4. **Wilson, B. G.** Metaphors for instruction: Why we talk about learning environments. *Educational Technology* 35(5): 25–30, 1995.
5. **Brigham, S. E.** TQM: Lessons we can learn from industry. *Change:* 42–48, May/June 1993.
6. **Gordon, O. E.** Pedagogical issues in Internet education. *Electronic Journal of the American* Association of Behavioral Sciences 3: 6, 2000.
7. **Dziuban, C. D., J. L. Hartman, and P. D. Moskal.** Blended learning. *EDUCAUSE Center for Applied* Research Bulletin 7: 1–12, 2004.
8. **Dziuban, C. D., J. L. Hartman, P. D. Moskal, S. Sorg, and B. Truman.** Three ALN modalities: an institutional perspective. In *Elements of Quality Online Education*, ed. J. Bourne and J. C. Moore, 127–148. Needham, MA: Sloan Consortium, 2004.
9. **Dziuban, C. D., J. L. Hartman, F. Juge, P. D. Moskal, and S. Sorg.** Blended learning: online learning enters the mainstream. In Handbook of Blended Learning Environments: Global perspectives, local designs, ed. C. J. Bonk and C. R. Graham. San Francisco, CA: Pfeiffer Publishing, in press.
10. **Oblinger, D.** Boomers, gen-exers and millennials: Understanding the new students. *EDUCAUSE Review*, July/August 2003. Online: http://www.educause.edu/ir/library/pdf/erm0342.pdf.
11. **Microsoft Corporation.** Unlimited learning: Preparation for a life of change and challenge. Higher Education Leaders Symposium, Redmond, Washington, February 4–5, 2004. Online: http://www.mcli.dist.maricopa.edu/ocotillo/retreat04/docs/ms_ed_summary_0414.pdf.
12. **AASCU.** Microsoft and EDUCAUSE Key to Competitiveness Conference. University of Central Florida, Orlando, June 9–11, 2004.
13. **Wendover, R. W.** From Ricky and Lucy to Beavis and Butthead: Managing the New Workforce. Aurora, CO: The Center for Generational Studies, Inc., 2002.

14. **Santos, S. R. and K. Cox.** Workplace adjustment and intergenerational differences between matures, boomers, and Xers. *Nursing Economics* 18(1): 7–13, 2000.

15. **Hagevik, S.** From Ozzie and Harriet to the Simpsons, generations in the workplace. *Environmental Health* 61(9):39, 1999.

16. **Hatfield, S.** Understanding the four generations to enhance workplace management. *AFP Exchange*: 72–74, 2002.

17. **Solomon, J.** Probe Ministries. *Generation X*. Online: http://www.probe.org/docs/genera-x.html.

18. **Cetron, M. and K. Cetron.** A forecast for schools. *Educational Leadership*: 22–29, 2002/2003.

19. **Lowery, J. W.** The millennials come to campus: John Wesley Lowery talks with William Strauss. *About Campus*: 6–12, July-August 2001.

20. **Marx, G.** Preparing students and schools for a radically different future. *USA Today*, March 2002.

21. **EDUCAUSE.** *The Pocket Guide to U.S. Higher Education*, 2003. Online: http://www.educause.edu/ir/library/pdf/PUB2201.pdf.

22. **Horn, L., K. Peter, and K. Roony.** Profile of Undergraduates in U.S. Postsecondary Institutions: *1999–2000* (NCES 2002-168). U.S. Department of Education, National Center for Education Statistics, Washington, DC: U.S. Government Printing Office, 2002.

23. **Webster's Revised Unabridged Dictionary.** Springfield, MA: C and G Merriam Co., 1913.

24. **Osguthorpe, R. T. and C. R. Graham.** Blended learning environments, definitions and directions. *The Quarterly Review of Distance Education* 4(3): 227–233, 2003.

25. **Garrison, D. R. and H. Kanuka.** Blended learning: Uncovering its transformative potential in higher education. *The Internet and Higher Education* 7: 95–105, 2003.

26. **Aycock, A., C. Garnham and R. Kaleta.** Lessons learned from the hybrid course project. *Teaching with Technology Today* 8(6): 2002. Online: http://www.uwsa.edu/ttt/articles/garnham2.htm.

27. **Waddoups, G. L., G. L. Hatch, and S. Butterworth.** Blended teaching and learning in a first-year composition course. *The Quarterly Review of Distance Education* 4(3): 271–278, 2003.

28. **Carroll, B.** Going hybrid: Online course components increase flexibility of on-campus courses. *Online Classroom*: 4–7, 2003.

29. **Young, J. R.** 'Hybrid' teaching seeks to end the divide between traditional and online instruction. *Chronicle of Higher Education* 48(28): A33–34, 2003.

30. **Johnson, J.** Reflections on teaching a large enrollment course using a hybrid format. *Teaching with Technology Today* 8(6): 2002. Online: http://www.uwsa.edu/ttt/articles/jjohnson.htm.

31. **Hopper, K.** Reasons to go hybrid. *Distance Education Report*: 7, December 15, 2003.

32. **Strambi, A. and E. Bouvet.** Flexibility and interaction at a distance: A mixed-mode environment for language learning. *Language Learning and Technology* 7(3): 81–102, 2003.

33. **Wingard, R. G.** Classroom teaching in web-enhanced courses: A multi-institutional study. *EDUCAUSE Quarterly* 1: 26–35, 2004.

34. **McCray, G. E.** The hybrid course: Merging online instruction and the traditional classroom. Information Technology and Management 1: 307–327, 2000.

35. **Waddoups, G. L. and S. L Howell.** Bringing online learning to campus: The hybridization of teaching and learning at Brigham Young University. International Review of Research in Open and Distance *Learning* 2(2): 2002.

36. **Story, A. E. and J. DiElsi.** Community building easier in blended format? *Distance Education Report*: 2–7, June 1, 2003.

37. **Cottrell, D. M. and R. A. Robison.** Blended learning in an accounting course. *The Quarterly Review of Distance Education* 4(3): 261–269, 2003.

38. **Schwartzman, R. and H. V. Tuttle.** What can online course components teach about improving instruction and learning? *Journal of Instructional Psychology* 29(3): 179–188, 2002.

39. **Willett, H. G.** Not one or the other but both: hybrid course delivery using WebCT. *The Electronic Library* 20(5): 413–491, 2002.

40. **Leh, A. S.** Action research on hybrid courses and their online communities. *Education Media International* 39(1): 31–38, 2002.

42. **Rovai, A. P. and H. M. Jordan.** Blended learning and sense of community: A comparative analysis with traditional and fully online graduate courses. *International Review of Research in Open and Distance Learning*, 2004. Online: http://www.irrodl.org/content/v5.2/rovai-jordan.html.

43. **Twigg, C. A.** New models for online learning. *EDUCAUSE Review*: 28–38, 2003.

44. **Utts, J., B. Sommer, C. Acredolo, M. W. Maher, and H. R. Matthews.** A study comparing traditional and hybrid Internet-based instruction in introductory statistics classes. *Journal of Statistics Education* 11(3): 2003.

45. **O'Toole, J. M. and D. J. Absalom.** The impact of blended learning on student outcomes: Is there room on the horse for two? *Journal of Educational Media* 28(2–3): 179–190, 2003.

46. **Hotelling, H.** Analysis of a complex of statistical variables into principal components. *Journal of Educational Psychology* 24: 417–441, 498–520, 1933.

47. **Hendrickson, A. E. and P. O. White.** Promax: A quick method for rotation to oblique simple structure. British Journal of Statistical Psychology 17: 65–70, 1994.

48. **Dziuban, C. D. and E. C. Shirkey.** When is a correlation matrix appropriate for factor analysis? Some decision rules. *Psychological Bulletin* 81(6): 358–361, 1994.

49. *Introduction to Answer Tree.* Chicago, IL: SPSS Inc. 2002.

50. **Hindman, M. and K. N. Cukier.** More is not necessarily better. *The New York Times*, August 23, 2004.

51. **Laing, R. D., H. Phillipson, and A. R. Lee.** Interpersonal Perception: A Theory and a Method of *Research.* New York: Harper and Row, 1996.

52. **Clark, R. E.** Motivating performance: Part 1—diagnosing and solving motivation problems. *Performance Improvement* 37(8): 39–47, 1998.

53. Major findings and observations from the Sloan-C Invitational Workshop on Blended Learning, Online: http://www.uic.edu/depts/oee/blended/findings.html

VIII. ABOUT THE AUTHORS

Charles Dziuban is Director of the Research Initiative for Teaching Effectiveness at the University of Central Florida (UCF) where has been a faculty member for the past 32 years teaching research design and statistics. He received his Ph.D. from the University of Wisconsin. Since 1997 he has directed the impact evaluation of UCF's distributed learning initiative examining student and faculty outcomes as well as gauging the impact of online courses on the university. Chuck has published in numerous journals including: Multivariate Behavioral Research, The Psychological Bulletin, Educational and Psychological Measurement, the American Education Research Journal and the Phi Delta Kappan. His methods for determining psychometric adequacy are featured in both the SPSS and the SAS packages. He has received funding from several government and industrial agencies including the Ford Foundation and the Centers for Disease Control. In 2000, Chuck was named UCF's first ever *Pegasus Professor* for extraordinary research, teaching, and service. Email: dziuban@mail.ucf.edu.

Patsy Moskal is the Faculty Research Associate for the Research Initiative for Teaching Effectiveness at the University of Central Florida (UCF) where she has been a faculty member since 1989. She received an Ed.D. from UCF specializing in Instructional Technology and Research Methods and holds BS and MS degrees in computer science. Since 1996 she has served as the liaison for faculty research of distributed learning at UCF. Patsy specializes in statistics, graphics, and applied data analysis. She has extensive experience in research methods including survey development, interviewing, and conducting focus groups and frequently serves as a consultant to school districts, industry, and government organizations. Email pdmoskal@mail.ucf.edu.

Joel L. Hartman is Vice Provost for Information Technologies and Resources at the University of Central Florida in Orlando. As the university's CIO, he has overall responsibility for library, computing, networking, telecommunications, media services, and distributed learning activities. Hartman has been an active author, and presenter at industry conferences. He previously served as treasurer and 2003 Chair of the EDUCAUSE Board of Directors, and currently serves as chair of the EDUCAUSE National Learning Infrastructure Initiative (NLII) Planning Committee. He also serves on the Florida Digital Divide Council, the Microsoft Higher Education Advisory Council, and the Board of Directors of Florida LambdaRail. Email joel@mail.ucf.edu.

ADDING CLICKS TO BRICKS: INCREASING ACCESS TO MAINSTREAM HIGHER EDUCATION

Raymond E. Schroeder
Office of Technology-Enhanced Learning
University of Illinois at Springfield

Burks Oakley II
University of Illinois

- The virtual campus of the University of Illinois at Springfield is designed to provide new access to public higher education.

- A range of degree programs and support services that are available to on-campus students are now available to a new population of previously under-served learners, no matter where they live or what time restrictions they may have.

- By providing a wide range of quality online degree programs to individuals who otherwise would not be participating in higher education, UIS truly is democratizing higher education.

- The implementation of the virtual campus at UIS involves moving online education into the mainstream via a process that is driven by the faculty and supported by the administration.

- Important features of this implementation include enabling the faculty to determine which degree programs are to be offered online, expanding the size of the tenure-track faculty to teach the increased number of students enrolled by the campus, offering online classes as part of the regular faculty teaching load, and providing online access to the full suite of student services.

I. INTRODUCTION

Since the release of the first graphical web browser, Mosaic, by the University of Illinois in 1993 [2], the internet has grown exponentially, permitting new and rapid access to information and improved interpersonal communication. Building upon the internet, online courses and degrees developed using the concepts and principles of asynchronous learning networks (ALN) have fundamentally altered the face of higher education in the United States, specifically in the area of distance education and lifelong learning. In just over a decade, ALN has become the predominant distance education medium, quickly outpacing and replacing other modes of delivery [3, 4].

A recent review of statewide online initiatives showed that Illinois ranks first in the nation in online enrollments on a per capita basis [5]. The latest report from the Illinois Virtual Campus found that there were more than 69,000 enrollments in over 4,800 online course sections offered by Illinois colleges and universities during the Spring 2004 semester [6]. In this same report, the University of Illinois at Springfield (UIS) ranked number one in enrollment in for-credit online courses of all public four-year institutions in the state.

The Springfield campus was established by the Illinois General Assembly in 1969 as Sangamon State University (SSU). It was created to serve as a regional capstone university, offering junior, senior, and master's level studies, and it provided new access to public higher education for individuals living in central Illinois. From its inception, the campus emphasized a wide variety of innovative teaching approaches, including the use of educational technologies. In 1995, the campus became a part of the University of Illinois, and its name was changed to the University of Illinois at Springfield (UIS). Since that time, the campus has expanded its reach across the state of Illinois and beyond. Originally through compressed interactive video, then beginning in 1998 through online courses and degree programs, the campus reached out to students at a distance, providing access to higher education where there had been none. By the fall of 2004, students in 36 different states as well as seven different countries located on five continents were taking online classes from the Springfield campus. A plot of the growth of online enrollments at UIS is shown in Figure 1 below.

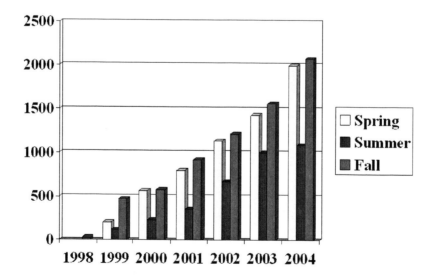

Figure 1: Growth of Online Enrollment by Semester at UIS

Since offering its first online class in the Fall 1998 semester, UIS has developed online baccalaureate degree completion programs in English, history, philosophy, mathematics, mathematics education, computer science, and liberal studies, an online master of science degree in Management Information Systems (MIS), and an online master of arts degree in education (Master Teaching and Leadership, MTL) targeted to in-service K–12 teachers. The enrollment in these online programs has grown steadily: the liberal studies online program enrolled its first students in 1999 and now has 236 online majors and is the second-largest major in the College of Liberal Arts and Sciences; the MTL program currently has an enrollment of 283 (this degree, which was first offered in the Fall 2000 semester, is only available in an online format).

To attract students from outside of Illinois, the Board of Trustees of the University of Illinois approved e-tuition for the UIS campus in the summer of 2003. Residents of Illinois automatically qualify for e-tuition, and out-of-state students qualify for e-tuition during a particular semester if they are enrolled in an online degree program and only take online classes that semester. For the Fall 2004 semester, e-tuition at UIS is $124.25 per credit hour (continuing undergraduate) and $140.00 per credit hour (graduate) [7]. Students enrolled in online courses also pay fees amounting to $25 per credit hour [7]. This fee is used to support the infrastructure associated with online education, such as the technology help desk and the Office of Technology-Enhanced Learning (OTEL), and it also provides a revenue stream to colleges and departments to support their online course offerings (including, but not limited to, hiring program advisors and developing new online courses).

During the Fall 2004 semester at UIS, the campus had approximately 4,400 students (headcount). Almost one in three of these students took at least one online course and more than one in six students took online courses exclusively; nearly 20% of all course credits were generated by enrollments in online courses. Retention in online classes at UIS in recent semesters has averaged greater than 94%, which is comparable with on-campus retention [8].

II. THE FUTURE OF ONLINE LEARNING AT UIS

In 2003, the UIS campus convened a National Commission on the Future of UIS, which engaged in a decentralized visioning process. It was intended to be a broad-based collaborative effort at dreaming "boldly yet realistically" about what UIS might become ten years into the future as well as a visioning process that would precede a more formal strategic planning process. Chancellor Ringeisen's summary of the commission's report [9] highlighted the importance of online learning at UIS: "We are already a national leader in providing online courses and online degrees. That trend will continue as more faculty and students use the internet to teach and learn online." At the same time, the chancellor emphasized the importance of a "vibrant campus" as part of the future vision for UIS.

More recently, Chancellor Ringeisen addressed the UIS faculty at the Fall 2004 Convocation [10]. Speaking extemporaneously, he made the following remarks about online education:

> And let me say once and for all relative to online: UIS is not going to become an online-only university. We wouldn't be building a $31 million building if that were the case. But we'll never neglect that important niche. … It is not that we are terrific at online or that we are terrific on-campus, what we really want to demonstrate to the world is that we can be really good at both, … to show that an institution such as UIS, which has strong, high-quality academic programs, can have strong, high-quality online programs. That is what it is all about. That is what we shall always be. That is why we have insisted that we don't have an online faculty and an on-campus faculty. That is why those of you who are

teaching online teach on-campus. And those of you teaching on-campus have the opportunity to teach online, if you so desire. That is the one way that we know when you [a UIS graduate] get UIS stamped on your forehead, saying that you have earned that high-quality UIS degree, we know that you have that same high quality, no matter which way you went to school here.

The $31 million building to which the chancellor referred is the new University Hall classroom and office building, which opened in July 2004. In addition, a 66,000-square-foot multipurpose facility campus recreation center is currently being designed, and new dormitories are under construction. A number of other initiatives are targeted to improve the quality of the on-campus experience at UIS and to increase the size of the residential student body.

Growing in parallel with the residential campus, the UIS virtual campus [11] will eventually include the breadth of academic degree programs on the campus, with many of the on-campus degrees available in a completely online format. These degrees will span the four colleges on the UIS campus (Liberal Arts and Sciences, Education and Social Work, Public Affairs and Administration, Business and Management). However, just as some degrees will only be offered in an on-campus format, additional degrees—such as the MTL master's degree or the philosophy bachelor's degree—will only be offered in an online format. These variances reflect student demand, the desire of the departmental faculty members, and the need for hands-on experiences in laboratories or studios. The virtual campus also must include the full range of student services, ranging from advising to library services to career services, in order to insure the same high-quality experiences for all degree-seeking students, no matter how they access their UIS education. By adding "clicks" to "bricks," UIS is providing new access to mainstream public higher education.

The decision was made early that online teaching must be integrated into the administrative mainstream of the university. Accordingly, online teaching has always been a part of regular faculty workload—it is not done as part of a separate continuing education unit. Online classes are located in the same academic structure of departments and colleges as the on-campus classes. Courses and sequences must pass the same curriculum committee and graduate or undergraduate council review as on-campus courses and programs. Many other institutions have separate continuing education units for their online programs, which often means that their online classes are taught by a largely adjunct faculty or by regular faculty as overload assignments. UIS has never had a separate extension office or a unit charged with distance education. In fact, online education at UIS really is not about distance—it is about providing access to educational opportunities. A single online class typically enrolls the full spectrum of students, ranging from traditional college-age students living on campus in residence halls, to commuter students who also take on-campus courses, to students in other states or countries who may never visit the campus until they attend graduation.

While other four-year public institutions have online programs, most of these institutions have not embraced the scale or breadth of program development that UIS has. Some institutions focus on a few high-demand programs, whereas others may concentrate their online offerings within one college. With online BA degree completion programs currently spanning the breadth of liberal arts, including history, English, mathematics, and philosophy, UIS is unique among all Sloan-C institutions. The virtual campus initiative will continue to increase the breadth of the online offerings at UIS as new online degree programs are developed in all the colleges on the campus.

III. IMPLEMENTING THE VIRTUAL CAMPUS

It is important to emphasize that the virtual campus at UIS must be driven by the faculty. UIS has only supported the creation of online degrees in cases where the departmental faculty has first chosen to offer those degrees online. No department at UIS has ever been required to offer an online degree without the formal support of its faculty members. Since the inception of the online program at UIS, faculty support for online teaching has evidenced itself through a measured growth of one or two new online degrees each academic year. With support from the Alfred P. Sloan Foundation, the UIS campus now plans to develop and deliver eight or more new online degree programs in the next three years. The process for moving forward with this implementation is clear: departments must first carefully consider the online option and vote in favor of creating the online degree before the college will consider such a move. The relevant governance committee—the graduate or undergraduate council—must review the proposal. A vote of the executive committee of the college (with representation from each department in the college) must accompany a recommendation by the dean of the college before such a proposal will be considered by the campus administration. A business plan detailing the anticipated enrollments and rollout of online classes must show that the program will be self-supporting in the long term. Only after all of these conditions are met will the administration consider the proposal [12]. In August 2004, a special assistant to the provost was appointed to help departments as they move forward through this process.

Although the decision to offer a degree online is clearly a decision to be made by faculty, it is equally clear that the implementation of the virtual campus could not take place without strong support from the senior administrative leadership on the campus. It is necessary to articulate a clear vision for the role of online education at the institution, and the ways in which an expanded online program can help the campus move forward. However, as UIS Chancellor Ringeisen has emphasized, it is imperative that the expansion of the online program be done with full support of the faculty and the campus senate, and that this expansion occur in parallel with the expansion of the residential campus—as noted above, "what we really want to demonstrate to the world is that we can be really good at both, ... to show that an institution such as UIS, which has strong, high-quality academic programs, can have strong, high-quality online programs." [10]

Online education is not just about providing high-quality online courses. It is critical that the campus also provide the full range of student services to off-campus students who are enrolled in online degree programs. Each of the online programs has a program coordinator who works primarily with students. This individual acts as a student recruiter and advisor. Over time, the success of individual online programs is critically dependent upon these program coordinators. The campus also provides a full range of library services to off-campus students [13]. The technology help desk supports on-campus and online students alike [14], as does the online bookstore [15]. Major campus events—such as the recent dedication of University Hall [16], commencement ceremonies, athletic events, and campus celebrations—are streamed live over the internet and subsequently archived, so that students living off-campus may enjoy these activities. While the campus is doing a fine job supporting distant students, additional services need to be provided. Over the next few years, it will be essential to develop online access to the full complement of student services, including the counseling center, the career counseling center, and the placement office.

A. Why Would a Department Want to Increase its Online Enrollments?

On a small campus with small departments like UIS, faculty members often seek to expand their enrollments in order to increase their budgets, hire additional colleagues, support more graduate assistants, and build the reputation of the department. By increasing the size of its faculty, a department is able to add colleagues to cover additional areas of its discipline. More faculty members means greater opportunities for collaboration in research and publication. In brief, the expansion of the department facilitates professional growth for the faculty members of the department.

Increasing the size of the campus faculty will enrich the faculty pool and will enable the campus to offer a broader set of elective courses to all students, both online and on-campus. The additional faculty will enrich the intellectual environment on the campus. Not only will new faculty develop elective courses in their specialties but also they will advise clubs and other student organizations, direct master's degree thesis research, and so on. Overall, the addition of new faculty as part of the virtual campus initiative is an exciting opportunity for the campus, and a very positive feature that has received widespread support from all audiences, from various constituencies on the campus, to the university-wide administration, and to the broader Springfield community.

B. How is it Possible to Increase the Size of the Faculty?

At UIS, the normal faculty teaching load is three courses per semester; each course at UIS typically equals four credit hours, although some equal three credit hours. Once a new online program is offered at UIS, the initial course offerings are covered by full-time faculty on overload payments, or by hiring adjunct faculty to teach on-campus to free up full-time faculty to teach the online sections. After a department is able to fill six new online course sections in an academic year, it is then given the authority to hire one additional full-time faculty member. The new faculty member teaches both online and on-campus courses. This process enables departmental growth without any increase in state funding, because the incremental costs of a new faculty member are more than covered by the increase in tuition revenue (the income fund) generated by the six new course sections.

C. Increasing Diversity at UIS

The relatively rural geographic isolation of the UIS campus in central Illinois limits the rich cultural opportunities that would appeal to diverse groups, meaning that the campus is always going to struggle to increase diversity on the physical campus. However, through an expanded online program, the UIS campus will be able to enroll diverse learners and engage diverse faculty members at a distance, regardless of the geographical limitations of the campus. Specific online initiatives are designed to increase the diversity of the academic experience at UIS. For example, in the fall of 2004, UIS and Chicago State University (CSU) began team-teaching selected online classes. CSU, located on the south side of Chicago, has a largely urban, minority student population, unlike UIS with its largely small city or rural white student population on campus. This arrangement features students from the two institutions working together in discussion forums and on group projects in the team-taught classes.

IV.   ENSURING SUCCESS AND LONG-TERM SUSTAINABILITY

Online education is continuing to expand at UIS. It is critical that online education be done with the same high quality as residential education so that the online degrees will have the same value as the on-campus degrees. This goal entails continuous quality improvement not only in academic areas but also in student support services as additional online programs are developed and delivered. As an example of a program designed to measure quality, U of I Online has provided a grant to UIS (administered by OTEL) to provide baseline studies of the outcomes of online and on-campus classes using the TaskStream e-portfolio system [17]. Using e-portfolios for assessment will enable course- and program-level assessments of quality, and will eventually permit qualitative comparisons of work by online and on-campus students.

A. Increasing Online Enrollments

Increasing both on-campus and online enrollments is critical to the long-term sustainability of the Springfield campus. The need for additional online enrollments points to a critical role of marketing, capitalizing on the University of Illinois brand name throughout the state, the nation, and the world. UIS currently employs a variety of marketing initiatives as part of a comprehensive strategy to increase awareness of its online courses and degree programs. In the interest of maximum efficiency, most of these marketing initiatives are online, where potential students for the online education market are most likely to be searching. Initiatives include comprehensive search engine optimization, the use of website traffic analysis software, and paid or pay-per-lead listings in various higher education portals, including GetEducated.com, Gradschools.com, and ClassesUSA.com. As evidence of the success of search engine optimization, the U of I Online website, which lists all UIS online programs and courses, is currently in the sixth position in results from a search of the phrase *online degrees* on Google (and there were over 1.5 million web searches conducted in July 2004 for this phrase, as determined using Overture's keyword selector tool [18]).

Another approach used to increase online enrollments is partnerships with community colleges. UIS has formal articulation agreements with more than thirty community college partners throughout the state and the nation. In recent months, new partnership agreements have been signed with colleges from California to New York. The community college partners promote the UIS online baccalaureate degree completion program to their students, while UIS agrees to accept students with AA/AS degrees as having met the lower division general education requirements of the campus. As a measure of the effectiveness of these marketing partnerships, nearly sixty percent of all enrollments in one online BA degree completion program (Liberal Studies) come from partner institutions. UIS sees these partnerships as a very effective mechanism to promote awareness of its online programs throughout the nation.

B. Sustaining the Momentum

As more and more departments meet with success through their online programs (expanded enrollments, enlarged faculty, and additional resources from a share of the online fee), more and more faculty members find the prospect of offering their degrees online to be attractive. Momentum is built through the success of the early efforts (which is why success with the first online degrees was so important). So far, all of the online degree programs at UIS are thriving. Confronted with large numbers of applicants, the English department now enforces higher entrance requirements in its online program than its on-campus program. The reputation of the online campus grows, attracting even more students (and more highly qualified students). The reputation also attracts support from other sectors. In the federal FY04 Omnibus Appropriations legislation that became law in January 2004, there was a $250,000 earmark for the UIS campus to develop an online math education baccalaureate degree completion program [19]. This earmark was supported strongly by U.S. Representative John M. Shimkus (R-IL), in whose district UIS is located.

C. How Large Will the Virtual Campus Get?

Will it be possible for the online program to grow to be comparable in enrollment to the physical campus? The answer to this question depends largely on student demand and faculty interest. The real goal is to provide all potential students with viable alternatives spanning the breadth of on-campus degrees (as long as faculty want to offer their degrees in an online format). The balance of enrollments will then depend upon student interest. Currently, all enrollments in MTL and philosophy are online (these programs are only offered online), enrollments in the Liberal Studies online program are much greater than those on campus, and online enrollments in history and English are smaller online than on the campus.

D. Student Support

The program coordinators at UIS provide a unique level of support to students in the online degree programs. Serving as initial entrance advisors, the program coordinators field questions from prospective students, disseminate literature, speak at community colleges, and serve as a constant source of support throughout the students' pursuit of their online degrees. Technology support is provided online, by telephone, and in person by the tech help desk. Wizards (peer tutors and mentors) are a new addition to many online classes at UIS [20]. The Wizards serve to model best practices in discussions, post exemplary assignments, answer student questions, encourage interaction, and facilitate the constructivist approach taken in the student-centered classes at UIS.

E. Faculty Support

Interestingly, the online students and faculty members receive greater support than their on-campus counterparts. This support comes through Wizards, pedagogical and technical workshops, instructional designers, and course developers provided by OTEL. Daily postings to the Online Learning Update blog provide a searchable accumulated resource of some 4,000 articles highlighting the best practices in online learning pedagogy and related areas [21]. The heavy emphasis on a student-centered constructivist approach is apparent in the bi-weekly workshops offered by OTEL. The OTEL home page highlights articles aimed at engaging the online student [22]. The success of this unit is exemplified by the dozens of presentations made by the OTEL director and staff at national and regional conferences. UIS faculty also have access to the award-winning faculty development program *Making the Virtual Classroom a Reality,* which is offered online by the Illinois Online Network (ION) [23, 24]. A number of UIS faculty members have earned ION's Master Online Teacher certificate [25].

F. How Will Progress be Monitored?

Metrics are in place to monitor the quality, scale, and breadth of the virtual campus at UIS. Briefly, these metrics include quantitative descriptions of the virtual campus in all five of the Sloan-C pillars (see below), including enrollment targets and number of new degrees (access pillar) and assessment of learning outcomes (learning effectiveness pillar). Regular review of these metrics will help to ensure that the goals for the virtual campus are met. Use of the newly acquired TaskStream e-portfolio system will enable careful and detailed monitoring of outcomes at the course and program level [17].

G. What are the Obstacles to be Overcome?

While there is a pathway to implementing the virtual campus, there also are obstacles to be overcome; certain issues become magnified in importance as online enrollments grow. One of the main challenges in scaling up the virtual campus is the hiring of new, full-time, tenure-track faculty. To hire these new faculty, the campus has to assume that online enrollments will continue to grow, which will produce a revenue stream from tuition and fees to support the salaries of these new faculty. Questions need to be asked, such as "What areas will grow fastest?" and "In what fields do we hire the new faculty?" Another important challenge is developing a campus culture that emphasizes the importance of scaling the online enrollments. To this end, it is important that the senior leadership be entrepreneurial, at least to the extent of finding ways to open additional course sections as student demand warrants. It is also important that the faculty and staff on the campus come to view the online students in much the same way as they view the on-campus students—that they believe that a student living in Los Angeles is just as important as a student living on campus in a townhouse. Another key hurdle to be overcome is convincing all constituencies, ranging from state legislators and university trustees to faculty, that online education can be as good as (or better than) on-campus education. Unfortunately, there still is a stigma associated with online learning in some quarters that it is not as good as the "real" thing. It is imperative that online education continue to be studied and analyzed if it is to continue to grow at UIS and other institutions, to demonstrate conclusively that it is in no way inferior to on-campus learning. These critical issues must not be allowed to become insurmountable obstacles, or online education will never fulfill its promise.

One of the concerns that has been expressed by some faculty is that online courses may cannibalize the on-campus class enrollments. Some students, when given a choice between an online and on-campus section of the same class, may choose to take the online class. This may mean that certain on-campus classes will not enroll sufficient students and that they will have to be cancelled. This concern has kept the online program from growing as rapidly as it could. In this case, online education may be thought of as a disruptive technology—one that creates entirely new markets and in so doing cannibalizes existing markets. One example of a disruptive technology was the personal computer.

> "Most mainframe and minicomputer companies walked away from PCs ... with the obvious results. IBM actually managed both business models for a while, before competition came in and crushed their PC business. But the destructive power of the disruptive technology was undeniable: in less than a decade, PCs went from being cheap toys for hobbyists to being powerful tools that started to cannibalize mainframe sales" [26].

It may well be that the virtual campus will cannibalize some existing enrollments from the traditional campus. To date, the experience at UIS has been that the clear majority of students taking online sections are doing so from a distance. Furthermore, there is anecdotal evidence that students within the commuting distance are taking more courses during a given semester than they had in prior years, availing themselves of the flexibility of the online classes to supplement their on-campus classes. This development is resulting in more efficient progress toward the degree by students who are mixing the online and on campus classes in their degree program. But if a segment of the student population currently being served by UIS prefers online courses to on-campus courses (for whatever reason), it certainly is much better that they take these online courses from UIS rather than from another institution. And by offering the online courses within the virtual campus, there will be synergies that should improve the educational experiences for all students. During the 2004-2005 academic year, the UIS campus will conduct a detailed study to determine the extent to which online enrollments are taking students away from on-campus programs.

H. Becoming a Model Institution for Others to Emulate

Overall, by implementing the virtual campus initiative described in this paper, the UIS campus will indeed become the prototypical twenty-first century institution, in which there is little distinction between online and on-campus teaching. It will demonstrate directly how ALN can serve as a change agent and can transform a regional institution into an institution with national visibility and reach. The UIS virtual campus will serve as a model for regional colleges and universities throughout the nation, and will show how these institutions, which are the plurality of higher education in the United States, can integrate ALN into their institutional missions in order to provide a broad range of high-quality educational opportunities on a scale never before imagined.

V. RELATIONSHIP TO THE SLOAN-C QUALITY PILLARS

In 1998, Mayadas first used the metaphor of the five pillars that support quality in online education [27]. The five pillars are learning effectiveness, access, student satisfaction, faculty satisfaction, and cost effectiveness. The Sloan Consortium has adopted these five pillars as part of its quality framework [28, 29]. It is worth examining the pillars in light of the implementation of the virtual campus at UIS.

A. Learning Effectiveness

The recent emphasis on the growth of the online program at UIS is supported by the 2003 Sloan-C Survey of Online Learning [30], which found that a majority of academic leaders already believe that the learning outcomes for online education are equal to or superior to those of face-to-face instruction. Even more compelling, nearly one third of these same academic leaders expect that learning outcomes for online education will be superior to face-to-face instruction in three years. But it is not just administrators who have this high opinion of online learning. Students now realize that online learning can be as effective as classroom-based learning (or, for some, more effective). Online students view their degrees to be completely equivalent to degrees earned on-campus—and perhaps more valuable, since earning degrees online demonstrates that they have the drive and determination to do all this from a distance, while gaining new knowledge about the internet and collaboration. The virtual campus must be grounded in the learning effectiveness pillar, and it will be important to the growth of the virtual campus to conduct research studies demonstrating comparable learning outcomes in on-campus and online courses and degree programs.

B. Access

The UIS campus (originally SSU) was founded to provide new access to public higher education, and that clearly is what is now driving the virtual campus—to have the same high-quality programs available online as on-campus (within faculty interest). Many online students today would not be enrolled in degree programs at UIS if these programs were not available online. These online programs make it possible for place-bound and time-restricted individuals to work towards a degree. Distant students have access not only to online courses and degrees but also to a wide range of online student support services (advising, library, help desk, etc.). The implementation of e-tuition at UIS has certainly given students throughout the nation and, indeed, the world new access to affordable online degree programs. But it is not just the distant student who benefits from the virtual campus. Commuter students report that, while they might only have time in their lives to take one class on campus, the scheduling flexibility of online classes allows them to add online classes and thereby make more rapid progress toward their degrees. Overall, by expanding the scale and breadth of the online degree programs at UIS, the virtual campus most certainly addresses the access pillar head on.

C. Student Satisfaction

Students are enrolling in online courses, semester after semester. They are completing online courses in which they enroll at a rate equivalent to those students taking classes on campus [8]. Students are telling their friends about the quality of online learning at UIS. They are very pleased with what they are learning and they are also pleased with the student support services to which they have access. As a measure of this satisfaction, a number of online students have contributed funds to the University of Illinois Foundation, to fund a scholarship for online students in the name of one of their favorite online professors [31]. Nevertheless, as part of the virtual campus initiative, it will be critical to provide even more student services in the future in order to keep student satisfaction high.

D. Faculty Satisfaction

Faculty are finding value in their online teaching. They enjoy getting to know their online students on a personal level through daily interactions, and they find positive benefit in having a more diverse group of students in their online classrooms. They also are enjoying the anytime-anyplace aspects of online teaching (as online teachers often joke, being able to teach from home while wearing pajamas). New faculty are now hired at UIS with the expectation that they will teach both on campus and online. It is critical, therefore, that the campus work to provide an environment in which faculty satisfaction with online teaching will remain high. This means that appropriate professional development opportunities in the area of online education must be provided for new faculty and that continuing faculty must have strong technological and pedagogical support on a continuing basis. To this end, OTEL plays a critical role in supporting faculty.

E. Cost-Effectiveness

Students certainly view online learning at UIS to be cost effective, and they comment that the UIS online education is indeed affordable to them. They realize that the UIS e-tuition is a very fair price to pay to earn a degree with the University of Illinois brand name, and the financial costs of earning their degrees online are good investments in their future [32]. The virtual campus must be self-sustaining based on e-tuition and fees, without new state funds. In the Fall 2004 semester, online courses generated more than $975,000 in tuition revenue and $185,000 in technology fees. The online program must be able to generate the revenues necessary not only to be able to continue to hire new faculty but also to develop additional new programs. To this end, creative, pedagogically effective approaches must be developed with the support of the faculty senate and employed (such as Wizards [20]) to expand enrollments in individual courses in order to maximize tuition revenue.

VI. CONCLUSIONS

UIS is significantly expanding its ALN program and positioning itself as a national leader in online education. If one considers the entire spectrum of higher education, it is clear that community colleges and large research universities have embraced ALN. The one stratum of higher education that has not effectively implemented ALN is the mid-sized public university that has primarily a teaching mission. UIS is an exception. By expanding its promising online initiatives even further, UIS can successfully deliver an online curriculum in a wide variety of fields that meet the needs of the full range of students, from those living on campus to those living far from campus. Developing the virtual campus is an ambitious goal for UIS but one that is anchored in the principles by which the campus was founded: using innovative teaching methods and educational technologies to provide new access to higher education. The virtual campus will impact the institution by bringing online teaching into the mainstream at a significant scale and breadth, showing that an institution can excel at both on-campus and online education. In so doing, UIS can become a national, and perhaps international, leader among colleges and universities that emphasize teaching and the scholarship of teaching.

VII. REFERENCES

1. **Democratic**–adj. "Of or for the people in general; popular: a democratic movement; democratic art forms." The American Heritage® Dictionary of the English Language, Fourth Edition Copyright © 2003 by Houghton Mifflin Company.
2. **Living Internet.** Web history — Mosaic. Online: http://livinginternet.com/w/wi_mosaic.htm.
3. **The Sloan Consortium.** Program for anytime, anyplace learning. Online: http://www.sloan.org /programs/edu_careers.shtml.
4. **National Center on Educational Statistics.** Distance education at degree-granting postsecondary institutions: 2000–2001. Online: http://nces.ed.gov/pubsearch/pubsinfo.asp?pubid=2003017.
5. **Mayadas, A. F.** personal communication, August 2004.
6. **Illinois Virtual Campus.** Distance education enrollments at Illinois colleges and universities Spring/Winter 2004. Online: http://www.ivc.illinois.edu/pubs/enrollment/Spring04.html.
7. **University of Illinois at Springfield. Tuition and fees.** Online: http://www.uis.edu/registration/ tuition /falltuition04.htm.

8. **University of Illinois at Springfield.** UIS online course completion. Online: http://online.uis.edu /info/retent.htm.

9. **University of Illinois at Springfield.** National Commission on the Future of UIS. Online: http://www.uis.edu/chancellor/commission/.

10. **University of Illinois at Springfield.** Convocation 2004. Online: rtsp://otel3.uis.edu:554/ convocation/ Convocation2004.rm.

11. **Virtual**–adj. "Created, simulated, or carried on by means of a computer or computer network: *virtual conversations in a chatroom.*" The American Heritage® Dictionary of the English Language, Fourth Edition Copyright © 2003 by Houghton Mifflin Company.

12. **University of Illinois at Springfield.** Online initiative proposal process at UIS. Online: http://online.uis.edu/info/process.htm.

13. **University of Illinois at Springfield.** Brookens Library. Online: http://library.uis.edu/.

14. **University of Illinois at Springfield.** UIS Technology Support Center. Online: http://www.uis.edu/campustechnologyservices/techsupport/.

15. **University of Illinois at Springfield.** The University of Illinois at Springfield Bookstore. Online: http://shop.efollett.com/htmlroot/storehome/universityofilliniosatspringfield193.html.

16. **University of Illinois at Springfield.** UIS Live. Online: http://www.uis.edu/technology /uislive.html.

17. **TaskStream.** Online: http://www.taskstream.com/pub/.

18. **Overture.** Online: http://www.content.overture.com/d/USm/ac/.

19. **University of Illinois at Springfield.** UIS receives federal funding to address math teacher shortage. Online: http://www.uis.edu/pressreleases/mar04PR/03_08_04.html.

20. **Sax, B.** The Wizards Program at Mercy College. *Journal of Asynchronous Learning Networks* 7(2): 2003. Online: http://www.sloan-c.org/publications/jaln/v7n2/pdf/v7n2_sax.pdf.

21. **University of Illinois at Springfield.** Online learning update. Online: http://people.uis.edu/rschr1 /onlinelearning/blogger.html.

22. **University of Illinois at Springfield.** Office of Technology-Enhanced Learning. Online: http://otel.uis.edu/.

23. **Making the Virtual Classroom a Reality.** Online: http://www.mvcr.org/default.asp.

24. **The Illinois Online Network.** Online: http://www.ion.illinois.edu/.

25. **Making the Virtual Classroom a Reality.** Master Online Teacher Certificate. Online: http://www.mvcr.org/ courses/MOT.asp?textonly=false.

26. **Hiler, J.** Blogs as disruptive tech: How weblogs are flying under the radar of the content management giants. WebCrimson Online: http://www.webcrimson.com/ourstories/ blogsdisruptivetech.htm.

27. **Mayadas, A. F.** Quality framework for online education. In Panitz, B., Learning on demand, *ASEE Prism*, April 1998.

28. **The Sloan Consortium**, Quality framework. Online: http://www.sloan-c.org/effective/ framework.asp.

29. **Lorenzo, G., and J. Moore.** The Sloan Consortium report to the nation: Five pillars of quality online education, 2002. Online: http://www.aln.org/effective/pillarreport1.pdf.

30. **The Sloan Consortium.** Online learning is as good as being there. Online: http://www.sloan-c.org/ resources/survey.asp.

31. **University of Illinois at Springfield.** Scholarships. Online: http://www.uis.edu/scholarships.

32. **Oakley, B. II.** The value of online learning: Perspectives from the University of Illinois at Springfield, *Journal of Asynchronous Learning Networks*, 8(3): 2004. Online: http://www.sloan-c. org/publications/jaln/v8n3/pdf/v8n3_oakley.pdf.

VIII. ABOUT THE AUTHORS

Ray Schroeder is Professor Emeritus of Communication, Director of the Office of Technology-Enhanced Learning at the University of Illinois at Springfield, and Faculty Associate at the University of Illinois Online. He has taught more than a dozen online classes. As Director of Technology-Enhanced Learning he leads the campus online initiative. As Faculty Associate, Schroeder is engaged in the formation of online learning policy for the University of Illinois. He is a Sloan Consortium Distinguished Scholar in Online Learning 2002-2003 and the recipient of the 2002 Sloan-C award for the Most Outstanding Achievement in ALN by an Individual. Contact: Raymond E. Schroeder, Director, Office of Technology-Enhanced Learning, HRB 78, University of Illinois at Springfield, One University Plaza, Springfield, IL 62703. Telephone: 217-206-7531; email Schroeder.Ray@uis.edu.

Burks Oakley II is the Associate Vice President for Academic Affairs at the University of Illinois and serves as the director of University of Illinois Online. Oakley received his B.S. degree from Northwestern University and his M.S. and Ph.D. degrees from the University of Michigan. He has received numerous awards for his teaching and innovative use of technology in education, including the Luckman Distinguished Undergraduate Teaching Award from UIUC in 1993, the Outstanding Teacher Award from the American Society for Engineering Education (ASEE) in 1993, the Educom Medal in 1996, the Major Educational Innovation Award from the Institute of Electrical and Electronics Engineers (IEEE) in 1996, the Meritorious Service Award from the IEEE Education Society in 1998, the IEEE Third Millennium Medal in 2000, and the Achievement Award from the IEEE Education Society in 2002. He is a Fellow of the IEEE and the ASEE, a former Vice President of ASEE, and a member of the Board of Directors of the Sloan Consortium. He recently received the 2003 Sloan-C award for the Most Outstanding Achievement in Online Teaching and Learning by an Individual. Contact: Burks Oakley II, 337 Henry Administration Building, University of Illinois, 506 S. Wright St., Urbana, IL 61801. Telephone: 217-244-6465; email oakley@uillinois.edu.

How Can the Two Worlds of Academia and Industry Cooperate to Contribute to a Tenfold Increase in Online Learning in the Next Ten Years?

INSTRUCTIONAL TECHNOLOGY GRADUATE PROGRAMS IN SUPPORT OF CORPORATE E-LEARNING

Barbara B. Lockee
Virginia Polytechnic Institute and State University

Michelle A. Reece
Certified Medical Representatives Institute

- Higher education and external enterprises can work together to collaboratively advance the field of e-learning through shared experiences.

- Instructional technology programs in university settings are uniquely suited to support the e-learning efforts of corporate and government organizations.

- Faculty are convinced that interactions with external partners are essential to stay current in the practice of instructional design and technology as well as to maintain awareness of real-world issues faced by practitioners in industry.

- When given the opportunity for practical experience in real-world settings, students develop skills in instructional design as well as valuable contacts for employment.

- Academia must find ways to weave interactions with business partners into the fabric of their missions and activities.

I. INTRODUCTION

Collaborations between higher education and external partners in private and government sectors related to e-learning are becoming more common [1]. Such partnerships may evolve for differing purposes, by various approaches, and through a variety of entities within a college or university. While support units such as outreach, distance education, and learning technology centers often work with outside agencies in the development of e-learning initiatives, academic program areas also directly interact with external clients for such purposes.

Instructional technology (IT) programs in university settings are uniquely suited to support the e-learning efforts of corporate and government organizations, particularly advanced degree programs that prepare IT professionals at the master's and doctoral levels. Composed of faculty charged with the primary missions of research, outreach, and preparation of the future professoriate and students ready to apply new skills and knowledge related to instructional design and technology, instructional technology programs provide natural partners for businesses seeking assistance with distributed learning efforts. Historically, IT programs have advanced the research base on human learning and the application of such research outcomes for the creation of effective mediated-learning environments. This paper describes the rationale for academic-business partnerships for e-learning, the qualities and characteristics of IT programs as e-learning liaisons, the state of such partnerships in Research I graduate programs, and finally, a case study of an ongoing collaboration between IT at Virginia Polytechnic Institute and State University (Virginia Tech) and a nonprofit educational corporation.

A. Existing Research

While a great deal of research has been conducted related to the design, development, and implementation of distance instruction in higher education (see *Journal of Asynchronous Learning Environments, Educational Technology Research and Development, American Journal of Distance Education, Journal of Open and Distance Learning,* and so forth) and also distributed training in business and industry (see *Training and Development, Performance Improvement Journal, International Journal of Training and Development,* and so on) a gap in the literature exists related to e-learning initiatives and interactions between higher education and corporate organizations.

However, while little has been published on e-learning partnerships across business and academia per se, literature does support the union of industry and higher education for the advancement of research in general. An impressive report conducted by the Business-Higher Education Forum [2] details the advantages, challenges, and critical issues involved in research collaborations between universities and industrial organizations. In this document developed by an array of top-level administrators from academia, corporations, and the government, the benefits of joint research initiatives are described for both industry and academia. For businesses, the advantages are access to external expertise, access to students as potential employees, and the growth of the industrial laboratory as a result of additional contacts through the university sector. For universities, the advantages include financial support for research efforts, engagement in the service mission of the institution, the broadening of the experience of students and faculty, and the enhancement of regional economic development. Additionally, the *Review of University-Industry Research Relationships* [3] developed by the University of Southern California identifies cost savings for both parties related to shared research efforts. As research and development budgets become the target of budget cuts, businesses can ally with universities to stretch research dollars and often seek government funding through programs targeted solely for such relationships.

More specific to e-learning efforts and partnerships, Katz [1] produced effective guidelines and considerations for selecting business models and external partners for an institution's e-learning objectives. Written from an administrative perspective, this report suggests several reasons why an institution may want to partner with an external organization, including: the generation of new ideas; the ability to leverage complementary skills, strengths, and markets; shared financial risk; and the acquisition of resources for new ventures.

While reports and guidelines have successfully identified the rationale for industry-academia relationships, the academic perspective related to such partnerships seems noticeably absent from the literature on e-learning. Instructional technology is a program area with extensive experience in collaborating with external partners for the purpose of distance education research and service.

B. IT Programs as Partners

As members of The Sloan Consortium have demonstrated, higher education organizations offer a wealth of knowledge, skills, and experiences related to the creation and implementation of distance education courses and programs. Why would an academic program area like instructional technology serve as an effective partner in corporate e-learning endeavors? The answer lies in both the nature of the IT field and the overarching missions of its home institutions.

The profession of instructional technology "encompasses the analysis of learning and performance problems, and the design, development, implementation, evaluation, and management of instructional and non-instructional processes and resources intended to improve learning and performance in a variety of settings, particularly educational institutions and the workplace" [4]. Faculty in IT graduate programs must therefore maintain skills in the two broad areas of IT and graduate education. Faculty must be well versed in the psychology of learning as well as skilled in the application of learning theory for effective instructional design—in other words, they must be instructional technology practitioners as well as teachers. Also, faculty serving doctoral students must prepare learners to engage in professional research and scholarship that examines the theory and practice of instructional technology. Students enrolled at the master's degree level typically engage in curriculum that prepares them to serve in applied settings in academia, industry, or government. Doctoral candidates are usually groomed for employment in higher education, both as academic faculty and as instructional support administrators. Also, graduates of IT doctoral programs are hired to provide leadership in corporate and government training organizations [5]. Therefore, IT programs offer an interesting mix of expertise related to the design of both e-learning resources and e-learning research.

Also, the tripartite mission of many colleges and universities—teaching, research, and service—rings especially true for many of the state-funded land-grant institutions that are host to some of the larger graduate IT programs. Faculty in such units are charged with teaching the instructional technology curriculum; the conduct of research related to the design, development, implementation, and evaluation of technology-mediated learning environments; and the provision of outreach and service to external agencies in support of their instructional development needs, often related to the creation and implementation of distributed learning systems. The combination of these programmatic and institutional goals explains the natural liaisons between IT academic programs and industry partners. The following section provides an overview of the types of relationships maintained between such groups and offers examples of partnerships based on each purpose.

II. METHODOLOGY

Recent e-mail surveys and follow-up phone interviews with instructional technology program faculty at Research I institutions found that most of them had relationships with external entities in support of training and instructional development, with many of these relationships specifically in support of e-learning. Participants were selected based on the size of their doctoral student population as indicated in the 2004 *Educational Media and Technology Yearbook* [6]. Those programs serving 25 or more Ph.D. level students were contacted via e-mail with a request for information related to e-learning initiatives with external clientele. Eight of the ten programs meeting the specified criteria responded to the request for information, providing information related to partner organizations, descriptions of collaborations, and benefits of engaging in such opportunities.

III. RESULTS

Table 1 identifies the responding institutions, their external partners, and the manner in which they collaborate on e-learning efforts. An interesting array of interactions and e-learning support relationships were prevalent among the IT programs and their external partners. Partnership approaches include student internships with external client groups, corporate participation in online IT programs, contractual work, course-related projects, and collaborative research projects.

Institution of Higher Education	External Partner(s)	Relationship
Arizona State University	Computer manufacturing corporation (non-disclosure agreement)	Course-related projects
Brigham Young University	TALL (Technology-Aided Language Learning)	Collaborative research projects
Florida State University	U.S. Navy	Contracted e-learning development projects
Georgia State University	Home Depot IKON UPS Cingular	Internships
Syracuse University	IBM Canada Time Warner Blue Cross Blue Shield	Corporate enrollees in online masters program Specialized certificate programs Internships
University of Georgia	Centers for Disease Control Delta Air Lines Home Depot	Internships Contracted e-learning development projects Collaborative research projects
University of Texas, Austin	Apple Dell Arc Media TeamCraft	Contracted e-learning development projects Collaborative research projects

Virginia Tech	Certified Medical Representatives Institute	Contracted e-learning development projects
	Volvo, Inc.	Course-related projects
	U.S. Army	Collaborative research projects
		Internships

Table 1. Academic-Industry Partners and Relationship Types

Also consistent among the respondents was the sense of importance for all parties involved in external collaborations. Faculty indicated that they and their students gain greater awareness of real-world issues as a result of these interactions, knowledge that can be used to inform both the teaching and practice of instructional design for the purpose of e-learning. Partner organizations benefit from the distance education and instructional technology expertise shared by faculty and students, along with the potential for increased productivity and improved learning performance in distributed training environments.

A. Internships

The most common support approach was the use of instructional technology graduate students as interns in corporate training departments. Corporate partners have the benefit of access to newly prepared professionals with knowledge of theoretical principles of instructional design along with awareness of current technological innovations for learning. Interns gain from this relationship through the acquisition of professional experience and the opportunity to apply new skills and knowledge to real-world situations. Internship experiences were more prevalent through universities either located in or in close proximity to metropolitan areas, such as the University of Georgia and Georgia State University, both of whom have alliances with several corporate entities in Atlanta. The Instructional Technology Department at the University of Georgia has a partnership with Delta Air Lines' corporate training division, the Learning Services Organization. Several projects have included an internship program for faculty as well as one for graduate students. UGA also has a 15-year relationship with the Centers for Disease Control where many of their students engage in internship experiences, six of whom now work there on a permanent basis. Also in the heart of Atlanta, Georgia State University's instructional technology department works closely with corporate partners such as UPS, IKON, AT&T, Home Depot, and Cingular to arrange internship opportunities for its students.

B. Corporate Participation in IT Online Programs

Another manner in which IT programs and industries join forces in e-learning development is through corporate employee participation in IT online programs. In some instances, industrial partners contract with IT programs for a group of employees to engage in the distance instructional technology curriculum. Syracuse University and Florida State University both have contractual arrangements with external partners for the matriculation of employees through the institution's online program. More commonly, individual training and instructional technology specialists from the corporate sector choose to enroll in online IT programs for their own professional development. Often, employees in corporate or government training groups have little to no academic preparation in the fields of training, instructional design, or instructional technology. Training specialists are usually hired for such positions because they have proven themselves to be leaders among their colleagues or have demonstrated above-average knowledge and skills related to their company's products or services. Participation in instructional design and technology curriculum helps advance their instructional development skills and improve their job-related performance. In order to meet more immediate professional development needs, Syracuse and Florida State University also offer certificate programs in instructional design and distance education.

C. Contractual Projects

In yet another partnership approach, IT programs often engage in contractual work with external groups, either independently or through departmental or college centers such as the Learning Technology Center at the University of Texas in Austin, the Learning Systems Institute (LSI) at Florida State University, the Learning and Performance Support Laboratory at the University of Georgia, and the Center for Instructional Technology Solutions in Industry and Education (CITSIE) at Virginia Tech. As an example of such contractual work, UT-Austin's Learning Technology Center (LTC) has engaged with Apple to build a prototype tool for online collaborative knowledge building. This project exemplifies both product development and applied research in e-learning development. Also, UT faculty and students are working with Dell to develop multimedia-based training modules for its employees.

Florida State's Learning Systems Institute maintains strong connections to the government sector, as evidenced in a current project with the U.S. Navy: to move all naval training online. LSI research faculty are working with naval training personnel to develop design guidelines and instructor competencies that will facilitate an efficient and consistent product.

D. Course-related Projects

What better way to learn effective e-learning development than to engage in its creation or in related research? Arizona State University's IT program offers a course in human performance technology, a class that focuses on the analysis and resolution of performance problems across various environments. Students in a recent section of the course worked with a large computer manufacturing corporation to determine the reasons for discrepancies between high and low performers in its newly developed online training programs. Students conducted a causal analysis, identified the key sources of problems related to the training, and proposed interventions to improve employee performance.

Virginia Tech's IT program offers a course entitled Trends and Theories of Professional Development. During the current semester (Fall 2004), students are working with the Volvo Truck Division in Dublin, Virginia, to identify solutions to changes in training needs. The company faces a variety of challenges related to the cross-training of current employees and wishes to shift to a more performance-support approach to training, likely requiring the design of online, just-in-time knowledge management systems. The IT students will work as a team to develop an appropriate plan for the transition to such technologies.

E. Collaborative Research

While much of the activity related to partnerships for e-learning centers on the design and implementation of instructional programming, at least some of the collaborations between business and academia result from shared interests in e-learning research topics. The University of Georgia is working on a joint research project with Delta Air Lines regarding the implementation of instructional systems design across all business units. The outcomes of this inquiry hold promise for organizations interested in streamlining training processes while maintaining learning effectiveness and consistency of results.

A unique example of collaboration between academic and private sector partners for the purpose of e-learning research can be found at Brigham Young University. The instructional technology program at BYU has a major emphasis in research related to second language acquisition, due in part to a large second language program at the university. The university endorsed the group's creation of a spin-off business as an entrepreneurial endeavor. The organization, Technology-Aided Language Learning (TALL), is completely external to the BYU academic program, yet employs IT faculty and students for the creation of automated second language tutoring programs based on empirical research. This initiative serves as an excellent example of technology transfer as well as applied research for the creation of effective mediated-learning systems.

IV. CASE STUDY: VIRGINIA TECH AND CMR INSTITUTE

A partnership between an instructional technology academic program and a nonprofit corporation serves as an example of an ongoing collaborative initiative related to e-learning. The partner groups are described, as well as activities, benefits and challenges, and future projects.

A. Instructional Technology at Virginia Tech

Preparing instructional technology professionals to be effective practitioners is a primary focus of the Instructional Technology Program at Virginia Tech. Housed in the Department of Learning Sciences and Technologies within the School of Education, the IT program offers graduate degrees at the master's, specialist, and doctoral levels. The program curriculum is theoretically based, pragmatically oriented, and addresses the skills and knowledge necessary for careers across a variety of venues, including higher education, business, and K-12 environments.

While the IT faculty concentrate on serving over 35 full-time doctoral students on campus, the group is also strongly engaged in outreach initiatives to develop IT competencies in a broad range of external constituents. The project is supported through the aforementioned Center for Instructional Technology Solutions in Industry and Education (CITSIE). CITSIE is an integral component of the College of Liberal Arts and Human Sciences at Virginia Tech. The center's mission is to conduct research that informs instructional practice as well as to provide outreach to clients in K-12 education, higher education, business, and government. Activities of the center include instructional design and development consulting, instructional technology research, program and product evaluation, and the development of technology skills for a variety of clients.

The projects of CITSIE provide excellent opportunities for IT faculty and graduate students to become involved in authentic problem-based learning experiences; the projects also serve as a milieu for instructional technology research and development. The guiding philosophy of the IT program is that its graduates will be well prepared to design and develop instructional environments based on both behavioral and cognitive learning theories in order to serve diverse clients with varying needs.

In 1998, the IT program faculty developed an online Instructional Technology Master's Program (ITMA) designed specifically for public school teachers in the state of Virginia and now being offered on a national level. The first group of 50 students graduated in Spring 2000 and the program is on its fifth iteration, currently enrolling over 200 students across the country and internationally. A cohort model focusing on the integration of technology in curriculum, instruction, and assessment was used in the first iteration, with each participant simultaneously engaging in a prescribed set of coursework. The program has evolved to become completely asynchronous, allowing students flexibility in the courses they choose to take and the sequence in which they take them. Program design emphasizes student inquiry into how various technologies can assist the learning process.

The lessons learned by the IT faculty from the design, development, implementation, and evolution of the ITMA program have informed teaching and research as well as contributed to the distance education knowledge base [7, 8, 9, 10]. Particularly challenging were the barriers encountered in attempts to scale the program to serve more students across a broader geographic reach and through more flexible experiences than the university traditionally supports. The faculty have developed web-based administrative systems to manage the tracking and assessment of learners and has collaborated with university support systems to change business processes to accommodate the needs of the program and its constituents. CITSIE has used the ITMA design and development model to transition other academic programs for online delivery. Also, the ITMA program has been revised for use in Malawi as professional development for the country's K-12 educators. Funded by the United States Agency for International Development (USAID), the Malawi project has facilitated research on the cultural and contextual considerations of the repurposing of American courseware for implementation in an international setting.

B. Certified Medical Representatives Institute

The Certified Medical Representatives Institute (CMRI) is an independent nonprofit educational organization dedicated to advancing the healthcare industry through education that builds better understanding among professionals in the healthcare industry and, ultimately, between those professionals and the patients they serve. A majority of the students enrolled in CMRI courses are sales representatives from various pharmaceutical companies. Upon completion of the targeted program strands, employees receive the designation of Certified Medical Representative (CMR), indicating to other healthcare professionals such as physicians and pharmacy personnel that the representative has demonstrated essential knowledge related to body physiology, disease states, and the most current innovations in pharmaceutical therapies. For over 40 years, CMRI has developed learning strategies and a flexible and evolving curriculum of more than 40 courses that have helped leading healthcare organizations and sales professionals stay current on critical industry-related advancements. The CMRI curriculum is delivered via distance learning to more than 13,000 students across the United States and Puerto Rico [11].

The CMRI curriculum is available through several delivery modes, including printed text, audio CD-ROM, and browser-enabled or CD-ROM multimedia formats. While all 40 courses are available via print and audio CD-ROM, the development of electronic versions of the courseware began in 2001 and a pilot test of the first seven e-learning courses was completed in the summer of 2004.

C. Partnership Activities

The partnership between the instructional technology program at Virginia Tech and CMRI began over five years ago and has evolved to encompass a variety of activities. Initially, CMRI contracted with a Virginia Tech IT faculty member to provide a professional development seminar on e-learning for its board of directors. The board, consisting primarily of training directors from major pharmaceutical companies, was interested to learn the process of e-learning start-up, the benefits of engaging in online training initiatives, and the challenges they would face in adopting this innovation.

Following that initiative, the faculty member joined CMRI's curriculum committee, an advisory group that meets twice a year to provide guidance to the organization related to its instructional content, approaches, and delivery systems. In this capacity, the faculty member has provided the committee with relevant information on recent trends and issues related to e-learning in both corporate and academic markets. Engagement in this role provides shared advantages as the participating academic also learns much from these meetings regarding the issues that industry professionals grapple with as they develop and implement online training systems.

AS CMRI has begun transitioning its courses to e-learning, CITSIE faculty have assisted with the formative evaluation of CMRI's e-learning pilot courseware (called CMR-Interactive), offering instructional and interface design feedback to the electronic course developers. Here again the experience is of reciprocal value as the faculty gain increased awareness of industry approaches to the design of mediated-learning environments, approaches that can be shared with graduate students to advance their knowledge as well.

Recently, a large pharmaceutical company contracted with CMRI to assess its in-house training curriculum and determine gaps related to the company's best practices for its sales personnel. CMRI recruited two CITSIE faculty members for that review to provide an academic perspective in the analysis process. This endeavor reflects another example of how faculty can become more aware of corporate e-learning instructional design and development strategies while sharing academic perspectives on the same issues with their industry colleagues.

In the past several years, CMRI leadership has been involved in class presentations on distance education and training to students enrolled in the IT graduate program. Conversely, the author has conducted instructional design and e-learning workshops with CMRI partners at professional meetings such as the Society of Pharmaceutical and Biotech Trainers (SPBT). Perspectives from both organizations have been mutually beneficial not only to the direct participants but also to the professional groups of both academic and industry collaborators.

D. Benefits and Challenges

The relationship between the IT program at Virginia Tech and CMRI can best be described as symbiotic, because both parties gain from the collaborative activities previously described. IT program faculty are able to apply expertise related to instructional systems design as well as lessons learned from their own distance program in order to provide instructional solutions to issues faced by CMRI in their transition to an online learning system. IT graduate program faculty are able to leverage the interactions with CMRI and the pharmaceutical industry whenever they teach courses that focus on the design, development, and implementation of distance education and training across a variety of venues. Students gain from exposure to professionals in the field of distance education and their work-related responsibilities and challenges. Additionally, when given the opportunity for practical experience in real-world settings like those previously described, students develop skills in instructional design as well as valuable contacts for potential future employment.

The challenges of relationships across the two worlds of academia and industry have been few in this particular example. Issues of timing and differences in organizational cultures are noted issues that IT programs have faced in partnerships for e-learning development. However, the partnership in this case study has not encountered such challenges.

E. Future Plans and a Challenge

The future holds great promise for continued collaboration between IT at Virginia Tech and CMRI. In 2005, Barbara Lockee will engage in a research leave to work directly with CMRI on research related to e-learning design and adoption in an international setting. This effort will draw from the aforementioned CITSIE project that examined the transition of American IT curriculum for use in a different country. Factors that must be considered in the repurposing of CMRI materials and delivery systems will be investigated, along with issues that may influence the adoption of e-learning in an international venue.

The experiences highlighted in this case study have demonstrated a successful example of the bridging of the two worlds of higher education and industry for the advancement of e-learning. CITSIE faculty are convinced that interactions with external partners are essential to stay current in the practice of instructional design and technology as well as to maintain awareness of real-world issues faced by practitioners in industry.

Higher education and external enterprises can work together to collaboratively advance the field of e-learning through shared experiences such as those described in this paper. Academia must find ways to weave interactions with business partners into the fabric of their missions and activities related to e-learning. Industry should seek to leverage the extensive empirical research and experience in e-learning that educational institutions have demonstrated over the past decade. Together, both worlds can meet their individual learning needs through more informed and progressive approaches.

V.   REFERENCES

1.   **Katz, R. N.** *Selecting models and external partners for e-Learning initiatives.* ECAR Research Bulletin (3). Boulder, CO: Educause Center for Applied Research, 2003.
2.   Working Together, Creating Knowledge: The University-Industry Research Collaboration Initiative. Washington, DC: Business-Higher Education Forum, 2001.
3.   *Review of University-Industry Research Relationships.* Technology Transfer Newsletter. Office of Patent and Copyright Administration, University of Southern California, 1995.
4.   **Reiser, R. A.** What field did you say you were in? Defining and naming our field. In: Reiser, R.A., and J.V. Dempsey (eds). *Trends and Issues in Instructional Technology*, 5–15. Upper Saddle River, NJ: Merrill Prentice-Hall, 2002.
5.   **Larson, M., and B. Lockee.** Instructional design practice: Career environments, job roles, and a climate of change. *Performance Improvement Quarterly*: 22–40, 2004.
6.   **Orey, M, M. A. Fitzgerald, and R. M. Branch (eds.).** Westport, CT: Libraries Unlimited, *Educational Media and Technology Yearbook 2004* 29: 2004.
7.   **Lockee, B. B., D. M. Moore, and J. K. Burton.** Measuring success: Evaluation strategies for distance education. *Educause Quarterly* 25(1): 20–27, 2002.
8.   **Lockee, B. B., D. M. Moore, and J. K. Burton.** Old concerns with new distance education research. *Educause Quarterly* 24(2): 60–62, 2001.
9.   **Lockee, B. B., G. P. Sherman, D. M. Moore, and J. K. Burton.** Framing the questions of distance education research. Paper presented at Distance Education Conference 2000, 115–125, Austin, TX, 2000.
10.   **Moore, D. M., B. B. Lockee, and J. K. Burton.** Developing and delivering an online master's program in instructional technology. In: M. Fitzgerald, M. Orey, and R. Branch (eds), *Educational Media and Technology Yearbook* 27: 27–32, 2002.
11.   **Reece, M. and B. B. Lockee.** Improving training outcomes through blended learning. *Journal of Asynchronous Learning Networks,* in press.

VI.   ACKNOWLEDGEMENTS

Many thanks go to the instructional technology faculty and research associates at the universities highlighted in this paper; your assistance and timely input are much appreciated. Thanks also go to Deyu Hu for her assistance in combing the literature related to academic-industry partnerships.

VII. ABOUT THE AUTHORS

Barbara B. Lockee is an associate professor of instructional technology at Virginia Polytechnic Institute and State University, where she has taught for the past eight years. She teaches courses in distance education, training, and instructional design. Her research interests focus on instructional design issues within e-learning environments. She currently serves as president of the Research and Theory Division of the Association of Educational Communications and Technologies, and she has written over 30 publications for books and professional journals on the topic of distance education. Email lockeebb@vt.edu.

Michelle A. Reece, MEd, is Vice President, Learning and Curriculum Development for the CMR Institute. She is responsible for managing the development and revision of a diverse curriculum of more than 40 courses delivered in print-based, audio, and multimedia format. She regularly writes and publishes articles on pharmaceutical issues for industry publications and is a past president and board member of the Valleys of Virginia Chapter of the American Society for Training and Development. Email mreece@cmrinstitute.org.

IMPLEMENTING CURRICULA USING A VARIETY OF LEARNING MODALITIES AT LIBERTY MUTUAL GROUP

Richard Benner
Liberty Mutual Group

- Liberty Mutual emphasizes training that is relevant to employees, helpful to business, and develops employee abilities via emerging instructional technologies.

- Five primary elements comprise Liberty's learning strategy
  - Manager involvement
  - Focus on job requirements
  - Program design
  - Multi-part curricula
  - Assessment of learning outcomes and job application

- The expectations of recent college graduates will promote greater use of ALN in corporate learning and training.

I. INTRODUCTION

Liberty Mutual Group is a diversified worldwide insurance service organization with a common mission of "helping people live safer, more secure lives." Founded in Boston in 1912, the company is one of the largest multi-line insurers in the property/casualty field. Liberty has more than 38,000 employees located in over 900 offices worldwide.

In 2003, the company realized over $16.6 billion in consolidated revenue, ranking 116 on the Fortune 500 list of companies. Liberty Mutual Group is currently the property casualty carrier. In 2001 and 2002, Liberty Mutual Group reorganized into a mutual holding company structure. This structure provided the company with better capital market access and greater strategic flexibility while aligning its legal structure with its operating structure and preserving the company's mutual status.

Liberty Mutual Group is structured to address the specific needs of its customers. At the highest level there is a distinction between personal and commercial lines. Several Strategic Business Units (SBUs) serve specific customer segments. Each SBU uses an operating structure aligned towards meeting the specific insurance and risk management needs of its customer base.

A. Liberty's Training Organization

Liberty's training organization mirrors the company's organization structure. Most operating units within SBUs have training managers and staff who are responsible for developing and delivering training specific to the business function. Examples of some of the departments are Personal Market Sales, National Market Loss Prevention and Business Market Underwriting.

Corporate Human Resource Development (HRD) is responsible for management and executive development, enterprise-wide employee training, and general business skills training. In addition to design and delivery of programs in those areas, Corporate HRD has been given a quality assurance role by senior management. Corporate HRD works with training managers in the departments to ensure that training is both relevant to the employee and helpful to business. This oversight role includes exploring and encouraging the use of emerging instructional technologies to support employee development.

B. Executive Support for Learning and Development

Employee development is a critical success factor for Liberty Mutual. Ted Kelly, President and CEO of the Liberty Mutual Group, emphasizes the importance of the company's learning framework for skill development and for aligning business around core principles. Kelly's leadership and active involvement in program design, development and delivery is a key reason why learning is implemented at all levels of Liberty's Business.

II. LIBERTY MUTUAL'S LEARNING INFRASTRUCTURE

Like other human resource development organizations in business, Liberty's training and development groups work to ensure that employees have the capabilities to support business goals and execute the company's business strategy.

Liberty's success in developing curricula relevant to the business and to its employees is based on these critical success factors:

- Strong, consistent management support from the highest levels of the company.

- Rigorous methods for identifying employees' skills and knowledge requirements.

- Adoption of multi-phase, mandatory curriculum models that provide structured development activities for an extended period of time.

- Expanded use of instructional technologies to deliver the right training at the right time.

- Increased emphasis on assessment methods to document the effectiveness of the training and employee learning.

Instructional technologies have allowed Liberty to:

- Improve the timeliness of delivery of structured learning activities to employees.

- Improve the consistency of learning activities for dispersed learning audiences.

- Extend learning throughout an employee's tenure in a job or role through the use of integrated curricula that incorporate a variety of delivery modalities.

A. Learning Strategy

In 1997, Liberty's Human Resource Development group introduced a new corporate learning strategy to develop and enhance managers' and employees' capabilities to perform well at their jobs. This strategy focused on ensuring learner and business relevance in its training programs. In general, there are five primary elements that comprise Liberty's learning strategy:

1. Manager Involvement

There is a strong emphasis on management involvement throughout all aspects of learning at Liberty. Managers help direct program design approaches, and they help designers get access to subject matter experts. Managers frequently take the role of faculty by delivering segments of employee and management training themselves. Line managers are responsible for helping employees apply new skills back on the job.

2. Focus on Job Requirements

The process for developing appropriate training programs begins by determining "what an employee must know and do" to perform well in his or her job. Critical knowledge, skills and behaviors are determined by systematically documenting those that contribute to effective job performance. The knowledge, skills and behaviors are displayed in profiles that drive the instructional program development for the targeted group.

In 2002, Liberty was introduced to the DACUM model of job task analysis by William Coscarelli as part of a criterion referenced test development project. Liberty has found the DACUM model to be a highly effective method for discovering the core knowledge and skill requirements of a job, and for mapping their relationships [1].

In summary, the specific knowledge, skills and behaviors define the outcomes desired from program-design efforts and instructional activities.

3. Program Design

A great deal of emphasis is placed on program design. Liberty's internal design approach helps employees transfer knowledge, concepts and skills acquired in training to their day-to-day responsibilities. A key aspect of Liberty's design is ensuring that program objectives are out-come based. Learning objectives are criterion-referenced. In the training and learning environments, Liberty tries to replicate real job conditions with the goal of increasing knowledge and skill transfer back on the job [2]. Liberty makes extensive use of scenarios, cases, and simulations that look and feel like actual Liberty business practices. This increases the relevance of the learning from the learner's perspective.

4. Multi-part Curricula

Through the development of multi-part curricula, employees are assisted over an extended period of time after they have entered a new job or role. Training is no longer limited to an employee's initial few weeks in a new job or role. Curricula extend structured learning and development activities to continue throughout an employee's career. Given the highly dispersed nature of Liberty's workforce, instructional technologies are critical to delivering multi-part curricula in a timely and cost effective manner.

5. Assessment of Learning Outcomes and Job Application

A number of assessment methods are used to ensure that employee learning is relevant and useful. First, posting program surveys of the employee's opinion of training effectiveness provides useful feedback regarding the program's effectiveness at meeting the stated program objectives as well as an overall assessment of the program. Second, criterion-referenced tests measure the degree to which learners can recall key concepts and terms. Test items based on case material and scenarios measure learner application in a realistic, application-oriented manner. Third, self and manager assessments measure the success of the training at supporting on-the-job performance. These levels of evaluation are the first three of four levels described by Donald K. Kirkpatrick in *Evaluating Training Performance* [3].

Information from these assessments is used to ensure that the structured learning activities are focused on helping employees perform well on the job. Assessment results may reflect a need to revisit the job analysis, to alter program or module objectives, or to consider different design approaches or alternative instructional methods and modalities. The relationship of job analysis, objectives, design, development and delivery and assessment is illustrated below:

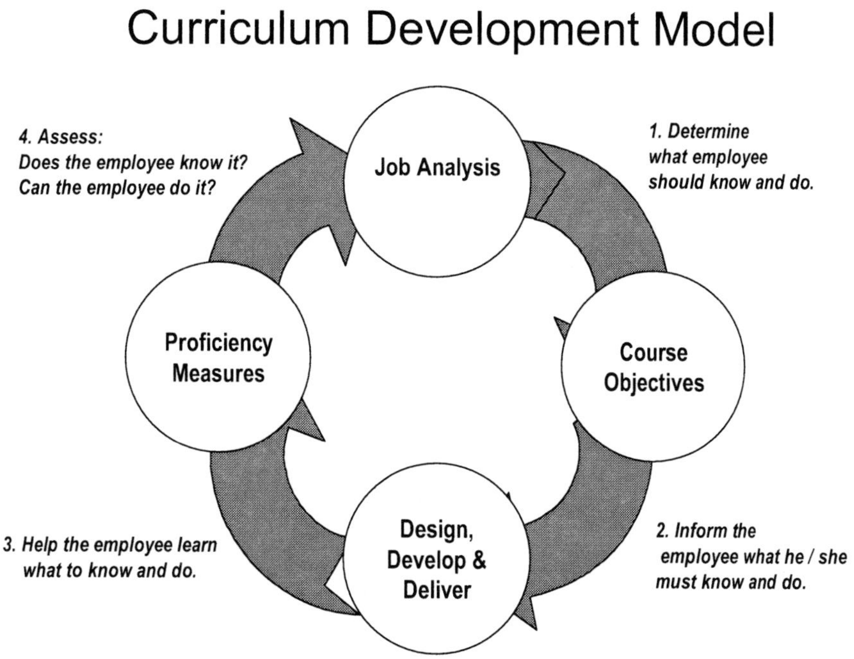

Curriculum Development Model

Figure 1. Curriculum Development Model

B. Enhancing Learning Relevance through Training Standards

Liberty places a strong emphasis on training design. However, training infrastructure is decentralized. To ensure that training is effective, Liberty has developed and implemented training design standards for its internal program designers. An initial set of standards was developed by a team of Liberty training managers in 1999, and were updated in 2001.

These standards, listed below, help to ensure that learning developed or purchased for employees in training programs is relevant and useful.

Table 2. Standards and Descriptions

Standard	Summary Description
Business and Learner Focus	Training programs will be driven by business and learner needs and have documented outcome-based objectives that are linked to business and job requirements.
	Documenting business needs helps to ensure that business-critical decisions and behaviors are emphasized.
	Objectives are written according to a criterion-referenced format including performance and conditions. This ensures that the training addresses critical business needs. (Example: When given a product and a list of the customer's insurance needs, participants will be able to identify the key features of the product that address each of the customer's needs.)
	Defining the characteristics of the training audience ensures that the training is understandable, focused, accessible and relevant to the employee.
Evaluation	Training programs will be evaluated for effectiveness in meeting objectives at

	three levels of the Kirkpatrick scale [3]: Reaction – Level 1 Learning – Level 2 Application on the job – Level 3
Continuous Improvement	There will be a process in effect to continuously improve program design and delivery after the initial rollout of each program.
Instructional Methods	The most efficient and effective instructional methods and technologies will be used, consistent with the audience and the learning objectives.
Training Personnel	Each unit will develop and implement plans for improving the skills of its training personnel.
Managers/Subject Matter Experts as Instructors	Experienced line professionals and managers will be used as instructors where possible to greatly enhance the learning experience for participants beyond the basics.
Vendor Standards	Define and implement a vendor qualification process

Training Managers in the various lines of business use these guidelines to assist program development. They also periodically assess their programs against these standards.

III.   FRONT-LINE MANAGER CURRICULUM

Liberty's management curriculum development effort started in 1997. The design effort was described by Richard A. Dapra in the September/October 1998 issue of *Corporate University Review* [4]. In this article, Dapra described the process of segmenting managers into major roles, identifying role-specific capabilities required for success, and creating the learning infrastructure. Dapra also described the extensive involvement of senior management teams in the design, development, and delivery of the management curriculum.

The management curriculum has expanded in recent years. The success of this model for management development has resulted in the expansion of a curriculum approach that leverages instructional technologies to other training areas at Liberty. The structured development available to managers now extends to two years after the new manager entered the role. The next section provides an overview the curriculum's evolution.

A. Audience and Curriculum Components

Each year about 500 employees are promoted or hired into a Front-Line Management role. Front-Line Managers are responsible for the day-to-day supervision of front-line staff and are responsible for hiring their staff, setting performance objectives, and evaluating the performance of their staff. They are also responsible for developing their staff by providing on-going feedback about job performance, coaching, and assistance with planning development activities that will increase knowledge and skills.

The Front-Line Manager Curriculum has the following curriculum components:

Table 3. Front-Line Manager Curriculum Components

Curriculum Component	Timing	Delivery Modalities Used	Mandatory or Optional
1. Front-Line Manager Orientation	First 30 days after being hired or promoted into a Front-line manager role	Self-paced, web-based Instructor-led web course Suggested on-the-job activities Manager coaching Online test (scenario and memory level)	Mandatory Program Completion is a mandatory prerequisite for attendance at the next phase
2. Building the Capabilities for Success (BCS)	Must attend the session within 120 days of hire or promotion	Physical Classroom	Mandatory Program
3. Continuous Learning	Post BCS attendance	9 physical classroom courses 4 Instructor-led web courses 30 Self-paced, web-based mini-courses	Optional Programs
4. Front-line Manager Assessment	1 year after Building the Capabilities for Success program	Online Assessment by employee and immediate manager	Mandatory Program Front-line Manager and immediate manager identify development activities to increase skill in targeted area

B. The Front-Line Manager Role Orientation

The Front-Line Manager Orientation curriculum component utilizes a "learn and apply" approach that supports the new manager through a series of web-based, self-paced modules and discussions with the participant's manager during the first 30-days in his or her new role.

The purpose of the program is to:

- Establish direction and familiarize the new manager with new management responsibilities and the knowledge and skills required to execute those responsibilities.
- Align the new manager with Liberty's management principles and beliefs.
- Increase the manager's awareness of critical management challenges.
- Provide the new manager with ongoing resources and job aids to help during the initial months as a manager.

The introduction of the company Intranet in 1998 provided a new distribution mechanism for learning. Since new Front-Line Managers have different start dates, the self-paced, web-based format was identified as providing the best access to learning. The web-based approach also allows Liberty to track learner completion and satisfaction with the program. Over the past several years, Front-Line Managers consistently rate the program as Excellent or Good (95% through the first half of 2004). Learners also provide feedback on the relevance and usefulness of each learning module.

Liberty has begun augmenting the self-paced instruction with live, instructor-led sessions. Last year a "webinar" was added to familiarize new managers with human resource management applications training on systems they use for recruiting and selection and for implementing new hires and promotions in the manager-self service portion of Liberty's Human Resource Management System.

While the first two Front-Line Manager curriculum components of Orientation and Building Capabilities for Success (BCS) started out as two distinct, but related, programs, Liberty believes that it can increase the continuity between the two programs and provide learners with increased support during their first 120 days on the job through the use of synchronous and asynchronous instructional technologies.

C. Building the Capabilities for Success (BCS)

The Building the Capabilities for Success curriculum component is a four-day, face-to-face management training program offered in the company's home office in Boston, Massachusetts. The objective of the program is to strengthen the new manager's capability to lead people and manage work units. Liberty Mutual content is specific to its business and emphasizes application and practice. Many of the activities covered in the class are introduced to the manager in the form of course pre-work. Each manager completes an assignment individually before class. Once the class begins in Boston, managers compare their individual analyses with other managers in small group discussions in peer break-out groups, compile their joint findings, and present them to a senior manager "faculty" member. Senior managers probe the learner assumptions, provide their own personal insights, and help pull together the key learning points of the exercise.

In addition to skill building exercises, the new managers meet with Liberty Mutual Group Chairman, President and CEO Ted Kelly, who engages them in discussion about the challenges of management, emphasizing the importance of their role in Liberty's success. One of the key goals of discussions between new managers and senior executives is to align managers' understanding of management philosophies and practices. When managers return to their offices, they indicate that they are better prepared to execute their management responsibilities consistent with Liberty's philosophies, policies, and best practices.

D. Continuous Learning

Once new managers return to their field offices, they can take advantage of a variety of instructional techniques that can increase their skills by covering in-depth treatments on particular management topics. This is accomplished through Liberty's continuous learning phase of the curriculum. Learning options include four modalities:

- Traditional one or two day classroom programs
- Self-paced, web-based modules
- 1-2 hour "webinar" courses
- Online performance support tools.

The table below lists the topics covered under each modality.

Table 4. Modalities and Topics

Delivery Modality	Course Names		
Physical Classroom Offerings	Feedback and Coaching Performance Management Selection	Making the Business Case Managing Projects Effectively Business Writing	Step-by-Step Problem Solving Principled Negotiation Customer Service
Virtual Classroom Offerings	Using Selection Tools	Evaluating Candidates for Selection	Setting Objectives Evaluating Performance
Self-paced Web-based Offerings	Behavioral Interviewing Developing People Giving and Receiving Feedback Hiring Communicating Performance Managing Troubled Employees Motivating and Recognizing Employees Coaching for Performance Pay and Performance	Making Business Decisions Managing Conflict Retaining Valued Employees Leading a Team Running a Meeting Capitalizing on Change Project Management Delegating Making a Presentation Leading and Motivating	Managing Your Time Working with a Virtual Team Negotiating Keeping Teams on Target Managing Difficult Interactions Managing for Creativity and Innovation Budgeting Finance Essentials Writing for Business Focusing on Your Customer
Online Performance Support Tools	Online Selection Tool	Online Performance Evaluation Tool	

Classroom programs are evaluated at Level 1 (Reaction) and Level 2 (Learning), and the three core management process programs (Performance Management, Selection and Feedback and Coaching at Level 3). Level 1 results for the classroom programs received overall satisfaction results of between 93% and 100% Excellent/Good ratings.

When the self-paced, web-based modules were created, Liberty did not have a corporate learning management system that would allow the company easily and cost effectively to track course evaluation results. In addition, the courses were designed as job aids, and there was no expectation for a manager to complete the entire program. Liberty does measure aggregate course use through a web metrics application that provides data on page hits for each of the programs. These web metrics demonstrate consistently strong use. For example, the Behavioral Interviewing module home page was accessed over 600 times in the first half of 2004. The implementation of an enterprise learning management system will provide Liberty with an opportunity for more in-depth tracking of use at the individual user level, as well as the ability to cost effectively gather learner satisfaction and test results.

E. Front-Line Manager Assessment

One year following a new manager's completion of Building the Capabilities for Success, the manager participates in the Front-Line Manager Assessment. This portion of the curriculum uses an online assessment independently completed by the Front-Line Manager and his/her immediate manager. The assessment is based on 17 Front-Line Manager capabilities, each containing three to four dimensions. These capabilities were identified through an extensive job task analysis in 2003. The analysis provided additional depth to the initial analysis that was conducted in 1997.

Once the assessment results are completed, the Front-Line Manager and his/her manager meet to discuss the results and reach agreement on the focus of future development activities. Managers can assess suggested development activities on the web to plan development activities mapped to capability areas.

F. Front-Line Manager Curriculum Results Mapped against the Sloan-C Pillars

1. Learning Effectiveness

Liberty measures learning effectiveness at three points in time. First, in each portion of the curriculum Liberty asks learners to rate their own ability to meet the course objectives. In some programs this is a pre/post session comparison. In other programs only a post-session evaluation is used. Second, criterion-referenced tests are used [1]. These tests help learners assess the degree to which they have acquired the targeted knowledge and skills. Finally, course participants are also surveyed three to six months after the classroom session and asked if they have applied the skills acquired in the course back on the job.

These results can be mapped against the core curriculum objectives to determine the success of the training. The table below presents 2003 results for the Front-Line Manager classroom program.

Table 5. Front-Line Manager Classroom Results

Building the Capabilities Session for Successful Program Objectives	Self-Assessment		Knowledge Test	OTJ Application
	Pre	Post		
Use tools for creating customer value	66%	89%	80%	60%
Practice Liberty's management principles and beliefs and management-leadership framework	52%	94%	82%	90%
Apply HR strategy	45%	89%	91%	76%
Use 4-step selection process	58%	90%	84%	53%*
Make valid performance decisions and communicate them to employees	60%	90%	93%	82%
Apply and communicate compensation philosophies	44%	87%	86%	92%
Use coaching and feedback techniques to address employee performance development	57%	90%	97%	97%

*Note: 39% indicated no opportunity to select a new staff member

Overall, these results document successful transfer of knowledge and skill from the instructional domain to actual on-the-job application. The on-the-job application results with lower application percentages generally reflect a significant number of managers indicating they had "no opportunity" to apply the designated skill.

2. Cost Effectiveness

Liberty periodically benchmarks the delivery costs of its programs against commercially based alternatives and consistently finds that costs are lower than off-the-shelf alternatives. In addition, instructional technologies can reduce the training travel budget. Given the size and dispersed nature of Liberty's workforce, instructional technologies can greatly reduce training expense when compared to the costs of airfare, hotel, parking and meals associated with a corporate training event.

3. Access

Use of the web provides managers with access to the role orientation courses immediately upon promotion. Individuals can begin to learn immediately, and they do not have to wait for a "critical mass" of attendees to begin a structured class. The web is also used for instructor-led sessions prior to the Boston-based BCS training. Instructional technologies allow for more in-depth skill building where the manager works.

An illustrative example of how critical timely access is for managers is the evolution of Liberty's Selection curriculum over the past four years. For many managers, selecting and hiring a new member of their staff is a critical activity, but one which is not frequently exercised. While initial training is effective at providing a basic overview, managers need "refreshers" when they actually have a need to fill a vacant position. And they need them quickly. The manager can't wait six to eight weeks for the next scheduled class.

Despite the acknowledged importance of this managerial skill, the company has had little demand and light attendance for traditional classroom training in selection skills. However, as instructional technologies were introduced to support Liberty's selection curriculum, usage increased and thus provided much more timely support for managers. These instructional technologies included:

- Self-paced web-based courses on hiring and behavioral interviewing skills.
- Online performance support tools that help managers create custom success profiles and interview guides.
- Instructor-led one hour "webinars" that provide managers with guidance on the overall process and on assessing a candidate's potential

Currently there is steady demand and usage for selection-related topics within all three online delivery mechanisms.

4. Faculty Satisfaction

In this environment, "faculty" are not similar to faculty in higher education. Liberty's primary stakeholders are the managers who are responsible for the development of their staff. One of the goals of every training activity is to ensure management satisfaction with employee learning. This is achieved through involvement in the design process, through management involvement in program delivery, and by providing managers with guidance as to how they can assist the employee in applying their newly acquired skills back on the job.

5. Student Satisfaction

Favorable evaluation results of overall program effectiveness are in the 90–100% range, regardless of delivery modality. The table below displays evaluation results for classroom training. Similar results have been achieved with online components.

Figure 2. Student Satisfaction Results for Building the Capabilities for Success

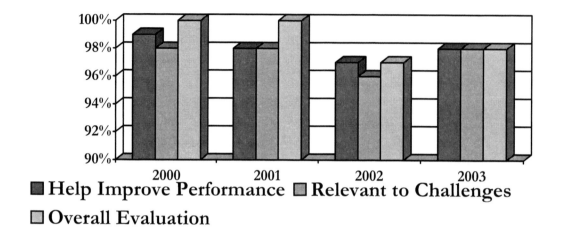

6. Next Steps

In 2005, Liberty plans to examine how it can better integrate the separate curriculum elements. The company would also like to expand the delivery of programs using synchronous and asynchronous learning technologies. Additionally, Liberty plans to examine how instructor-led, web-based instruction can be used to introduce additional core concepts and to facilitate peer-to-peer learning prior to the physical classroom component of the curriculum.

IV. ENTRY-LEVEL PERSONAL MARKET UNDERWRITING TRAINING

Based on the success of the management curriculum model, Human Resource Development has started to work with the training managers to develop curricula in other lines of business that support key functions of Liberty's business. This work began in 2003 and now involves four business units. For example, two curricula under development are geared toward entry-level underwriters in Liberty's Personal and Commercial Markets organizations.

Each year the Personal Market hires about 25 new underwriters who are assigned to underwriting offices located across the country. There are two hiring periods (December/January and May/June), with underwriters starting on different days at different offices. Historically, underwriting training used a structured apprenticeship model, with each center providing some prescribed job-shadow activities as well as individual self-study. New underwriters attended a 4-day session at Liberty's headquarters within six months after their hire date.

A. Job Analysis

In 2003, a new underwriter curriculum was designed. The work started by conducting a job task analysis with a team of experienced underwriters and underwriting managers to identify and describe the specific underwriting knowledge and skills that a new underwriter must master to perform effectively.

The output of this analysis is a description of critical skill areas in criterion-referenced format. The relationships of various job components are mapped.

As noted in Figure 3, two primary technical/functional skills were identified for the Personal Market Underwriter:

- Portfolio Analysis
- Individual Risk Analysis

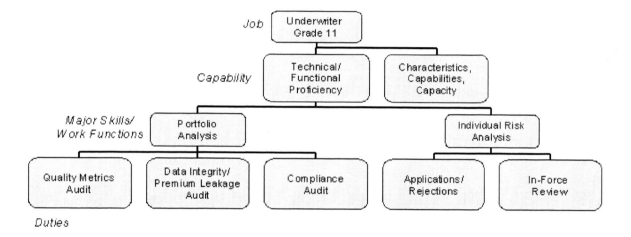

Figure 3. Personal Market Underwriter

The table below includes the descriptions for Portfolio Analysis and the description, tasks and knowledge elements for the Quality Metrics Audit duty.

Table 6. Major Functions and Knowledge Elements

Major Skills/Work Functions	Duties	Tasks	Knowledge Elements
S1 - Portfolio Analysis Given regional objectives/projects, home-office initiatives/projects, assignments/requests from portfolio underwriter and/or self-initiated projects, the underwriter will conduct	**S1D1 - Quality Metrics Audit (home & auto)** Given a scheduled assignment, manager request, region request, home office initiative, or self-initiated project, the underwriter will obtain relevant data using BRIO (e.g. query RDC characteristic, credit characteristic, and other	Task 1 – Review quarterly office historical loss data from Actuarial, four-year loss information (benchmark with command, state, region,	K1 – Understand calculations behind financial metrics (e.g. calculate loss and expense ratio, combined ratios) K2 – Interpretation of financial metrics. K3 – Current regional/state/country-

| quality metric, data integrity/premium leakage and compliance audits to ensure compliance with state laws and Liberty procedures, and business profitability according to score-card metrics. | quality-related POSU characteristics) and review other sources with compatible data (e.g., UW/actuarial reports, industry data), to analyze data for trends and to compare against benchmarks (e.g., other carriers, sales command, state/region/countrywide) to identity potential problems/opportunities (e.g., validate RDC percentages, identify best practices, etc.) and validate requests to make recommendations based on findings and ensure recommendations are implemented with agreed upon action plans and monitor progress. | countrywide) and other financial reports (e.g. expense ratio information, combined ratio) looking for fluctuations, trends (with regard to regional objectives), drivers of trends to determine initial assessment of loss history. | wide objectives (e.g., score card metric). |

After the core skills were identified, the curriculum development team surveyed incumbent underwriters and underwriting managers to determine the sequence of skill development for the curriculum.

Figure 4 displays the curriculum elements for the new curriculum.

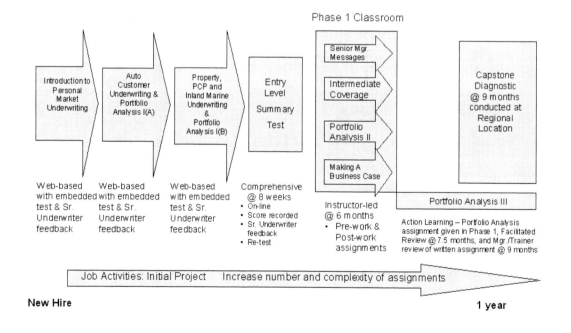

Figure 4. New Underwriter Curriculum

The table below describes the new entry-level underwriting curriculum components.

Table 7. New Entry-Level Underwriting Curriculum Components

Curriculum Component	Timing	Delivery Modalities Used
1. Personal Market Underwriting Orientation	First 2 weeks	Self-paced, web-based On-the-job activities with coaching Online test (scenario and memory level)
2. Auto Customer Underwriting and Portfolio Analysis	2–4 weeks	Self-paced, web-based On-the-job activities with coaching Online test (scenario and memory level)
3. Property Customer Underwriting and Portfolio Analysis	4–6 weeks	Self-paced, web-based On-the-job activities with coaching Online test (scenario and memory level)
4. Summary Test	8 weeks post hire	Online Test
5. Phase 1	6 months post hire	Physical Classroom
6. Portfolio Analysis	6–8 months	Action Learning - underwriters identify a state for analysis and identify trends, recommend actions to improve business results and present both the results and recommendations underwriting center management
7. Capstone Diagnostic	9–10 months	Case, scenario and memory level test items

The goals of this new curriculum are to:

- Prepare new underwriters with increasingly challenging responsibilities to encourage professional growth.
- Provide additional context about the Personal Market and Liberty's business goals.
- Use instructional technologies and methods to ensure timely and cost effective delivery of structured learning activities.
- More effectively assess the learner's acquisition of underwriting skills and provide support and re-direction to help the new underwriter attain the desired level of job proficiency.

B. Personal Market Entry Level Curriculum Results Mapped Against the Sloan-C Pillars

The development work for the program started in 2003. Liberty has started to pilot each of these curriculum elements in 2004. Initial pilot results are promising.

1. Learning Effectiveness

Assessments are built into each one of the curriculum components to ensure that the core concepts and terminology have been assimilated by the learner. The self-paced web components also have numerous scenarios to help learners test their decision-making, simulating the underwriting decisions they will make on the job. Managers feel that that the additional content, context and ability to practice will speed assimilation into the new job. Pilot results indicate that learners feel the new programs are effective at meeting the objectives.

2. Cost Effectiveness

In this case Liberty was able to add six new curriculum components without the additional training travel expenses associated with traditional classroom programs.

3. Access

The new curriculum model provides greater consistency of key messages about the context and importance of the underwriter's role. Since new underwriters come online at different start dates, the self-paced web approach provides them with timely access to relevant training.

4. Faculty Satisfaction

The new curriculum model continues to involve line managers in the development of the new underwriter. The web-based components relieve the line manager from content delivery. The practice exercises built into the web-based components better prepares the new underwriter.

5. Student Satisfaction

Initial pilot results of all elements have been positive to date, with positive learner reaction to the new web-based and classroom components. As the new curriculum components are implemented throughout this year, additional changes will be made to further enhance the various programs to increase student satisfaction.

V. COMMERCIAL MARKET-WIDE UNDERWRITING

Each year the four business units in Liberty's Commercial Markets (National Market, Business Market, Wausau Commercial Market, Specialty Risks) hire about 25 new underwriters in total. These underwriters start work in their offices located across the country. There are two hiring periods (December/January and May/June), with underwriters starting on different days at different offices.

Prior to Liberty's involvement, underwriting training used a variety of training methods, including a structured apprenticeship model, with each market providing prescribed activities as well as individual self-study for insurance coverage, i.e. Worker's Compensation and Auto Liability. Training was unique to each market. Commercial Markets Human Resources and Management wanted to accelerate underwriter development, increase underwriter familiarity with aspects of the business outside of their specific market and line of business assignments, and improve the consistency of underwriter development. Management felt that a common, Commercial Markets-wide underwriting curriculum could improve bench strength. This would, in turn, facilitate increased movement of underwriting talent between businesses.

A. Job Analysis

In 2002, the curriculum development work began with separate job analyses of underwriters in each of three businesses: National Market, Business Market, and Wausau Commercial Market. The team worked throughout 2003 to determine core knowledge and skills that were pervasive across all four businesses (Specialty Risks group joined the project). The 2003 efforts resulted in a "know, do and decide" document reflecting the critical knowledge, activities and decisions for entry level underwriters, regardless of their market and line of coverage assignments.

This document became the basis for a Commercial Markets Wide curriculum that works in concert with market-specific training to increase the breadth and depth of Liberty's underwriting capability. The skill areas identified in the original job analysis are displayed below:

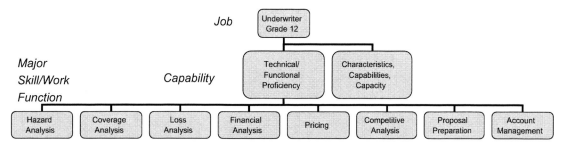

Figure 5. Commercial Markets Underwriter

The core underwriting skills identified were:

- Hazard analysis
- Coverage analysis
- Loss analysis

- Financial analysis
- Program structure
- Competitive analysis

- Pricing
- Proposal preparation
- Account management

There are two interesting points about the job task analysis work. First, while the experienced underwriters and managers came from different backgrounds, they reached a remarkable level of agreement on the skill, tasks and knowledge under each skill area. These skills applied to all lines of coverage (with some variation).

Second, while Liberty's training staff anticipated that it would be able to leverage commercially available training that directly addressed these skills, the team found that off-the-shelf materials provided spotty coverage of what were identified as core skills.

Accordingly, while the curriculum is able to leverage some commercial materials, much of the content is being developed using Liberty subject matter experts. These experts are also able to provide further context to the new underwriter by incorporating Liberty's business strategies and corporate competencies into the underwriting training.

Curriculum development efforts started in late 2003, and continue with the development of Liberty-specific underwriting training. This new curriculum has the following components:

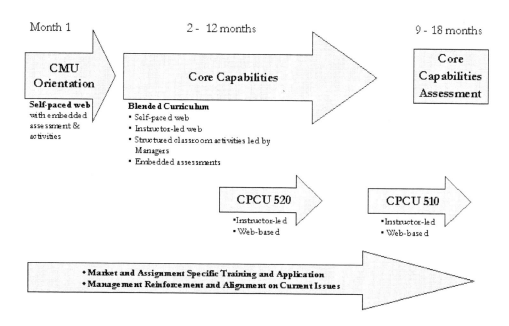

Figure 6. Commerical Market Entry Level Underwriting Curriculum

The following table provides additional information about these programs:

Table 8. Timing and Delivery for New Curricula

Curriculum Component	Timing	Delivery Modalities Used
1. Commercial Market-wide Underwriting Orientation	First 2 weeks	Self-paced, web-based On-the-job activities with coaching Online test (scenario and memory level)
2. Hazard Analysis	Between 2 and 10 months	Virtual Classroom On-the-job activities with coaching Online test (scenario and memory level)
3. Loss Analysis and Forecasting	Between 2 and 10 months	Virtual Classroom On-the-job activities with coaching Online test (scenario and memory level)
4. Financial Analysis	Between 2 and 10 months	Physical classroom with pre-work
5. CPCU 510 - Foundations of Risk Management, Insurance and Professionalism	Between 2 and 10 months	Asynchronous and Synchronous Instructor-led
6. CPCU 520 Insurance Operations, Regulation and Statutory Accounting	Between 2 and 10 months	Asynchronous and Synchronous Instructor-led
7. Capstone Diagnostic	End of 1st year	Case, scenario and memory level test items

B. Commercial Market Entry Level Curriculum Results Mapped Against the Sloan-C Pillars

Initial pilots have been promising and development work continues.

1. Learning Effectiveness

Assessments are built into each one of the curriculum components to ensure that the core concepts and terminology have been assimilated by the learner. The self-paced web and instructor–led web-based components include assignment and activities to help learners test their decision-making, simulating the underwriting decisions they will make on the job. Pilot results indicate that learners feel the new programs are effective at meeting the objectives.

2. Cost Effectiveness

In this case Liberty was able to add new curriculum components without incurring significant travel expenses, and the associated drop in productivity.

3. Access

The new curriculum model provides greater consistency of key messages about the context and importance of the underwriter's role. Since new underwriters come online a different start dates, the self-paced web approach provides them with timely access to the relevant training. The Virtual Classroom sessions provide learners with a greater degree of structure to their learning, while reducing time and expense involved with travel to a central training location.

4. Faculty Satisfaction

The new curriculum model continues to involve line managers in the development of the new underwriter.

5. Student Satisfaction

Initial pilot results of all elements have been positive to date, with positive learner reaction for the new web-based and classroom components. As the new curriculum components are implemented throughout this year, additional changes will be made to further enhance the various programs to increase student satisfaction.

VI. CONCLUSIONS

Liberty plans to examine other methods for delivering instruction. Members of Sloan-C might ask, "Why doesn't Liberty Mutual Group use ALNs to deliver its programs?"

Early experiments with ALNs failed. Liberty's Business and National Markets both tried to deploy Blackboard to support its sales training for several years. This modality failed to take hold. Training managers reported that both trainers and sales staff liked the idea of continuing their learning using Blackboard. However, the sales staff found it difficult to stay engaged in the moderated on-line discussions given their busy schedules.

ALNs have recently re-emerged as part of a mix for program delivery. Liberty is currently using Blackboard through a license agreement with the American Institute for Chartered Property Casualty Underwriters and Insurance Institute of America, the Property/Casualty industry's, professional designation provider. Liberty introduced exam preparation courses to help its employees prepare for their CPCU designation exams and is experiencing very heavy demand for these ALN courses.

More than 70% of Liberty employees have stated that they were pleased with this method of learning. Participants in the pilot who took the CPCU exam also had a high pass rate of close to 100%.

This success rate indicates that this method of training delivery will become a larger part of Liberty's delivery mix. As mentioned earlier, Liberty's Commercial Market Underwriting group is incorporating two CPCU exam preparation courses delivered through Blackboard into the core Commercial Market-wide curriculum.

The company is also seeing increased demand for and use of Virtual Classroom technologies. The Commercial Market training groups, in particular, are looking at instructor-led, synchronous delivery to reach its highly distributed learner population.

The implementation of a new learning management system will provide Liberty with improved capability to deploy online and blended programs and blended curricula, track learning results and report on learning results across the organization.

The company is also looking at ways to enhance its ability to deliver rich media on its corporate networks, while staying within the bandwidth constraints developed by Liberty's Information Systems group, ensuring that web-based applications do not disrupt front-line employee customer interface applications.

An important additional factor is the changing expectations of Liberty's newly hired population of recent college graduates. As online learning becomes more of the fabric of the undergraduate and graduate college experience, the new hires will expect the corporate world to offer similar capabilities and opportunities. This expectation will be a driving force for greater use of ALNs in corporations.

VII. REFERENCES

1. **Sharon, S. and W. Coscarelli.** International Society for Performance Improvement, 53–75. Washington, DC: 2000.
2. **Mager, R. F.** *Preparing Instructional Objectives.* Atlanta, GA: Center for Effective Performance, 1997.
3. **Kirkpatrick, D. L.** *Evaluating Training Performance: The Four Levels.* San Francisco, CA: Berrett-Koehler Publications, Inc., 1994.
4. **Dapra, R. A.** *Corporate University Review*: 24–35, September/October, 1998.

VIII. ABOUT THE AUTHOR

Richard Benner is the Director of eLearning and Instructional Design Services for Liberty Mutual Group. Email Richard.Benner@LibertyMutual.com.

What do We Need to Learn About the Business of Education?

BUSINESS ISSUES IN ONLINE EDUCATION

Stephen Schiffman
Babson College

- Standard measures across institutions, or among different programs at the same institution, have not been fully developed.

- The drivers for online education include institutional mission and Carnegie classification, organizational structure, audiences served, leadership, and for-profit and not-for-profit status.

- There is a thirst for knowledge of business models and methods and for benchmarking.

- Competition, or the effects of competition, was an issue that was seldom raised by interviewees.

- Defining marketing broadly to include product development, as well as communications activities, the range of marketing budgets spans from zero to over 20% of budget.

I. INTRODUCTION

This report summarizes and synthesizes wide-ranging information about business issues in online education drawn from interviews with more than fifty people working in the field of online education at eleven not-for-profit higher education institutions during the winter and spring of 2004.

These eleven institutions have different motivations for pursuing online education, as well as different goals, success measures, and organizational structures. Each institution's online initiative can be defined as being driven by an educational organization comprised of people and systems that regulate online courses and degrees; control its resources for investing, planning, designing, developing, marketing, managing, teaching, and implementing online education; and support students.

Institutions are developing ways to better understand costs and set tuition and fee levels, but standard measures across institutions, or among different programs at the same institution, have not been fully developed. Additionally, institutions with online initiatives are struggling with rationalizing work flow and funding processes within parts of their educational organization, including academic departments, student services, and a variety of other support-service areas. Some institutions are grappling with this problem by collaborating with external partners, such as sister programs or university systems.

Marketing is another area in which institutions with online initiatives have different processes and approaches to budgeting. Defining marketing broadly to include product development, as well as communications activities, the range of marketing budgets spans from zero to over 20% of budget. Depending on an institution's specific goals for online education, some providers do little formal marketing. Other institutions have developed formal, controlled, and more integrated approaches, with activities spanning from market research to product (e.g. course or program) selection, to marketing communications. Also, business-to-business marketing techniques are employed by some programs, with interest expressed in affinity and coalition marketing.

As institutions try to build sustainable business models, they seek revenue for continued program development, with funding originally coming from foundational or institutional grants. In addition, institutions are developing tools and processes to aid in the building of more effective business planning and cost models for online programs.

There appears to be a thirst for knowledge of others' models and methods, and for benchmarking. As a result, four ideas are presented for future research or other activities:

- Collect and publish business case studies and best practices.
- Conduct a survey of customer experiences and expectations.
- Create a cross-institutional project to develop comprehensive business and cost models and performance metrics.
- Conduct a research project to develop a structural/predictive model of factors that correlate with success measures.

II. PURPOSE OF RESEARCH

This research looks at cost structures, compares and contrasts business practices, and initiates a cross-institutional analysis. Overall, data was collected and compared within the context of the following question: What is the motivation for developing an online learning program, and how is work organized and implemented? For example, the wide variance in the dollar amounts budgeted for marketing—from zero to 20% or more—begins to make sense only when one understands that some institutions are looking to online education to serve new markets and others to help handle the overflow of demand for courses by existing, captive, residential learners.

All these issues were addressed through interviews with faculty, staff and administrators working in the field of online education at these institutions:

Table 1. Institutions and Carnegie Classification

Institution	Carnegie Classification
University of Maryland University College	Master's College and University I – public
University of Baltimore	Master's College and University I – public
Stevens Institute of Technology	Doctoral/Research Intensive – private
New York University – School of Continuing and Professional Studies	Doctoral/Research Extensive – private (NYU)
University of Massachusetts Lowell	Doctoral/Research Intensive – public
New England College of Finance	Associate's Colleges – private
University of Illinois at Chicago	Doctoral/Research Extensive – public
University of Illinois at Urbana Champaign	Doctoral/Research Extensive – public
University of Illinois at Springfield	Master's College and University I – public
University of Central Florida	Doctoral/Research Intensive – public
Pennsylvania State University – World Campus	Doctoral/Research Extensive – public (PSU)

The purpose of this document is to describe, explain and raise questions—not to draw conclusions. It elucidates points of similarity and difference among business practices at institutions that are generally recognized as successful in online education. Its goal is to sharpen up points for future research, to frame issues so they may be studied in a way that admits a more systematic and thorough analysis, to spark debate, and to find the issues that people care to learn more about. "Hard" data are included where they can be provided in a meaningful way. In the interest of confidentiality, practices and data are not attributed to specific institutions.

Through cross-institutional reporting and analysis, and by drawing attention to relevant practices and issues of concern, a conversation can continue among those especially interested in these business issues. Through such a community of interest, and out of such a process, consensus may be gained about how best to move forward in research and other valued activities as it relates to business issues in online education.

III. METHODOLOGY

There was no "scientific" formula for choosing and interviewing the eleven aforementioned institutions. Each was chosen in part because of its prominence in online education as evidenced by its size, historical longevity and reputation. The eleven institutions represent a cross-section of different kinds of not-for-profit, four-year colleges and universities. Representatives from approximately twenty-five different online programs were interviewed, ranging from continuing professional education and certificate programs to master's degrees, as well as programs geared toward serving existing student bodies to those attempting to attract new markets, and individual programs championed by one or two persons in isolated academic departments to whole schools or campuses charged with integrating and expanding online education.

Overall, the more than 50 people interviewed were deans, provosts, controllers, data managers, marketers, faculty directors and instructors, instructional designers, strategic planners, student services directors, support staff, faculty, administrative champions, visionaries, and budget directors. This helped present a view of the business of online education as a multifaceted integrative activity and a deep understanding of motivations and expectations.

Interviews were general and wide-ranging. These interviews did not attempt to define online education in a specific way (e.g. blended, asynchronous, etc.). Instead interviews were geared toward allowing each institution talk about what they are doing online as a broadly defined teaching and learning modality. Therefore, business issues that might be unique to certain modalities were not segmented. Also, discussions did not focus on educational quality, but, occasionally, there was some overlapping.

One key challenge in writing this report was deciding what level of granularity to use in analyzing the broad data collected. At what level of organization does it make sense to compare and contrast business practices? This is an "apples to oranges" question. Can one usefully compare the business model of a relatively small support organization driving online education at a public research-extensive university to one for a large school of continuing studies that has control of its own degrees and faculty? Can one compare the business growth strategy for an online graduate degree coming out of an academic department to one for an entire institution focused on providing education for employees of the financial services industry?

The answer proposed is that comparisons among business practices at different institutions' online initiatives are most valid when they are put in the context of each institution's comprehensive educational organization as defined earlier.

IV. WHAT DRIVES ONLINE EDUCATION?

Each institution was asked what motivates the growth of online education. Some interviewees had longer perspectives than others. Overall, it became clear when interviewing multiple people from different parts of the same institution that no one person had the full answer and that people's professional motivations were bound up with the mission and goals of the particular units they worked in.

The organization structures for planning, developing and delivering online education varied considerably from institution to institution. Rarely were all the necessary pieces and resources brought together as a single organizational entity, with unanimity of goals and reward structures. A useful way to think of each of these online education organizations is as a collection of nodes in a network. Together, these nodes act as a coalition. Some of the nodes might be units charged with driving the growth of online education, and these might occur within organizations (such as schools of professional studies) or support organizations (such as an information technology support arm). Sometimes there are multiple nodes within the same institution driving online education. Other nodes might control the resources necessary to deliver online learning, including faculty resources and student and infrastructure support. Some nodes, usually the traditional academic departments, control the regulation of courses and degrees. Some nodes might report up a common organizational channel (such as to provost's office, or a school of professional studies), but usually multiple channels are involved, each concerned with their own specific goals and rewards, even if connected by a common institutional mission. Finally, there are some nodes, external to the day-to-day operations of an institution, which nevertheless must be taken into account. For example, boards of trustees at private and public institutions, and various state boards at public institutions, may play key roles.

For these reasons, it is important to examine all the nodes at any particular institution when trying to understand what drives online education. Plus, one cannot easily separate drivers from organization structures.

A. Institutional Mission

To understand what drives online learning, one can start by examining an institution's mission. As a first filter we can use the Carnegie classification to get an objective categorization of mission. As noted, of the eleven institutions studied, three are Doctoral/Research Extensive - public, one is Doctoral/Research Extensive - private, one is Doctoral/Research Extensive - private, two are Doctoral/Research Intensive - public, three are Master's College and University I - public, and one is an Associate's College - private.

An institution's Carnegie classification is relevant to understanding online education because it ties into an institution's overall mission, which typically comes into play as a force that affects at least some of the nodes on an educational organization. Two of the institutions studied illuminate this point.

For instance, at one of the public doctoral/research-extensive universities, the unit charged with developing online education is referred to as a separate campus and is viewed that way by other parts of the state system. One might conclude that the Carnegie classification of the university as a whole would be irrelevant to the models and strategies of that "campus." However, from a practical standpoint, it works with traditional academic units at the university to gain permission to offer degrees and courses and to obtain faculty to teach them.

On the other hand, at the private doctoral/research-extensive institution studied, its school of continuing and professional studies contains all the nodes necessary for an educational organization providing an online learning environment. Although the school does have some restrictions on degrees it can regulate (e.g. it can not offer degrees similar to those at the other traditional academic schools of the university), it does have enough control of degrees and other resources (including ability to hire its own faculty) to consider it as an educational organization in its own right. It does not have to seek approval from institutional regulatory bodies and garner resources from academic departments, which have goals more closely related to institutional mission (e.g. gaining research grants, traditional academic scholarship, rankings of professional schools, etc).

Institutions where all the nodes of an online initiative fall into a proper subset of the institution (such as the school of continuing and professional studies mentioned above), typically spread online education efforts faster and farther than at other doctoral/research-extensive institutions where online education depends on the cooperation of nodes lying within the more mainstream parts of the institution. Repeatedly, interviewees responsible for growing online learning at institutions relying on such mainstreamed factors talked about the challenges of garnering faculty attention, approval and resources.

1. Audience Served

Beyond the Carnegie category, a second filter can be applied in understanding institutional mission as it relates to online education: the primary student audience served, as evidenced by the institution's own mission statement. For example, one private institution studied has as its mission to serve the needs of a particular services industry; it offers "a wide variety of offerings for all levels of ... financial services personnel". A second, public, institution has as mission "to provide higher education opportunities to adult, part-time students". These two institutions, at the level of the institution as a whole, have missions which would seem amenable to the modality of online education, independent of other drivers.

2. For-Profit or Not-for-Profit Status

A third filter to be applied in understanding the mission of an institution would be whether it has for-profit or not-for-profit status. Although no data was collected from for-profits, there is reason to believe that business issues arising in the for-profit world should bear some points of intersection with that of the not-for-profits. For example, to the extent that a for-profit is regionally accredited, it must also allow its faculty some voice in governance and generally be seen to follow standards "appropriate to an institution of higher learning."

B. Internal and External Drivers of Online Education

Beyond institutional mission, there are other internal and external drivers of online education particular to an institution, including:

Cost reduction or avoidance. Three institutions that were located in metropolitan areas cite lack of, or the expense of, real estate in growing face-to-face course offerings, or in maintaining throughput for existing students.

Two public institutions faced a trend of decreasing student enrollment due either to location, demographics and/or a perceived competitive threat by for-profit institutions.

One public institution was dealing with a loss of faculty lines, or at least non-growth of faculty lines, and was of significant concern to the academic deans. They worked collaboratively with the unit promoting online education, as well as with the upper administration, to construct a deal whereby the deans gain faculty lines when they demonstrate (according to a formula) increased enrollment from new student audiences via online sections of courses.

Two private institutions said overall enrollments were not decreasing, but revenue generated from corporate/industrial education was down due, in part, to poor local economic conditions. Institutional budgets may rely on contribution margin generated by units responsible for professional, corporate, continuing, or extension education, even if this is not the central mission of the institution.

Pressure on budgets of public institutions means they look to units responsible for professional, corporate, continuing, or extension education as desirable alternative sources of revenue.

One of the public institutions faced a trend of significantly increasing student enrollments, in part due to favorable demographics. Although the state legislature had allocated funds for increasing faculty, the institution was struggling to meet student demand for class sections. The ability for departments to increase student throughput by offering online courses was cited as a key driver of online education.

Government or professional/industry requirements for education present specific opportunities for certain institutions. For example, at one public institution located in a rural area, an online math certification and degree program was launched to respond to a federal act. At another institution an online program covers portions of courses for medical residents required by an accrediting body. Some courses are outsourced through a collaboration of in-and-out-of-state medical schools. It helps that the dollars generated by this program stay with the department.

The two programs just cited are examples where the targeted student would be difficult to reach effectively onsite. Perhaps even more significantly, dynamic changes in the structures of certain industries are leading to shifts in employee demographics, shifts which exacerbate the difficulty of educating employees only by face-to-face modalities. For example, one institution has a core student-enrolment base of employees who are working in the local financial services industry. That industry is consolidating nationally; local banks are losing headquarters out-of-state. That institution would no longer be the educational provider of choice (to the banks) if it could not serve students outside of the local region.

Where state regulation may block an institution from offering an existing degree program at an off-campus location, online education may be used as a means to deliver the program instead. This is documented in the case of a professional masters program which was denied the request to open a 'branch' campus; rather, the masters program was "mirrored" in an online modality, available now to current (and, also, new off-campus) students.

Deans and department heads benefit from revenue from online programs in cases where the institutions have worked out such arrangements. The arrangement may be complex, involving revenue sharing among schools, departments, and units.

Several institutions are finding that online education can work in a collaborative setting as a way to more efficiently fill class sections. One flagship masters degree program is in a collaboration with other web-based providers of its degree; schools within the collaboration are able to offer and share specialty courses.

Key individuals were cited in a number of these institutions as catalysts for the growth of online education at that institution. Words such as "leader," "visionary," "entrepreneurial," and "innovative spirit" were used to describe these individuals.

Institutional or foundation grants were instrumental in providing funds to start or continue development of new online programs.

C. Organizational Structures as Drivers

Organization and reporting structures for the planning and delivery of online education vary widely by institution. Control of resources and regulatory processes are often not in the hands of the units charged with driving online education, and the organization for online education is best described as a network of internal organizations with potentially conflicting goals and missions. Chief among these internal organizations are traditional academic departments; continuing, extension, corporate or professional-education schools or programs; information technology units; and special units set up to drive online education. Additionally, in the case of public institutions, the state has a voice in authorizing new degrees.

The balance of power among these units also varies widely among the institutions studied. The traditional academic departments or schools, with their ability to regulate courses and degrees and to control the teaching resources, have strong power. At only three institutions, the goals of the key nodes of the educational organization managing online initiatives appeared to be more or less congruent. Two of the three have institutional missions to serve the non-traditional student, with academic departments acting as strong advocates for online education. The third institution is one where the school of continuing and professional studies has the ability to regulate its own courses and degrees and hire its own (part-time) faculty.

However, congruence of organizational mission does not seem to provide a sufficient or even necessary condition to assure predominance of online learning as an educational modality. At two of the institutions whose mission is to serve more traditional students, the percent of online courses or enrollments is over 15%, and one of these institutions is doctoral/research intensive.

Seven institutions have separate continuing, extension, corporate or professional-education schools or programs. In all but one case, these units play instrumental roles in supporting and driving online education institution-wide. These units, with respect to online education, were responsible for managing student services, setting and managing budgets and collecting and dispersing tuition, helping to facilitate the institutional regulatory processes, and marketing.

Two institutions that do not focus on "non-traditional" students, nor do they have continuing, extension, corporate or professional-education schools or programs, support other organizations that play instrumental roles in driving online education. For example, an IT organization is the driver at one institution, and a special "technology learning" organization at the other. The IT organization devotes approximately 20% of its budget for training, stipends and support for faculty that will teach online. This institution is growing in student body and faculty size, and student demand for courses exceeds supply. Currently approximately 80% of this institution's courses are delivered face-to-face, with 20% delivered via other modalities (including online). The institution with the technology learning organization is small in size and budget; it has been effective in working across much (but not all) the rest of the organization to introduce online courses and programs. It has approximately 18% of its course credits being delivered though online courses.

V.   BUSINESS MODELS AND PROCESSES TO SUSTAIN ONLINE EDUCATION

Business models show how an organization captures value by offering a product or service and turning it into a revenue stream that can sustain and grow business. This section discusses how institutions turn their online initiatives into sustainable endeavors. It involves understanding three concepts:

1.   How a chain of value-adding activities work together to implement a business model.
2.   What leverage points are used for generating funds for sustained operations.
3.   How costs are managed.

A. What are Value-Adding Activities, and How do they Work Together?

From a business context, activities performed at different nodes of an institution's education organization that manages its online initiatives add value to the final online product by directly converting raw material into finished goods or by providing logistical or other support. This subsection presents information about what these activities are, the value they provide, and what processes exist to manage them. This is not a complete list of value-adding activities. The focus is on issues relating to business rather than educational value (as championed by the Sloan Consortium), but these are clearly bound together.

1. Regulation of Courses, Degrees and Programs, and of the Teaching Resource

Eight institutions have primarily full-time faculty housed in "home" academic disciplines and departments working within online initiatives but not reporting directly to the unit responsible for online education. These faculty and departments act as gatekeepers both in regulating courses and degrees, and in being the providers of the teaching resource. Two institutions have part-time faculties hired by the units responsible for online education to teach most, if not all, of the online courses. One institution, whose mission is to serve nontraditional students, uses a mix of full and part-time faculty.

One of the most common incentives discussed was paying faculty stipends. Stipends for developing online courses or for attending training in how to develop online courses ranged from $2,000 plus hardware, to $7,000 per faculty. One institution gives its faculty first right of refusal to teach online courses they develop, and to receive a royalty if another faculty teaches it, or even a small royalty if they never teach it again. A number of programs share revenue with the departments and schools themselves. This may allow the chairs or deans to hire other faculty to teach the courses they wish to offer, or use that revenue in other ways for budget relief. Intellectual property rights policy is another lever for providing an incentive to faculty. At one institution, intellectual property rights depended on whether the online course was commissioned intentionally, or not, by the unit driving online education.

From the vantage of providing value to the online educational "product," the gatekeeper role played by traditional faculty can give rewards as well as incur drawbacks. On the reward side, a number of interviewees talked about the value the marketplace puts on for-credit versus not-for-credit courses and programs. "Non-credit programs are a tough business because they don't support price levels that for-credit programs do," said one interviewee. Others talked about the value of regular degree programs, especially from "brand-name" schools, as supporting price levels for their online degrees. Finally, others talked about the market placing value in the degree itself, rather than the specific online modalities. One interviewee said an online program can be thought of as a "scheduling option" rather than a "separate degree."

Interviewees also talked about the drawbacks of having to engage traditional faculty and departments along with their distinctive governance processes in order to regulate degrees and gain teaching resources. An interviewee at one institution that does not rely on traditional faculty commented that a source of their competitive value is "very fast time-to-market (weeks!) when business is found." Typical of comments from online program managers (or even some visionaries), with respect to working with traditional faculty who have other priorities, included "unanticipated resistance from faculty and chairs." Another interviewee, who works in a research institute (across departments) where the online program is not mission-driven, wonders "what would happen to my programs if I leave?" A different example, from a public doctoral/research intensive institution, reveals that "developing and teaching online courses seem to count for promotion and tenure," and "the chancellor supports online programs."

2. Processes for Planning and Developing New Online Courses and Programs

Value can be created by using effective and efficient processes for planning and developing new courses and programs is evidenced by some of the following comments:

"Need to provide courses to other programs that will incorporate them."

"Use a model of creating online courses across different groups that are used in multiple programs."

"Get customers to follow a natural progression: non-credit then for-credit."

"A basic strategy has been to 'web-ize' most popular existing courses and programs."

"Key is class size."

A number of institutions have developed their own business templates and processes to plan for new online courses and programs, including: a 5-year pro forma template, a program description/intake form and rate card [for development and marketing services], and/or a student services roles matrix. Another institution follows a model taken from the publishing industry. If institutions are willing to share these templates and processes, they can be used as jumping off points for the development of cross-institutional models and processes; they would be useful in constructing the value-chain of activities, costs and other aspects of an effective business model.

3. Student and Other Support Services

The business model for aligning student support services with online education appears to be evolving and is an area of concern to those involved in a wide range of related activities. Comments illustrate some issues:

"Revenue split [between program deans and campus] doesn't really work well—doesn't pay for support services."

"What is the business model impact in student support?"

"What is "rationalizing student services role online? Who does what?"

One large state institution is developing a matrix of student service roles by course/program type. It looks to rationalize the locus of responsibility for each of the following areas: tuition setting, marketing, recruitment, admissions, registration and payment, orientation, records and advising. At another public institution, where online education is being viewed as a way to rationalize and share specialized upper division courses among campuses, there is discussion about how to separate the flow of tuition and fee revenue into student versus academic support dollars.

Other support activities mentioned are: help desk support (both to students and faculty), other tech support, other student retention support, alumni services, career services, data management, legal support, and financial aid. The overriding question is who provides these services, at what level, and what are the mechanisms that fund them? For example, should online education at a given institution have a separate records and registration system (a legacy system) or not? To what degree is alumni or career services support desirable? There is evidence from at least one institution that alumni of an online program have demonstrated financial support by contributing to a scholarship fund especially for online students of the program. Financial aid is of particular concern in another way, too: one institution stated that if more than 50% of their enrollments go online, the institution will lose assistance for financial aid.

Listed below are three basic models for distributing tuition and fee revenue, at least among internal nodes (sometimes multiple models occur at the same institution):

1. A unit charged with driving online education (e.g. outreach, external education, tech support) manages the distribution of online tuition and fees revenue, and takes some of this revenue to fund its activities. Examples of other units that share in the distribution of revenue are: the

institution as whole, individual schools, departments, individual faculty, and/or other support organizations such as student services or IT. This distribution may be standardized across all programs, or there may be individual agreements with different schools, departments or programs. Sometimes tuition and fees are standardized across an institution, in other instances they are negotiated program by program.

2. The unit charged with driving online education does not manage the distribution of revenue but instead pays stipends and other monies out of its annual budget to departments and faculty for development and training, and for other expenses such as marketing and infrastructure.

3. Individual academic programs fund their own development and delivery of online programs.

4. Marketing

See section VI.

B. What are the Leverage Points for Raising Funds for Sustained Operation?

When asked about challenges or limits to growth, a lack of funding for new course and program development was raised as an issue at roughly half the institutions. Foundation (especially Sloan) and institutional grants were singled out as important contributors of capital in efforts to start online education at their institutions. These grants still play a major role in funding development at some of these institutions today. Several of the large public institutions rely on presidential/institutional grants in the $1 million to $2 million a year range. Particularly in the arena of developing online education for traditional students, a number of interviewees cited the lack of foundation or institutional support as slowing or halting progress. At one public institution, where foundation grants played a role in early years, funds for new course development is limited by tech fees generated as part of the revenue stream from online course tuition and fees; roughly twenty-five new courses are being developed per year on a base of approximately 150 online courses offered during this past semester.

Even for online courses developed for corporate or professional markets, the issue of insufficient funding for development was raised. This is a problem especially for non-degree-credit courses. Yet one interviewee thought that development monies might be raised from industry, particularly industries that have an affinity for the target student market, e.g. pharmaceutical companies for continuing medical education.

There does not seem to be agreement across institutions as to whether tuition for online course should be pegged at a rate higher or equal to that of face-to-face courses. Some courses were priced as follows:

*   Online priced the same as onsite.

*   Charges a tuition premium for online.

*   Charges higher off-campus tuition to out-of-state online students.

*   Tuition is same as face-to-face except for a $25 per credit tech fee.

The majority of the institutions have either higher tuition or charge special fees for online courses. One institution did not have any incremental tuition or fees for its online courses. Three of the institutions charge "tech fees" for online courses that vary from $5 to $25 per credit hour. At one of these institutions, 70% of this fee goes back to the college and academic department deans, who use this money to pay stipends to faculty who develop online courses; the remaining 30% is used by the unit supporting online education for technology infrastructure and to fund its budget (i.e. for staff to support faculty developing online courses).

At the public institutions, there is the added complication of setting online course tuition in the environment of differentiating between resident and non-resident rates. At some institutions, where each program may set or negotiate its own tuition and fees, there is not yet intra-institutional standardization. For example, one online master's degree has tuition set at a rate between resident and non resident, another program features a master's degree at a different campus of the same state university and charges off-campus tuition to out-of-state-students. A few institutions are in the process of tackling this issue by clarifying a notion of "e-tuition."

The issue of how high to set tuition for online course speaks directly to the "capture value, and turn it into a revenue stream" part of the business model. At one institution which charges a "tech fee" for online courses, the associate provost/budget director expressed his opinion that e-tuition should be higher—maybe quite a bit higher than face-to-face tuition. He wants to understand what that increment should be.

C. How are Costs Understood and Managed?

Using the language of for-profit accounting, the units devoted to online education operate as cost centers. Sometimes they are also revenue centers with clear revenue targets. None seemed to regard themselves as operating as profit centers in the sense they could invest and distribute monies as they wish in order to return an agreed upon profit or margin. Institutions with schools or programs of continuing or professional education usually did look to these units to return an agreed upon contribution margin. That the units driving online education are not profit centers may be explained in part by the fact that many, if not most, rely on continuing "external" funding in the nature of institutional or foundation grants to provide the investment necessary to develop new online programs. Some rely on this funding to recover costs, even just direct costs. Also, the notion of "profit center" with its implication of making decisions to maximize 'profit' (net cash) may be at odds with the values of not-for-profit educational institutions.

That an understanding of costs is an issue of significant concern to many is evidenced by such typical comments as:

> "We now run as cost recovery and need to be self-supporting."

> "Cost avoidance [real estate costs] is key to justifying a model for pursuing online programs."

> "What is the true cost of development? What is the cost to handle a faculty 'client' for life?"

Not surprisingly, there was no common way that institutions conceptualize and account for costs associated with online education. However, there is a desire to develop a cross-institutional way to conceptualize cost components, and some attempts among groups are already being made. Such a project might be undertaken as part of the business models study. Below are some of the related challenges:

- Budget structures and models are not standardized across educational institutions.
- Costs relating to online education are not separated out cleanly within institutional or unit budgets.
- Individual educational units have limited control over how costs are allocated by the institution; what are considered direct costs to some units are indirect costs to others, although there do exist standards for this.
- Granularity of cost components would have to be commonly agreed to. To take an example from one institution, the following 5 components account for 81% of unit expenses:

instructional design and development, student services, marketing, data management, and program planning and management.

- Because "cost avoidance" (e.g. for classroom real estate) may be a key part of the value proposition for online education, the model would have to encompass this in some way.

Different metrics to calibrate and compare costs were raised in the course of discussions: e.g. cost per student, cost per enrollment, percentages of total costs, etc. If this project was attempted, it would seem useful to do it in the context of constructing the value-chain of activities for online education, as aforementioned. Institutions were willing to share their costs to develop new online courses, with costs ranging from $10,000 to $60,000 per course.

D. Some Final Points Related to Business Models

It needs to be noted that the question of "granularity" is relevant when talking about business models and cost issues. Business models can be developed at the level of the individual online program or at the level of growing and sustaining online education at an entire institution. This fact became apparent when comparing and contrasting, cross-institutionally, elements of business models that were discussed by interviewees.

One, perhaps controversial, conclusion drawn from the information collected from interviews pertaining to business models, is that it cannot be stated unequivocally that any institution interviewed had a comprehensive model for online education that showed it making a sustainable "profit." However, it may be the case that the online education endeavor is totally self supporting across all nodes of the educational organization involved in planning, developing and delivering online education. Also, beyond that, it generates enough net cash for investment or reinvestment for infrastructure and growth. Indeed, one institution claimed that it earned back within 18 months the initial grant that funded the online program, and at least one other institution now requires new online courses to come up with a plan, using a standardized business template that shows positive contribution margins after a fixed number of years. But until a systematic way can be developed to account for all the activities involved in online education (the value-chain) and understand their costs, it would be difficult to verify these claims.

Construction of a complete value chain, and a way to conceptualize costs components cross-institutionally, might be the focus for future research or interest-group activity. It would be a challenging project to undertake, considering the different basic business models that underpin private and public education, not to speak of the differences in state systems. What is meant by sustainability and growth for online education would need to be defined carefully and be put in the context of educational missions as well as other "products" such as undergraduate, graduate, or professional programs. On the positive side, institutions are now in the process of building and refining business models for online education and that a variety of persons, in different positions, are interested. There appears to be a thirst for knowledge of others' models, methods, and for benchmarks.

VI. MARKETING: HOW ARE PRODUCT CHOICES MADE AND COMMUNICATED?

Marketing is a source of concern to many but not all programs and institutions visited. Here are two typical comments that emphasize marketing issues:

"Does every [separate] program need its own marketing? Very expensive."

"Do I cut costs or do more marketing?"

For the purpose of this report, marketing activity is construed in its broadest sense as a set of value-added business activities ranging from understanding customer needs, to shaping the product and services to meet those needs, to communicating with the target audience.

A. Three Marketing Process Models

Three general models of the marketing process seemed to predominate among the institutions interviewed. These are listed from least to most structured:

Marketing activity is not significant enough to warrant common or formal methods or budgeting processes across the institution's various online educational initiatives. At the very least, most institutions appear to produce a catalog of online courses and programs. Most, but not all, of these institutions promote their online programs using free or low-cost methods, either promoting them at professional meetings, as appropriate, and by using inexpensive web or print-based communications. Marketing may be done mostly at the level of the individual program manager or faculty member. The activity is centered on marketing communications.

Some level of marketing activity is controlled by a "central" marketing arm at the institution (or shared by a number of collaborative institutions), and this is budgeted for in some formal way, but other marketing activity, sometimes significant, sometimes not, is done by individual online programs. Five of the institutions had such structures: sometimes they handled marketing for online programs only; sometimes they served as marketing arm for face-to-face programs as well. The activity of the central group includes marketing communication, but may extend beyond that to issues such as rationalization of products and services.

A formal, controlled, more integrated marketing approach, with activities spanning from market research to product (e.g. course or program) selection to marketing communications, is taken in a more or less uniform manner across all online programs. This does not necessarily mean that a significant degree of marketing is done for all online programs, but at least there is an intentional process to determine the desirable marketing effort. Only a few institutions appeared to have evolved this integrated marketing process.

1. Example of a Formal Marketing Approach

This third model is best explained by illustrating how it works, in general, at one doctoral/research-extensive public institution. The unit responsible for online education organizes its curriculum and programs into segments according to broad subject areas (e.g. management, education and health, etc.). To each segment is assigned a team consisting of a program manager and a marketing strategist; these teams work with the institution's academic departments who regulate programs and control the teaching resources. As characterized by one team interviewed, in the early days they worked with whichever academic departments would work with them, and went after the "low hanging fruit." Today, they claim to be more "in the driver's seat," more marketing-research driven, and have better shaped the process. They employ a "rate card" which attempts to budget a specific dollar-per-enrollment charge for institutional marketing as well as other marketing charges, depending on the service level agreed upon (there are three named levels of service). From overall data provided by this unit, marketing accounted for 22% of FY02–03 expenses.

2. Constructing a Proforma

Formal methods like this, even if not so extensive, were described at two other institutions. They are part of a more general business planning process that involves constructing a "standard" pro forma for any new online program that is being considered for development. Marketing costs and needs are but one component of this pro forma, which generally considers cost and revenue estimates out over a number of years.

The dollar amounts spent or budgeted for marketing online programs varied from zero up to over 20%. These numbers are difficult to define and compare because sometimes marketing dollars are paid for indirectly through a tax (or split of tuition or fee revenue) to units that do some marketing activities. At one of the large public institutions, an estimated 15–20% of the budget of the unit driving online education is spent on marketing activities. At the other extreme, marketing did not appear to be a priority at one institution and in several programs at other institutions.

3. Affinity Marketing

One specific marketing technique employed by three of the institutions (or at least by some programs at those institutions) is what has been described as affinity marketing. According to this concept, organizations with some sort of customer affinity can play a role in marketing a product or service to its "members" and benefit in some way. Here are examples of affinity marketing:

- An institution that focuses on corporate education gets onto catalogs and mailing lists of professional societies, and splits some revenue from non-credit courses with these organizations.

- An institution that focuses on serving the needs of the financial services industry appoints "college advisors" at the financial organizations whose employees it serves. These advisors recruit and look after students. No tuition revenue is shared with the company employing the student.

4. Coalition Marketing

Affinity marketing may be considered one example of the more general concept of business-to-business (B-to-B) marketing. Another example mentioned was the concept of coalition marketing. According to this concept, groups of online educational providers would band together to jointly market their services. The idea is that it affords a way to enable a number of different institutions to serve the specific regional needs of a national group buyer of services. Coalition marketing could, as described, be a way that relatively small educational providers could compete against large ones. So, for example, under this theory a coalition of not-for-profit institutions might have been able to compete successfully against a relatively large for-profit educational provider to meet Wal-Mart's educational needs.

B. Discovering Market Value

One of the primary purposes of the marketing process is to shape and make explicit the value proposition. Specifically, what are the attributes of online education (product and ancillary services) that attract customers? Customers can be users (e.g. individual learners) or groups, such as corporations or coalition partners that contract for educational services for its employees or individual learners. Several interviewees expressed interest in getting a better understanding of student experiences and expectations. This survey could be expanded beyond individual students to get an understanding of experiences and expectations of groups that contract for services in bulk.

Here are some attributes, putting educational quality aside, which emerged. Beyond interviewees' observations based on business they have generated, there is no hard data to back-up the assertion that these product attributes translate into certain dollar value to customers. This should be viewed as a partial, emerging list:

- Time to market (i.e. the time it takes to develop and implement the educational product): From the customer's standpoint this would include the ability to be efficient and flexible in adding new degrees and programs.

- Scalability.

- Standardization across geographies (e.g. national financial services company is able to offer a uniform educational product to its employees no matter where they are located, or national professional accreditation body requires courses for all medical residents).

- Access (as defined as one of the five pillars of Sloan-C).

- Demonstrated quality control (e.g. through standardized assessments).

- Brand (e.g. premier name).

One final note about discovering value: Marketing textbooks stress the importance of market segmentation. Because online education may be viewed as a still new and evolving technology, the classic segmentation into innovators, early adopters, early majority, late majority and laggards is probably relevant. Discussions did not reveal a sense of whether or not institutions understand how far into these segments their market has penetrated. They may have understood it, but that information did not emerge.

More than one interviewee decried the "lack of appreciation" of marketing by colleagues, and other interviewees described marketing as one of the challenges they faced; there was interest in obtaining benchmarking data and for best practices to be shared.

C. Marketing Communications

A number of interviewees interpreted questions about marketing as being about their marketing communications activities, exclusively. Generally, there were levels of marketing communications efforts consistent with the three models of the marketing process defined at the beginning of this section. For example, one public institution has both a university-wide organization supporting exclusively online education as well as a campus-wide academic outreach organization that does promotion (self-reportedly approximately 15–20% of its budget). Nonetheless, five online programs interviewed on that campus showed their own approaches to marketing communications. Three related that they did no or little activity (these are a math program for rural students, a for-credit continuing education in dairy science, and a masters program in library science). Their marketing activities were mostly limited to word-of-mouth, and advertising in professional journals. The other two programs (continuing education in veterinary practice, a new program; and an online master in education, an established program) reported higher levels of marketing activity, using a combination of methods such as outsourcing and marketing with ASTD. The program that did extensive outsourcing reportedly spent approximately 20% of its budget on this. Three of the five programs talked about marketing as a challenge.

While it was clear that central units which drive online education play an important role in working with individual programs, there may be little communication among the programs themselves, associated with different schools or faculties, who may or may not communicate with each other.

Perhaps because of the extraordinary variety of online educational activity, there no "rules of thumb" about marketing communications that could be discerned as applied across all programs. But a few issues were raised that were of concern to multiple institutions:

- Because of the proliferation of online programs at some schools, a challenge posed is how to balance between "point" marketing of programs and marketing of an entire institution.

- Rising levels of customer sophistication in the use of online search tools means that marketing communication techniques need continue to evolve.

- Not a concern, but rather several institutions pointed out the marketing communications value to them in their having won major awards for quality online education (e.g. Sloan-C).

VII. THE ROLE OF EXTERNAL COLLABORATORS AND COMPETITORS

A. Collaboration

Evidence of collaboration at four levels can be broadly defined as follows:

1. Collaboration among programs within an institution: These collaborations took various guises, from shared marketing to shared use and re-use of courses across different online programs.

2. Collaboration among similar programs across multiple institutions: Examples of this are collaboration among library science programs, and collaboration among medical schools for the purpose of providing graduate education to medical residents.

3. Collaboration at the institutional level across multiple programs at multiple institutions: Typical of this are the university-system-wide online programs at some state universities. Levels of collaboration can vary from mainly marketing activities all the way to revenue sharing.

4. Collaboration between educational institutions and industry, professional or government organizations: These may be collaborations between a single institution and industry or industry groups. Examples include outsourcing of technical and support infrastructure, providing education for corporations, and affinity marketing. Or they may be collaborations between several academic institutions and an industry or professional partner, such as offering workers in an industry the opportunity to complete educational degrees by sharing courses across multiple educational institutions.

1. Sharing Revenue

Institutions are developing models for sharing revenue (tuition and fees) externally among institutions that engage collaboratively in online education. Under model 2 above, there is the example of the consortium of library school programs that are sharing "virtual seats" at no cost or reduced rates. The idea behind this is that courses can be offered, and student demand met, in cases where the individual program could not offer or fill the course on its own. Under model 3, a large state university is in the process of working out a model of accounting for inter-campus revenues so that online courses can be used by students common to all institutions in the system. Questions they are considering include how to split the tuition and fees stream into one channel that would go to one institution to cover student support services and another channel which would flow to the campus offering the online course to cover the academic costs.

2. Inter-organizational Process

The collaboration of one institution with regional financial services providers has yielded some interesting inter-organizational business processes and resources. Member companies provide guidance and operational support by appointing "college advisors" to look after students from their companies (a kind of outsourcing of student services). Member companies also provide staff, gratis, who serve on task forces with the educational institution to recommend and even develop new programs.

3. International Collaborations

Although there was not a lot of discussion about international collaborations, there were some significant examples, including the offering of online degrees in partnership with international educational institutions. One institution has its roots in providing education to military personnel around the world. Though overseas enrollment in all courses is approximately 50%, overseas enrollment in online-only courses appears to be much lower.

B. Competition

Interviewees expressed business issues as they saw them at their particular institutions and did not often turn to concerns about competition and competitors. It did not even come up when asked about "challenges" or "limits to growth" of their online educational programs.

However, there were exceptions. At one Master's College and University I institution, this was an issue as expressed by more than one interviewee. Unfavorable demographic trends, coupled with potential competition from other online programs, including the for-profits and "name brand" not-for profits, caused concerns about continued erosion of student body. At this institution, online education is looked at as a way to extend the demographic range served by traditional academic programs (albeit by offering some new programs, too) —as a way to reverse the declining student population.

The other area of concern about competition, more generally mentioned, is in the not-for-credit or at least non-degree-credit arena. One interviewee discussed the problems of a yet-to-be-launched program geared for professionals who may or may not need continuing education credit, depending on their home state. The program is significantly behind schedule, and has now lost "first mover" advantage to one from another state. The potential target audience of these programs is seen to be about 60,000 professionals U.S.-wide. Another interviewee, from a different institution, but again in the professional continuing education space, talked about the difficulty of competing with all the "free stuff" out there that could count for continuing education. Finally, some interviewees who looked into programs for corporate markets talked about the difficulty of competing with schools that have "premium" names.

Sometimes, collaborators can also be competitors. One public institution relies on community colleges as a source of students; another, in a different state, sees community colleges as a source of potential competition.

Why was competition, or the effects of competition, an issue that was seldom raised by interviewees, unless asked directly? There are several possibilities, including that online education is still in its early stages of growth, that access to education via online is increasing, and that the market is not saturated. No matter, it seems logical to conclude that at some point, given the very nature of the modality of online education, institutions will compete with each other for students at a distance. As noted by the interviewee from the institution concerned about unfavorable demographic trends, when this institution was created by the state, it and peer institutions were placed geographically so they would serve their own mutually exclusive "commuting" communities. Obviously, geographic isolation is not likely to serve as well as barrier for competition in an online educational environment, except, of course, in programs and markets where physical proximity is still an important component of the education.

In the future, how will institutions collaborate and compete with respect to online education? What parameters will form the basis for sustainable competitive advantage? Some hints may be given by the information provided in this report, but this can well be an area for focused study. Ways to measure trends and effects need to be constructed, and data collected and analyzed systematically.

VIII. SUCCESS MEASURES

An institution's venture into online education is shaped by its own mission, and institutional-specific internal and external drivers. The business model it evolves for its online educational initiatives, the particular value it wishes to create and capture through online modalities, needs to support institution-specific goals, as well as provide value to "customers". There is no reason to assume that for-profits would not also shape their business models in the light of goals arising from mission and other environmental drivers. It follows that to measure success of the online venture, institutions will create metrics that reflect, at least in part, their own goals.

In this section of the report, a short list of potential business-related (not educational quality) metrics is proposed. A future project might be to flesh out the list and to see if within every institution's unique set of metrics, a cross-institutional common core set could be constructed, and data collected and published for benchmarking purposes.

1. Penetration and growth measures to include percent of "market" captured and rate of growth for:
   - Courses/degrees/programs online
   - Students/enrollments online
   - Faculty teaching online, or trained in developing and/or teaching
   - Market segments (e.g. demographic, psychographic, or geographic segmentation)
Note that some of this data is already being collected through the Sloan Consortium.

2. Financial and operation measures to include:
   - Top line measures of revenue (e.g. tuition, fees, other revenue)
   - Bottom line measures (e.g. costs)
   - Surplus or deficit (e.g. net cash, contribution margin)
   - Investments (e.g. in infrastructure)

3. Other measures, including:
   - Satisfaction (e.g. faculty, student, alumni, business partners)
   - "Repeat" customers (e.g. students who take follow-up courses, progress from individual courses to certificates, certificates to degrees)
   - Retention
   - Rankings, awards, grants, giving

- Measures of competition (traditional academic measures include inquiry conversions, cross-applications, and yield)

IX. POINTS FOR FUTURE RESEARCH OR ACTIVITIES

In this final section, a summary of ideas for future projects or activities that emerged from discussions is provided. Although each project many have its own set of persons most interested in it, driven by job, experience and the like, an overall special interest group in business issues might be formed to help prioritize, guide, coordinate and communicate results.

1. **Case studies**. An interviewee, early on, when asked what information she would find most useful in a study of business issues, remarked that a series of case studies of different types of online education programs would help establish some baseline data. Others echoed this theme including the idea of writing and sharing case studies on best business practices. Sloan-C already does work on effective practices. This might be expanded to include an emphasis on business issues. Here are examples of potential cases collected: Affinity marketing, B-to-B marketing, outsourcing, publishing as a business paradigm, models for faculty organization and deployment, customer service issues, the demise of a major effort in online education at a not-for-profit institution. Many more potential topics exist.

2. **Customer experiences and expectations**. Several interviewees expressed interest in obtaining data that would help prioritize resource allocation among support options. They wish better to understand customer expectations with respect to education delivered through online modalities. The term "customers" includes individual learners as well as group buyers of services (such as companies or industry groups that contract for education). It was pointed out that some institutions already are doing some of this work.

3. **Business models and processes, cost models, performance metrics**. As discussed in section V, models for business planning and costing online programs already exist or are being evolved at various institutions. Many interviewees expressed interest in knowledge of others' methods and benchmarks; some, but by no means all, interviewees expressed interest (or were optimistic) that common, cross-institutional models and metrics could be established. Beyond the writing of cases about best business practices, other means might be created to allow those with interest to develop and communicate models collaboratively, or define and prioritize cross-institutional performance metrics (see section VIII above), that could be collected and disseminated for benchmarking.

4. **Structural/predictive model of factors correlated with success measures**. I stated at the outset of this report that the business issues I set out to study could be compared cross-institutionally only if understood in the context of the individual institutions' missions and goals. But as cross-institutional costs and performance measures are developed, and data becomes feasible to collect, it becomes possible to test to what extent certain factors correlate with particular outcomes. So a model could be developed and tested that might further our understanding of how business practices and resource allocations correlate with different possible success measures. This project would require assistance from individuals adept at building statistical models and collecting data.

X. ABOUT THE AUTHOR

Stephen Schiffman is dean of the undergraduate program at Babson College in Wellesley, Mass. A faculty member in Mathematics and MIS since 1986, he is also the architect of the new undergraduate curriculum, which was launched in the fall of 1996. In 1997, the Pew Charitable Trusts recognized this effort by selecting Babson for a Pew Leadership Award for renewal of undergraduate education. Steve holds a Ph.D. in mathematics from Dartmouth College as well as an M.S. in management from Sloan School, MIT. He has taught at the University of Colorado and Colorado College, and, prior to joining Babson College, he worked at Digital Equipment Corporation. Email stephen.schiffman@olin.edu.

XI. APPENDIX B: INTERVIEW GUIDE, GOALS OF STUDY

Interview Guide

Institution_____**Name**_____

One of our key goals is to understand what specific information/data we are likely to be able to collect successfully (via survey) that will be of use to the community who cares about the business of online education. What information would be important and useful to you, and, (how) could we collect it? Some areas of information are:

1. Costs (total costs, costs of components such as development, delivery, marketing etc): costs now and your sense of future costs. Relative costs, but can we meaningfully get absolute costs (by what metrics)? Would the difficulty of collecting absolute cost information be worth it in terms of being able to provide benchmark data?

2. Target Audience (who do you develop courses for and why? Who actually takes your courses and why? New audiences or old? Does the data exist for you to be able to glean the characteristics of your online learners and compare it to your "traditional" learners? Would this (aggregated, shared) information be of value to you?)

3. Product Offerings (what courses make up your "product offerings" now, and why? What do you think this portfolio will look like in the future?)

4. How do you most successfully market your products?

5. Business Barriers (What are the major barriers to growing your business?). What would be of value to you that we could do to help you in solving them? (e.g. best practices, training, providing models,....)

6. Other

Beyond these, we are interested in listening to "your story" in the hopes of better understanding what we might do to provide you information.

B.2 Version 2.0

Trip interview guide v2.0

Overview: Three goals of our study on the business of online education are:

1) Learning what factors lead to success in on-line programs.

2) Understanding what specific information/data we are likely to be able to collect successfully (via survey) that will be of use to the community who cares about the business of online education.

3) Uncovering and sharing best business practices.

At this preliminary stage of research we are very much still in "listening mode". Hence we are trying to visit about a dozen institutions to understand their own "stories".

A little more about each goal:

1) We are trying to develop a model that explains program success (dependent variable) as a function of business factors and decisions (independent variables). We need to develop an understanding of what variables come into play, and how they might be measured. This breaks down into two parts: 1) what is "success" and how do you measure it? and 2) what are likely factors/decisions that contribute to success and how might they be measured. At this point in our research, we are casting the net wide to try to uncover as many variables as we can. In particular, for each institution we visit we would ask: How do you define success in your own context? How successful have you been? What factors or decisions have contributed to or against your ability to succeed?

2) Here are some possible examples of data we can try to collect and share about the business of online education for benchmarking and other purposes: Costs (absolute numbers or percentages: costs of components such as development, delivery, marketing etc.); Customer demographics (who takes courses and why? service level expectations etc.); Marketing techniques; Policies (admissions, tuition, credit, partnerships etc.); Organization structures.

3) So far in our interviews, the idea has emerged that we might collect and publish cases about businesses practices. Some topics already mentioned include: Affinity and B to B marketing, customer service issues, outsourcing, re-establishing oneself in a market you lost, use of full-time versus part-time faculty, the tension between traditional academic program control versus control of online degrees and faculty. What other ideas do you have for cases? Either best (or interesting) practices or key issues that you have faced? Would you be willing to write a case?

THE BUSINESS OF ONLINE EDUCATION: ARE WE COST COMPETITIVE?

Rob Robinson
University of Texas System TeleCampus

- A consensus has not yet emerged in answer to the question of whether online efforts are cost-effective.

- Cost-effectiveness is normally defined as the ratio between inputs and outputs or performance.

- Differences in size, mission, and structure (public vs. private) translate to fundamental differences in cost structures.

- Properly designed and constructed, online courses, when compared to traditional face-to-face courses, can better engage learners, increase retention, improve student outcomes, and greatly increase access to higher education.

- Average or lower-than-average delivery cost is an additional argument in favor of this mode of delivery.

I. INTRODUCTION: QUESTIONS WITHOUT ADEQUATE ANSWERS

In the current era of rising tuition and falling state support, colleges and universities (particularly public institutions) are looking to a variety of measures to cut costs, increase revenue, or more cost-effectively deliver their programs and courses.

A. Costs and Revenue

While overall revenue to colleges and universities has increased over time, costs have risen at a proportionally faster rate, representing what Bowen terms "the revenue theory of costs" [1]. This well-known dictum reveals that institutions of higher education (IHE) will not only raise as much revenue as possible, but will spend all that is raised. Traditional sources of revenue (tuition, fees, legislative appropriations, returns on investment), however, have become increasingly difficult to tap into, which lead IHEs to turn their focus to increasing productivity wherever possible without increasing costs.

As Johnstone states, "… the major remaining productivity problem in higher education may not lie in excessive costs but in insufficient learning—a function of such features as redundant learning; aimless academic exploration; the unavailability of courses at the right time; excessive non-learning time in the academic day, week and year; insufficient realization of the potential of collegiate-level learning during the high school years" [2].

Fundamental to the ability to examine productivity and efficiency issues, however, is the ability to examine the underlying costs structures of higher education. There has been resistance to attempting to undertake "business-style" examinations of costs and productivity on most campuses. As Newman points out, "…higher education institutions simply do not analyze their cost structure, particularly on the academic side. They do, of course, know the cost of the Geology Department or the Admission Office but not the cost of mounting different courses, or the efficiency of using faculty time in varying ways, or whether a redesign would improve the effectiveness and the efficiency of a large introductory course" [3].

B. Online Instruction = Increasing Efficiency?

Much has been written and discussed about the evolution (some say revolution) represented by online learning. Properly designed and constructed, online courses, when compared to traditional face-to-face courses, have the ability to better engage the learner, increase retention, and improve student outcomes [4]. Online learning also represents the opportunity to greatly increase access to higher education. Geographically and temporally isolated students can continue to pursue their educations via online learning.

Moreover, online instruction presents opportunities that do not exist in the traditional classroom. Duderstadt comments that "[online] learning has a deeper significance than simply relaxing the barriers of space and time. Because of its interactive nature, it transforms learning from simply absorbing new knowledge to the creating of knowledge. It provides new mechanisms for rich social interactions that simply could not exist if restricted to face-to-face contact. It provides both students and faculty with access to learning resources far beyond the boundary of the campus itself" [5]. Certainly, then, it can be said that online learning breaks down barriers and presents new learning opportunities. But at what cost? Is online delivery cost-effective?

Finding the true costs of online learning is a subject that has been examined closely since the late 1990s. As online moves from the experimental "toe-in-the-water" stage to being mainstreamed at many institutions, cost elements take on new importance. However a consensus has not yet emerged in answer to the question of whether online efforts are cost-effective. Cost-effectiveness in higher education as a whole is itself a murky area because higher education operates (as an economic entity) less like a business than other labor-intensive "productivity immune" organizations, such as live theater, symphony orchestras, and social welfare agencies [6]. Cost-effectiveness is normally defined as the ratio between inputs and outputs or performance. Given that there is no agreed upon method for measuring the outputs of higher education, establishing cost-effectiveness is a dicey proposition. Rather than attempting to measure student learning, student enrollment (being easily measurable) is a common proxy for output.

Comparing higher education costs across institutions can also be problematic. Differences in size, mission, and structure (public vs. private) translate to fundamental differences in cost structures. Large public, research-intensive institutions will have higher per-student costs than smaller teaching-intensive institutions. Private institutions generally spend significantly more per-student than public institutions [7]. Given this diversity, online education as a tool will likely be used in very different ways, and very well may not fit into the mission of a given institution.

If we define the mission of colleges and universities as providing a quality education to as many qualified individuals as possible, then we have a foundation on which to build our cost-effectiveness analysis. On the surface, offering online courses would seem to make great sense: build high-quality, high-enrollment courses and offer them as frequently as possible. The latter is a promise of a very cost-effective delivery of higher education. The potential is there, but how does this promise play out in reality?

Early thinking regarding distance education in general and online in particular fostered the idea that these delivery methods would lead to huge decreases in marginal costs. In other words, "develop once/deliver (to) many" would allow great cost efficiencies when compared to the "guild" process of most traditional instruction, unchanged in many ways from the founding of University of Paris and Oxford in the 11th century [5, 8]. In fact, many institutions have approached online delivery as a way to generate quick profits. The profit potential, in most cases, has failed to materialize in the ways envisioned.

Rather than offering low-cost/high-enrollment courses, online practitioners quickly learned that class sizes needed to be kept small in order for faculty to manage the class and to ensure a high-quality, interactive student learning experience. However, small class sizes, particularly for undergraduate general education courses, do not necessarily sit well with business officers on most college campuses. When focusing on the costs of online courses, there are many variables that must be examined, some of which are not observed when costing traditional higher education. Quality of the course (however defined) itself can be a major determining cost factor, and yet it is often overlooked.

In addition, discussions about online costs tend to focus heavily on the typically high costs of course development. While it is difficult to separate the costs to develop higher education courses and the costs to deliver those same courses, it is the only true way to compare costs for face-to-face and online.

II. THE TELECAMPUS COST STUDY

The University of Texas (UT) TeleCampus is the University of Texas System's "virtual campus." It works with all of the member institutions within the system to build and offer collaborative online degree programs, certificate programs, and individual courses. In pursuing degrees, TeleCampus students may concurrently take courses from as many as eight of the various institutions. These programs have been very successful in bringing new opportunities to students across Texas, in offering new options to on-campus students, and in increasing the enrollments at the participating campuses. It has not been immediately clear, however, if these efforts are fiscally on-par with traditional methods.

In early 2002, the Board of Regents of the University of Texas System asked the TeleCampus about the cost effectiveness of online courses. Specifically, the Board wanted to know if it cost more or less to deliver online courses in comparison to face-to-face courses on campus. A study was conducted to uncover the answer to this question.

In constructing the study, the decision was made to separate the development costs of courses from their delivery costs. Development costs for new online courses are actually fairly easy to quantify, and would include faculty release time costs, technical support, design team support, and some portion of hardware and software costs. In contrast, however, it is very difficult to develop a comparable cost for traditional face-to-face courses, which, in the case of veteran faculty, have evolved over many years. For example, what is the value of those yellowed class notes in the hands of the instructor on the first day of class? It is probably safe to say that the development costs for online courses are significantly higher than those for face-to-face development, but it is very difficult to quantify that gap. Therefore, the TeleCampus cost study did not address development costs, but focused rather on delivery costs only.

A. What to Compare?

It was important to seek the most useful and measurable proxy for student outcomes. In this study, the most useful measure was "one unit of education," for which the Semester Credit Hour (SCH) figure was used, as reported by the institutions to the Texas Higher Education Coordinating Board. The SCH is beneficial as a unit of measure because it corrects for the diversity of size and mission of the various institutions. Those campuses focused on undergraduate teaching reflect a different total budget/SCH than the larger research and graduate education oriented institutions, and it was important to capture this diversity in the study.

The table below demonstrates the wide variety of size and mission of the UT academic campuses. These figures are of interest when assessing costs of educational delivery.

Table 1. Institutions in Study

Institution	Code	FY 04 Budget ($m)	FY 03 Enrollment	Carnegie Class. (2000)
UT Arlington	UTA	$266.7	24,979	D/R Extensive
UT Austin	Austin	$1,444.6	51,438	D/R Extensive
UT Brownsville	UTB	$89.5	10,705[1]	Master's I
UT Dallas	UTD	$192.9	13,725	D/R Intensive
UT El Paso	UTEP	$217.7	18,542	D/R Intensive
UT Pan American	UTPA	$178.8	15,889	Master's I

UT Permian Basin	UTPB	$31.1	3,044	Master's I
UT San Antonio	UTSA	$243.6	24,665	Master's I
UT Tyler	UTT	$46.5	4,783	Master's I
UT TeleCampus	UTTC	$2.8	1,200[2]	N/A

[1] Brownsville's enrollment is combined with South Texas Community College

[2] The TeleCampus counts its enrollment as seats in classes. It is a tally of the number of students taking courses offered from TeleCampus courseware and supported by TeleCampus student services. For the FY 2003 year, course enrollment was 8,345, which represented a headcount of 6,371. For this chart, TeleCampus enrollments for FY03 have been converted to an estimated FTE number

B. Investigating On-Campus Cost Structures

The study began with an examination of the published budgets of the nine academic institutions within the UT System, as well as the budget for the UT TeleCampus as base data. The budgets of the system institutions use common categories and nearly-common allocation methodologies. This allowed us to identify specific and pertinent cost categories that can be attributed to educational delivery. The line items from those budgets that were included fully were:

- Academic Support Services, which includes line items for non-instructional staff and materials.
- Student Support Services, primarily a salary and wage category.
- Institutional Support Services, again, primarily a salary and wage category.
- Operations and Maintenance of Plant—in addition to staffing, this item includes a significant materials cost.

In addition, a portion of the depreciation and amortization cost category was included in the total cost derivation. Deriving the appropriate portion of the depreciation and amortization was an interesting question and one that was decided only after much discussion with administrative, accounting, and finance staff. The final algorithm captures the ratio of the educational and general expenditures (those that are directly attributable to instruction) to the total university expenditures. For those with the finance mindset, the formula used, quite simply is:

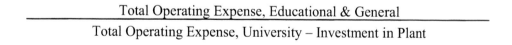

$$\frac{\text{Total Operating Expense, Educational \& General}}{\text{Total Operating Expense, University} - \text{Investment in Plant}}$$

This ratio, ranging from 0.5 to 0.7, is then applied to the depreciation and amortization line item and included in the campus' total cost of delivering instruction. Identified costs were then distributed across each campus' reported number of semester credit hours for the year, resulting in a "cost per SCH." This became the unit of comparison for the study.

C. Investigating Online Cost Structures

Because the TeleCampus and the campuses work together to bring quality online courses to life while also supporting the student, some costs are shared (for example, library) while some are borne by either the TeleCampus (for example, delivery platform) or the institution (for example, instructional costs). This makes it difficult to perform a straight item-by-item comparison.

The TeleCampus does not operate as an academic unit. It is, in fact, a department within the Office of Academic Affairs at the system administration level. As such, the TeleCampus does not capture or report its costs in the same fashion as the campuses. Being a relatively small operation, however, it was relatively easy to assign analogous costs to the line items identified for the institutions above.

TeleCampus cost categories:

- Specific TeleCampus staff salaries, those directly involved in the support of the faculty and students. Marketing, for example, was excluded.

- Infrastructure costs. Represents both in-house and contracted services (course management system, hosting, help desk, academic services).

- TeleCampus Digital Library—database subscription and staff costs. The Digital Library is used to "level" access to resources across all the institutions' digital holdings.

- Training costs for faculty and technical support on the campuses.

Again, after calculating the cost for TeleCampus course delivery, it was spread across the SCH represented by the total number of courses offered.

It is important to note that the TeleCampus does not directly employ faculty. The courses offered via the TeleCampus are taught by the faculty of the offering institutions. The vast majority of TeleCampus courses are taught in-load by campus-based faculty. This means that instructional costs will be the same whether the course is taught face-to-face on the traditional campus or online through the TeleCampus. Thus, for the purposes of this study, instructional costs have been netted out. This is an important point as many studies of this type indicate an additional cost for instruction in the online environment due mainly to overload or other compensation for faculty. The UT System campuses do not typically provide additional compensation for teaching a course online. Also note that this study did not seek to compare the amount of hours spent teaching, but rather focused only on the instructional costs as represented by salaries.

D. Findings

This cost study was conducted in both FY 02 and FY 03. The study shows that, when compared to the academic components of the UT System, the TeleCampus has a cost of delivery that is within the range of what was found for delivery costs of face-to-face, but it is close to the lower end of that range.

Table 2. FY 2002 Cost/SCH

Campus	Total Costs/SCH
UTPA	$93.00
UTTC	$101.75
UTSA	$106.22
UTA	$116.78
UTEP	$123.54
UTD	$130.73
UTPB	$157.75
Austin	$164.06
UTT	$165.00
UTB	$347.99

Table 3. FY 2003 Cost/SCH

	Total Costs/SCH
UTPA	$78.68
UTTC	$88.18
UTSA	$104.01
UTA	$107.34
UTD	$108.47
UTEP	$115.37
Austin	$145.60
UTPB	$159.91
UTT	$163.13
UTB	$293.13

Figure 1. 2002 Costs per SCH, by Institution

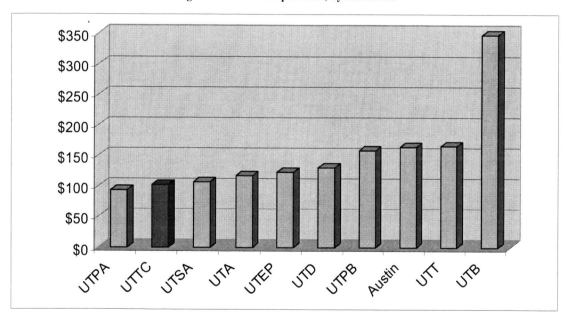

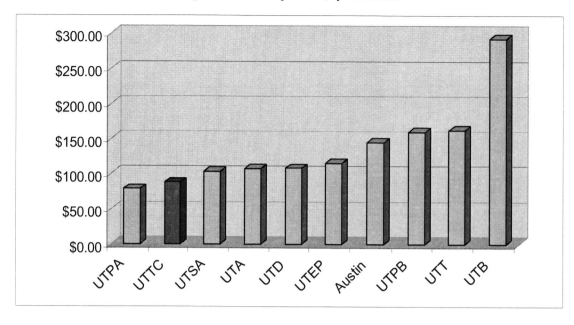

Figure 2. 2003 Cost per SCH, by Institution

III. TRENDS AND IMPLICATIONS

This study is by no means wide or broad enough to be conclusive for generalizing online and face-to-face delivery costs. However, if it's assumed that this study is indicative of a common cost structure in online programs, then several interesting points may emerge. First, an average or lower-than-average delivery cost is an additional argument in favor of this mode of delivery and can play into a return-on-investment calculation when amortizing development costs.

Second, while this study focuses solely on delivery costs, development costs must not be ignored. There are significant labor and technology costs in building a quality online course. In some cases, this initial cost can be enough to dissuade a real commitment to quality online delivery. As noted, several institutions which ventured into online from a profit perspective have changed their model or closed their online operations. Institutions that have taken a more measured approach to online have found various degrees of success, and some are indeed generating revenue.

It is worth pointing out that the TeleCampus courses are offered with an average faculty-student ratio of 1:25. As we endeavor to increase class size (while continuing to maintain quality), the cost/SCH will decrease, and, since the TeleCampus enrollments are growing at a faster rate than on-campus enrollments, the TeleCampus cost/SCH should decrease faster than the on-campus costs.

The cost study also indicates that online courses may have a role in mitigating, or at least delaying, on-campus construction costs. According to the Texas Higher Education Coordinating Board, in the State of Texas there is a documented need to enroll 500,000 new freshmen by the year 2015. If online instruction is assumed to be deliverable at a lower cost/unit than face-to-face, there is then an argument to be made for increasing online offerings. Hybrid courses could be used to make more efficient use of existing facilities while completely online courses could defer or delay the need to construct additional classrooms.

IV. REFERENCES

1. **Bowen, H.** *The Costs of Higher Education—How Much do Colleges and Universities Spend Per Student and How Much Should They Spend?* Jossey-Bass, 1980.
2. **Johnstone, B.** "Financing Higher Education: Who Should Pay?" Chapter 1 in the *ASHE Reader on Finance in Higher Education*, Second Edition, Pearson, 2001.
3. **Newman. F., L. Couturier, and J. Scurry.** T*he Future of Higher Education: Rhetoric, Reality, and the Risks of Market.* Jossey-Bass, 2004.
4. **Russell, T.** *The No Significant Difference Phenomena.* North Carolina University Press, 1999. Online: http://www.nosignificantdifference.org/nosignificantdifference/ and http://www.nosignificant difference.org/significantdifference/.
5. **Duderstadt, J., D. Atkins, and D. Van Houweling.** *Higher Education in the Digital Age: Issues and Strategies for American Colleges and Universities.* Praeger, 2002.
6. **Baumol, W.** as quoted in Johnstone, B. "Financing Higher Education: Who Should Pay?" Chapter 1 in the *ASHE Reader on Finance in Higher Education*, Second Edition. Pearson, 2001.
7. **Clorfelter, C., R. Ehrenbery, R., M. Getz, and J. Siegfried.** *Economic Challenges in Higher Education.* University of Chicago Press, 1991.
8. **Texas Higher Education Coordinating Board.** *Closing the Gaps.* 2000. Online: http://www .thecb.state.tx.us/ClosingTheGaps/.

V. ABOUT THE AUTHOR

Rob Robinson is the Associate Director for the University of Texas System TeleCampus. He heads up the budget and strategic-planning functions of the TeleCampus. At the state level, Robinson serves on the Distance Education Advisory Council of the Texas Higher Education Coordinating Board and recently served on the Telecommunications Planning and Oversight Council for the Department of Information Resources. He holds a B.S. degree from the University of Texas at Austin, an M.B.A. from St. Edward's University, and is currently pursuing a doctoral degree from the University of Texas at Austin. Email rrobinson@utsystem.edu.

SUCCESS VERSUS VALUE: WHAT DO WE MEAN BY THE BUSINESS OF ONLINE EDUCATION?

Doug Lynch
University of Pennsylvania

- There is a need, a market, and a moral imperative to be entrepreneurial when it comes to developing and delivering online education.

- The old model is utterly irrelevant to the vast majority of students.

- Educators can apply some business principles in creative ways that help maximize mission rather than profits.

- Competitors can find stable places from which it makes more sense to cooperate.

- Working cooperatively with employers, higher education can be available to any employee.

"Try not to be a man of success, but rather one of value" – A. Einstein

I. INTRODUCTION

Given the diminishing resources of colleges and universities and the increasing complexity of the demands placed on them, those of us who lead online programs and institutions are joining our face-to-face peers in exploring how to make our schools more like businesses. However, the goal of education as a business, at least as it is widely understood, is not the path to take. We need to understand, to paraphrase Clark Kerr, what the uses of online learning are [1]. Therefore, before this paper begins to describe the skills that can make us better educators, I will put forth a sort of manifesto about the business of education.

We need first to define *business* and then explore whether a university meets the definition. Milton Freidman argues that the primary responsibility of a business is to maximize its profits [2]. In contrast, Derek Bok outlines the social responsibilities of a modern university to make two points: "universities are concerned with education," [3] and "like churches, universities experience the constant tensions that result from embracing transcendent goals and ideals while having to exist and be of service in a practical, imperfect world" [3]. Henry Hannsmann explores the rationale for exempting nonprofit organizations from corporate income tax on the basis of the public good [4]. Hank Levin has written about the inefficiencies of teaching and learning [5]. Although many have argued eloquently that Freidman's notion is not a good fit for universities because we are different from businesses, yet we feel compelled to talk about the "business" of online learning as if to justify our existence.

At the 2003 Association for Continuing Higher Education annual conference, the central focus of the town meeting was the "attack" on adult education [6]. Ortman notes that while nonprofit colleges are closing, for-profit education is on the rise [7]. Simultaneously, there is a rise in corporate universities [8], and more recently we have learned that these entities are applying for accreditation and that fourteen can already confer degrees [9]. Despite research from economists that consistently demonstrates the value of higher education, we sense that non-profits are under the gun to justify our existence and the public's allocation of resources to our institutions.

To paraphrase Langston Hughes, to prevent dreams from being deferred, we need to redefine who we are and what we mean. We are accountable to many more stakeholders than Friedman's shareholders, and as Bok notes, we serve many purposes, thus he uses the term *multiversity* [3]. The service a business offers is a means to an end, which is profit. For higher education, education is seen as an end in itself. There are logical reasons for having universities behave like universities rather than corporations.

In higher education, what we really mean when we refer to the value of business principles is more in line with the notion of entrepreneurship, a notion more closely analogous with *champion* than with *business*. Because the public entrusts us with its resources and because we are concerned with providing the best education to the broadest number of people given the constraints both of our mission and our budgets, it is time for us to explore where we might apply some business principles in creative ways that help us champion and maximize our mission rather than our profits.

When using the business analogy, online educators should note that we have already solved the biggest issue faced by business: collectively, we have created a new way of learning, a new production function. That is the most valuable contribution we have made, and quality should continue to be our central focus. A wide body of literature exists that helps us think of learning in economic terms. Researchers such as

Hank Levin have promoted the idea of conceptualizing learning in terms of economic production [10]. Educators take a host of inputs and create an output or outputs. For a long time, there was only one way to teach, and the primary driving force on what we could do was really budget constraints—that is, what we could afford to pay faculty and how small we could afford to make class size. Online learning has enabled us to conceive and deliver learning using a new "business" production process that combines the essential elements of learning in a different way. Putting aside costs for a moment, educators are more advanced than we realize because we have the right product from an educational standpoint. We know that there are no significant learning outcome differences between face-to-face and online learning; we have a good product. Now we must figure out how we can convey the importance of that product and sustain its impact outside our walls.

To continue the analogy, the business principles we want to explore can be thought of as skill sets that map to any college's MBA curriculum. A fundamental part of the MBA curriculum is the admission process, where students opt to study business; the choice implies interest as well as talent, or what we might call acumen. The history and culture of higher education is based on the notion of conservation and preservation, which is squarely juxtaposed to the history and culture of business. Educators need to maintain our values and also cultivate a sense of urgency and a child's sense of both tenacity and wonder, all traits that make for the successful entrepreneur. Although suggestions for cultivating these talents and values are beyond the scope of this paper, I believe that without them, honing business skills will do little to change the shape of higher education.

Before I explore the skills that will help us do more with less, I want to comment briefly on structuring for purposeful innovation. The first is structure, and I will only mention it in passing because another paper in this book will explore the issue at length. New York University has a structure that facilitates entrepreneurship; the way the school is set up allows NYU's School of Continuing and Professional Studies to be the incubator of new ideas within the university. More important, though, the dean embodies entrepreneurship, and having a leader who "gets it" is more important than any structure. Nonetheless, we need to rethink how we organize ourselves in ways that allow us to meet students' needs. Whether you like the term *market* or are more comfortable with being *student-centered*, we should explore restructuring ourselves in order to respond better to student (market) needs.

The downside to innovative structure, however, is the risk of marginalization. We need to ensure that when we restructure ourselves in order to be nimble and innovative, we don't cut ourselves off from the core mission of the university. While it may be bureaucratic and inefficient, we need to be tethered to the university in order to maintain our relevance; we must take on the much harder task of pushing our agenda through the current structure. We should be concerned when colleges, in the name of flexibility, distance themselves from their online programs by creating separate institutions in which to house them.

A final word of caution in our journey toward innovation: we must keep the "why" in mind in whatever we do, and we must also be moral in the "how" of what we do. In these tough times, and particularly in education with its focus on outcomes, we must remember that the process by which we do things must be in line with our mission and have inherent value. Corporations are learning that the exclusive focus on outcomes advocated by Friedman and others is not viable and that doing the wrong thing (for example, polluting or manipulating numbers) in order to increase shareholder value is simply the wrong thing to do—people lose jobs and life savings, and people go to jail. The lesson is that we should not do the wrong thing simply because it will allow us to reach more students. I mention this because I see so much outsourcing of what I would view as core competencies (teaching and learning). What do I mean? A number of schools offer educational "product"—faculty, content, platform, and so forth—sold by a vendor that simply rebranded for that particular school's audience. This trend should worry us deeply.

Turning now to "business" skills, the first set of skills involves the production of education. Discovering a new, more efficient production process—combining the inputs in new ways—is a fundamental way of improving quality and reducing cost. However, there are other business skills that can assist in us in better serving our institutions and students. Specifically, these skills include financing online education, using process/project management to maximize efficiency in designing and delivering online education, and using principles of marketing to ensure that what is developed meets student needs.

According to Merrill-Lynch's *Book of Knowledge*, while the education sector is responsible for some 10% of GDP, it receives less than 0.2% of private capital formation [11]. This means that we are severely constrained when it comes to investing in our future; we essentially have to use whatever percentage of net tuition dollars is left over after we pay our provost tax to invest in new programs.

With respect to online education, several approaches have been used to secure capital. Certain institutions have restructured their budgets and allocated the additional resources needed to finance online learning. Others have obtained funding from government and foundations. Other institutions decided to venture directly into the capital markets and spun off separate for-profit ventures. Most of these approaches, such as Fathom and NYUonline, did not bear the fruit anticipated and were written up both in the academic and popular press as failures.

I have three fundamental concerns about how these ventures were viewed by the press. To chastise higher education on the one hand for not keeping up with the times and then to criticize it when it takes risks sends conflicting messages. Indeed, I am not sure that experiments like NYUonline could actually have been said to be failures. (As people we all cease to exist, but I hope when I am eulogized my life won't be viewed as a failure.) During the time that NYUonline existed as an experiment, NYU's online learning program had a 96% retention rate; NYU became the first college in New York State to be given blanket accreditation and was a test site for the U.S. Department of Education. NYUonline's beginning and end did not affect substantively NYU's online offerings in any way. Today, NYU continues to enroll students in its online programs and deliver quality education. Perhaps equally important, NYU learned some valuable lessons that are relevant to all of us. If we are to access capital markets, the quid pro quo associated with that money would mean that often we would cede at least some control over our institutions. We also now know that technology is a red herring and that what is important is quality learning, which is associated with our institutions and not with new brands such as Fathom. We also know that there are significant markets out there (international students and corporate training programs, for example) that crave access to quality education and that online learning may meet these needs. The point here is threefold: that there were valuable lessons learned, so the experiments shouldn't be perceived as failures; that there are needs that are not being met; and that the market would like higher education to meet those needs as opposed to our reinventing ourselves to the point where we are not recognized as universities.

Another set of skills involves using the best practices that have emerged from the field of operations management. Whether or not we subscribe to a particular approach such as Project Management Body of Knowledge (PMBOK), we should recognize that the production and delivery of online education is a complicated process. Historically, many of us have simply dumped added responsibilities onto our faculty—to make them, in addition to being experts in their subject area, experts in instructional design, graphic design, and technology. We do this all in a pedagogical approach that could best be defined as sink or swim.

The production accreditation requirement in AACSB (Association to Advance Collegiate Schools of Business) could help us improve efficiency while maintaining quality and allow us to explore opportunity costs of substituting one process for another. The analogy I like to use when discussing online learning is the performing arts in that it is, first, a group effort and people bring different sets of expertise to the table. Second, it requires us to understand our audience and medium in order to be effective. The script (content) can change depending on whether we are making a movie, reading it in a book, or seeing it performed as an opera. The sequencing component of operations management, combined with the iteration of tasks and the cost and time associated with them, will allow us to standardize quality while looking for efficiency savings. We need to professionalize and standardize the development of online learning rather than providing faculty access to technology and hoping that they are successful.

The final set of skills that may help us better serve our students and our institutions are marketing skills. We tend to use this word pejoratively in higher education as a synonym for *selling*, but marketing is much broader conceptually and can help us to understand students' needs, to find those students, and to enable them to access higher education.

We know that the old model—what Don Stewart and others have referred to as the great sorting [12], in which students and colleges participated in a sort of clearinghouse that allowed them to match their interests and talents with an institution's admission criteria and programs—is utterly irrelevant to the vast majority of students. The National Center on Education Statistics (NCES) tells us that today's average student looks more like what we used to call the nontraditional student in terms of age, background, and employment status. We also know from the U.S. Department of Commerce that higher education is this country's fifth largest service export and from the Institute for International Education (IIE) that the vast majority of students who want access to U.S. higher education can not attain it for legal and economic reasons. Indeed, it could be said that our two largest potential markets—the working adult and the international student—are essentially unable to access traditionally designed higher education. These two markets (and they are just examples) would be served tremendously by the promise of effective online learning. In online learning, the barriers to trade that exist in either bringing students in or in setting up branch campuses disappear and the challenges of reaching the working adult also vanish. If you are interested in barriers to trade in education, there is an organization, National Committee for International Trade in Education that has written extensively on the issue. I find it interesting in the whole exporting of skills debate that no one is thinking about comparative advantage. Because we have the comparative advantage in education, we could, in theory, outsource a job but get the contract to provide the training for that job. The countries to which we are exporting jobs are the very ones that have the highest demand for U.S. education; unfortunately, our policy-makers do not see the connection and opportunity.

However, we must recognize that we have failed to realize this revolution. First, we are not particularly good at selling our services. Compare most colleges' web sites or publications to any retailer's web site, and it is obvious who knows more about the selling of services. We must also recognize that, historically, our "business" is retail. We offer services and then try to convince students to purchase those services. We decide what we are going to offer regardless of what is needed and wanted by our students.

What we should recognize is that in learning there are many stakeholders and that, by and large their interests align. Government, industry, individuals, and colleges benefit when people enroll in our institutions. Therefore, we have an opportunity to implement business-to-business models and to follow the corresponding marketing strategies. In these models, one college might get 10,000 or even 100,000 students with one qualified lead. Obviously, the only way to even begin contemplating these sorts of numbers is to look at scalable online learning.

In addition to new markets for existing services, there are also competencies and resources that we have that are in demand. We need to recognize the market need and bundle our resources in ways that make sense for these markets. Some examples of what some companies might demand of us include the following:

Content. This is the most self-evident service that we can offer. It is the catalogue of existing courses that we have. We also have the intellectual capital within our walls to design and build custom courses.

Conversion to E-learning. Research on the average cost of developing an online course at a university demonstrates that while there is wide variance, universities convert at rates far lower than the costs that companies pay. If we captured all the costs (and we probably haven't) to convert a face-to-face course to an online format, then we have a huge comparative advantage over what organizations other than universities spend on designing and developing a class.

Consulting. Why doesn't academic consulting to industry on online learning become a greater revenue source to our institutions? Outside of higher education, organizations spend considerable amounts of money trying to understand how to deliver effective learning to adults distributed geographically. Since educators know about both learning and online learning, the array of consulting services we could provide is extensive. Consulting services could range from needs assessment to summative evaluation. Depending on institutional mission, they could even resemble the services that the Council on Adult and Experiential Learning (CAEL) advocates colleges should provide to adult students, a sort of codification of content in which we review the learning developed and delivered by a company or a country and then see if it is delivering what it intended to deliver. If so, we certify that learning.

Access to Technology. Many organizations are looking to implement e-learning but are daunted by the start-up costs. For most of us, those costs are sunk and probably not even capitalized. Consequently, we could rent space on our platforms and share authoring tools, which would allow others contemplating the move to online learning to both experiment with the medium as well as focus on the substance rather than the technology. In our world, talk of open source code and freeware are gaining momentum while many companies spend seven figures purchasing systems and software and still have no idea how to use them effectively.

Teaching Teaching and Teaching Learning. By definition, successful organizations know how to produce their product or service. However, in a knowledge economy, teaching new employees the business and developing current employees is a fundamental strategy for success. Given the geographic dispersion of employees in the global economy, online learning is a potentially valuable tool. Yet developing and delivering online learning is not within the core competencies of the vast majority of companies, even those who have great expertise in technology. Higher education has been developing and delivering online learning successfully for years. We can teach organizations how to do it successfully themselves, or at least how to overcome the caveat emptor that we all caution consumers of purchasing outsourced learning technology.

Access to Funding. The world outside our walls is challenged with respect to resource access. By partnering with each other, we may be able to help each other. Examples include fairly traditional models such as jointly securing government contracts or grants to more innovative approaches. Many companies have tuition remission programs that are separate line items from professional development accounts; if an accredited institution offers the professional development, the training department can use the tuition benefit to further its own goals. Even more novel is the notion of corporate loan programs. If an accredited institution provides, as an example, sales training, the company could guarantee a student loan. This has several interesting benefits. A third party (bank) provides the capital; the company (assuming its bond rating is sufficient) serves as guarantor. The company services the repayment of the debt assuming that the employee is retained. Should the employee leave (say to a competitor) the employee takes the learning expense with them. Companies only pay for the learning that benefits them. In addition, this approach moves the item from an expense to a liability on the company's books.

Customized credentials. We should recognize that there may be instances in which it is educationally appropriate to explore ways of customizing a body of knowledge to meet a particular company or industry's need. The range of customization is wide and could include admission policies, enrollment procedures, course format, the development of case studies relevant to a given industry, or simply a focus by faculty on a particular industry to demonstrate a particular salient point. It may also include recognition of work-based learning or non-formal education (for example, the army and ACE/Ponzi); or a customized curriculum offering a new credential (Pace's NACTEL Program is probably one of the most innovative examples). Clearly we should be guided by principles of academic integrity, but I would point out that the modern curriculum for most undergraduate education is a result of Harvard's 1945 Red Book and that most disciplines are fairly recent constructs. So, while we should value our integrity, we should recognize and welcome opportunities to review curricula. We also must grapple with the pedagogical question of diversity. For many of us, building a diverse cohort is paramount, but in this model, all the students might be from a single company, even a single division of a company. While we should and need to explore the learning consequences of such an approach, we shouldn't patently rule it out.

II.   CONCRETE EXAMPLES

Because each of these examples involves New York University's School of Continuing and Professional Studies (which is where NYU houses its online learning), I will provide some background on the school as part of the context, and then as I introduce each example, I will give background on the scenario, the specific opportunity, the strategy implemented, and the results and lesson learned. Each of the examples demonstrates a different approach, a different market or educational offering, and different outcomes.

NYU (www.spcs.nyu.edu) is viewed as one of the flagship institutions of adult and continuing education. It offers some 2,500 courses each semester in a broad array of options from conferences and short seminars through master's degrees. The university would characterize itself as expert in adult education, and professional education is one of its main strengths, with most adult ed course offerings focusing on industry-specific credentials and content. The university also focuses heavily on international markets and views itself as a leader in online learning, with a long successful history in the medium. During my tenure at NYU, I had responsibility for three main areas—new initiatives, international initiatives, and corporate learning.

Some examples discussed here were not successes. It is important to note that, while we want to mitigate and manage risk, risk is part of the plan and can have unavoidable effects even when one mitigates all reasonable risk. The greater goal is to make educators comfortable with ceding some control to the market.

The first opportunity involved a new program for a new online audience and emerged when two CEOs— one from a leading publishing company, the other from the music industry—asked to meet with NYU to explore partnering for some sort of online venture. The initial meeting took place in 1999, and both industries were concerned about how the internet was going to impact their core business and were looking for new services to provide. The thinking was that NYU knew how to deliver learning on the web and that the two companies each knew both their industry and how to market. The potential partners did not have anything more concrete other than a sense of urgency and internal resources.

During the conversation, NYU suggested offering two certificate programs online modeled on *Inside the Actors Studio* but much more substantive and interactive (since the medium can be two way and is much more cost effective than a television broadcast), focusing on the business of music and the business of writing. The companies liked the initial concept, and a team was formed to develop the concept into a formal proposal.

What emerged was a partnership whereby NYU would design the curriculum and provide the faculty, and the companies would provide access to talent (some of the best writers and musicians in the world) as well as capital (eight figures) to get the program off the ground. Because they owned print media as well as television and online media, the companies would also market the program. (As I mentioned, marketing is not a strong suit of education.) The programs would be noncredit and targeted at "generation Y" students. In addition to getting the opportunity to interact with their idols in a substantive way, the students would receive a certificate of completion and, if they had an interest, they could submit a writing sample to the publishing company, which would guarantee its review and would sign the author on the spot if the writing was of sufficient quality. A similar arrangement was made with the music company for demo tapes. The proposal included no capital investment on the part of NYU and a net tuition revenue share of 60% to NYU, with the 40% going to the two corporate stakeholders. A demo was made and the capital was secured from the boards of the two companies.

The deal provided both capital and access to market—two things that the school was lacking. It also brought to the table intellectual capital that was not previously available to the university. The end result of the program was that, after eighteen months of negotiations between the parties' lawyers, the parties agreed not to move forward. The two companies were frustrated with NYU, which they viewed as slow to make decisions and reluctant to take risks. Of paramount concern to NYU was the protection of its academic integrity and nonprofit status, and a reluctance to be "co-branded" with two entertainment companies. The lesson here is that if we as educational institutions are going to explore a partnership with others, we must first make sure that we do not over-commit and that the university structure is both philosophically in agreement with and logistically able to execute the opportunity. After eighteen months, even if NYU had wanted to salvage the relationship, there was so much frustration that it probably would have been impossible to make the program work.

The next opportunity was building on an existing program directed at a new audience. American Express, which has a longstanding and mutually beneficial relationship with NYU, reached out for assistance in ensuring that its employees were "best in class" when it came to direct marketing. An online program in direct marketing already existed through NYU's direct marketing institute, and American Express had sent some employees to the program in the past. American Express, a diversified worldwide travel, financial, and network services company founded in 1850, is a leader in charge and credit cards, travelers' checks, financial planning, investment products, insurance, and international banking. It also happens to view itself as one of the leading experts globally on direct marketing. In addition, American Express wanted the program to focus on its business units in Europe, which have different regulations as well different cultures from those in the U.S. Finally, American Express did not have a critical mass of employees needing training in any one particular site and so needed a distributed learning solution.

NYU agreed to leverage the existing material in the certificate program and then supplement it with customized content developed by faculty who worked with American Express internal experts. All the necessary technology and production processes were already in place at NYU. To keep costs to American Express at a minimum, NYU used PowerPoint with voiceover IP technology. Because the program was launched in Europe, faculty had to be amenable to teaching the synchronous component early in the morning.

The program was successfully piloted four months after development. Certain problems needed to be resolved with respect to European privacy laws as well as firewall issues, but in the end, a cohort of twenty students from seven different countries successfully completed the six-course program. From both the university's and the company's perspective, a high-quality customized program was delivered online successfully at a fraction of the cost of developing a completely new one either in-house at American Express (which did not have either the technology or the pedagogical expertise) or from the ground up at NYU. The relationship continues, and discussion of taking the program global is underway. NYU faculty are able to engage with an industry leader to keep the subject matter up-to-date, and at the same time, American Express is able to cost-effectively customize its internal learning based on market segment and deliver it to its employees without having to internalize any of the technology or instructional design expertise. And, of course, for NYU it is a source of tuition revenue with little administrative paperwork and zero cost to recruit students.

Another example focuses converting an existing program for an international audience. NYU was approached by the Spanish telecommunications giant Telefónica's Argentinian subsidiary to see whether NYU would be interested in delivering online education to Latin America. Telefónica is the leading operator in the Spanish and Portuguese-speaking markets and the sixth biggest operator in the world in terms of market capitalization. The company has operations in forty different countries and has more than 100 million customers worldwide.

The company had acquired a subsidiary—Terra Lycos—and was interested in content and programming to drive use of the internet in seventeen different Spanish-speaking markets globally. At the time of the initial approach, no Spanish-speaking university had online offerings except for the University of Monterrey, which has been very aggressive. Telefónica had identified two programs that NYU offered online—a certificate in e-commerce and one in business—that it believed would be viable in its markets. However, in order to be viable, the programs needed to be offered in Spanish.

An agreement was reached whereby NYU would convert both its learning management system (LMS) and all of its courses in each of the two programs into Spanish. NYU also committed to finding bilingual faculty who could teach the synchronous portion of the courses (each course had a voice-over IP component). Telefónica was responsible for marketing the courses, and because it overwhelmingly dominates both the internet and telephone markets in these countries, this responsibility was not seen as a problem. The company also would be responsible for three key components when operating in a foreign market: procuring the requisite government permissions, collecting student fees, and converting them to U.S. dollars. Consequently, Telefónica was assuming all credit risk, exchange rate risk, and inflation risk.

NYU spent a great deal of time working out the business flow processes in such a way that the relationship between student and institution remained sacrosanct. The university had a stringent and conservative approach to the Family Education Rights Privacy Act (FERPA) that required not having a third party involved in the process once the student matriculated. Concurrently, NYU invested heavily in converting its LMS and translating its fourteen courses into Spanish as well as recruiting qualified bilingual faculty. The NYU team went down to Buenos Aires to finalize the program and officially launch it, and the next day the Argentine government as well as its banking industry collapsed. Several years later, the program has yet to be resurrected. The lesson here is that you can do everything right both as an academic institution and as a business partner, and there is still no guarantee of success. But NYU learned a lot from the experience, and its boldness and initiative got the attention of the U.S. Department of Commerce, which awarded NYU with a presidential e-Award for innovation, the first time a college was ever awarded for exporting education (even though it is the country's fifth largest service export). So even failure can bring some accolades.

JetBlue, a low-cost/low-fare airline that provides high-quality customer service primarily on point-to-point routes, offers another example, one involving neither students nor courses. It is an interesting company because it is one of the few airlines currently operating at a profit and expanding. Unlike the cases above in which the opportunity came to NYU, NYU reached out to JetBlue. Because it flies the same routes as other carriers, JetBlue's fundamental business strategy is to compete on customer service and therefore to emphasize employee learning. This focus puts severe stresses on JetBlue for two reasons. First, because it is hiring thousands of new people each year, keeping up with training is incredibly difficult and the trainees are geographically dispersed. Second, the talents and backgrounds of the employees vary tremendously. To address these challenges, JetBlue created JetBlue University, which centralized training functions. While recognizing the appeal of e-learning, the company did not have either the technology or expertise in-house; it teamed up with NYU to gain access to learning technology and to tap into NYU's expertise in designing and delivering e-learning. The partnership began with NYU helping JetBlue design and deliver assessment modules required by the FAA of all pilots. Under the old system, pilots had to report to one central location and take a paper-and-pencil test, which then had to be scored and forwarded to the FAA. Using NYU's technology and learning from NYU's team of instructional designers, JetBlue was able to automate the process so that pilots, wherever they where, could take the assessments virtually and then have the LMS tabulate scores and develop reports that JetBlue could forward to the FAA. The program has been successful in its initial stage, and JetBlue is exploring other opportunities with NYU.

An example interesting because of its sheer size involves WorldCom, once one of the world's largest telecommunications companies. In 2002, it came to light that the company had failed to account for and inflated income by some twelve billion dollars. The result was an SEC investigation and the largest Chapter 11 bankruptcy filing in history. Tens of thousands of employees lost their jobs and life savings. As part of the settlement with the SEC, the company agreed to provide ethics and finance training to all of its senior management. The company issued an RFP asking for solutions that would meet the SEC's aggressive timeline. Concurrently, a new CEO was brought on board who felt very strongly that, for WorldCom to survive, it had to become the gold standard for business ethics and adopt a zero tolerance policy toward unethical behavior. Consequently, the original RFP, which called for the training of some 2,000 employees, was expanded to include every single WorldCom employee globally. NYU won the contract to provide the training by advocating two strategies: using voice-over IP to reach the finance and accounting professionals, and using asynchronous self-directed learning to reach every single employee globally.

The program as designed by NYU and WorldCom called for a year-long rollout. That timeline was accelerated when, in order to demonstrate its commitment both to the bankruptcy court and the U.S. government (which was a big client), WorldCom committed to speeding up the delivery of the program exponentially.

This gave NYU six weeks to design the program with WorldCom and another three weeks to deliver it. The program had to be delivered in nine different languages all over the world. The company needed to be able to demonstrate not only 100% completion of the program but that each employee understood the lessons learned. Once that program was delivered, NYU then had to develop a more in-depth eight-hour program that would begin an ongoing executive learning component for more senior employees, and deliver that to the 1,200 finance professionals within three weeks of finishing up the asynchronous program.

NYU was honored to have been chosen to help ensure that 60,000 people would retain their jobs but a little daunted by the timeline and the slew of technological challenges associated with delivering the program. The strategy was to bring together a wide team of experts in technology, instructional design, ethics, finance, and law together to jointly develop a custom program that NYU felt met the standards that WorldCom was setting for itself while complying also with what the SEC required. The program was designed so that each module had an embedded assessment, and an employee could not move forward until demonstrating competency in each learning module. The program was housed on NYU servers and in its learning management system. The university built and delivered a high-bandwidth prototype while developing a low bandwidth version to reach hearing-impaired employees and employees who had firewall challenges. NYU concurrently translated the program into the other eight languages and delivered that program as well, launching it two weeks later. The university had to provide nightly reports to WorldCom to let them know how many employees had started and completed the program. At the end of the three-week implementation cycle and despite the severe tax on the technological capacity of the university, NYU was able to report to WorldCom that every single one of its employees globally had taken and passed the course. In six weeks it was able to design and build ten different iterations of an asynchronous module, and in one three-week period the module was delivered to 60,000 employees globally.

At the same time the NYU team developed the synchronous part of the program, which was less daunting because it used a voiceover IP solution that WorldCom had internally developed. Consequently, NYU had only to bring together faculty experts in the disciplines and have them work cooperatively with WorldCom to ensure that the program fit with WorldCom culture and met SEC requirements. This program too was launched and delivered successfully, running virtual lectures of 250 students at a time. The end result was that WorldCom became MCI, emerged out of bankruptcy, kept its government contracts, and the SEC approved the settlement. NYU continues to develop additional ethics, finance, and law training for MCI employees globally.

The final example is one that was funded by the Sloan Foundation and presents a different way of thinking about marketing online learning. After 9/11, the Fire Department of the City of New York (FDNY) approached NYU to help it both think through its internal training and to provide access to higher education. FDNY has 16,000 employees who spend their time either saving lives or training. They also have the responsibility of training firefighters from other counties, cities, and countries. Their schedule does not lend itself to learning, and they have a history of internal training that is completely ad hoc and experiential (although FDNY does provide some 7,000 hours of formal training). Historically firefighting has been a blue-collar profession, and most firefighters did not go to college. The terrorist attacks made it abundantly clear that, in this complicated world, FDNY needed to standardize its internal training and provide access to higher education to their employees—not only to prepare them for retirement (firefighting is a young person's profession) but also to help them be better firefighters.

NYU initially worked with Herkimer County Community College to develop an articulation agreement whereby firefighters would complete their first two years online and then matriculate at NYU. However, with 16,000 employees, Herkimer and NYU could not ultimately handle the capacity. More important, the tuition costs at NYU would have bankrupted the city. Most important to us as educators, channeling all employees through one institution was not the right thing to do.

FDNY had three needs: it wanted to explore the possibility of standardizing its internal training and putting it online when appropriate, it wanted access to higher education, and it wanted a way for employees to get credit for their on-the-job training. NYU provided training to FDNY teams so that they could learn how to build their own courses, and CAEL built an online course designed to teach FDNY employees how to present their work to colleges for review for advanced standing and credit.

The beauty of the U.S. system of higher education is its diversity. No matter who you are, you can find at least one college that meets your interests and talents as a student. From community colleges to state universities to private institutions varying in mission and focus, there is something for everyone. It is this model that has led to our greatness as a country and, unfortunately, it is this same model that the working adult is often excluded from. However, online learning can right that wrong because working collectively with employers, higher education can be available to any employee.

The conceptual model is based on Nash's equilibrium point in general dynamic theory. He taught us that those who compete can find stable places from which it makes more sense to cooperate. Since the Sloan Consortium represents quality online learning that reflects the diversity of institutions that make up our system of education, collectively we are the best that the country has to offer, even if individually we compete for students. We should recognize that we are all better off if we all get students as opposed to what we currently do, which is buy the same direct mail lists and send out email blasts to the same narrow range of potential consumers. Instead of spending a fortune fighting over the same students, we can reach new markets of students (often fully funded) without cost to ourselves—we do not change our admission strategies, we do not discount our tuition, we simply agree to play.

FDNYU, as it is now called, is ready to launch and, although the pieces are in place, it is unclear whether the culture of FDNY will lead to massive enrollments. However, a technological framework exists that allows FDNY employees to design and develop their own online courses. The methodology and learning module allows them how to work with colleges to get credit for their on-the-job training, and a database of eighty Sloan-C member colleges offers several hundred programs that can be searched based on interest and talents so that any firefighter—if he or she wishes to access higher education—can find an outstanding online program that meets individual needs, all from the comfort of the home or firehouse. The implications for such a model to us are quite profound, in that entities we could never support individually we can now collectively support holistically.

III. CONCLUSIONS

The most important lesson that emerges from the cases above is that there is a need, a market, and a moral imperative to be entrepreneurial when it comes to developing and delivering online education. Within that lesson, we must recognize that while we have a duty to mitigate risk in order to serve as stewards of our institutions, we must try new things and become comfortable with failing. To quote Browning, our "reach should exceed [our] grasp—or what's a heaven for?"

To help mitigate the risks inherent in trying new things, we should look for partners to share that risk. In certain instances, it makes sense to partner with our traditional competitors (other schools). But if we are going after new markets, then it may make sense to partner up and down the value chain with very nontraditional partners such as publishing companies, technology companies, and consulting firms. If we are to be successful in partnering, we must have the processes and the culture in place to allow us to keep our autonomy but share risks and rewards.

We must also understand where the students are and what they need. Since the vast majority of today's students—especially potential students who are not being served—do not look like the brick-and-mortar students of a generation ago, we must be comfortable developing new services and thinking of new ways of delivering those services. Recognizing that there is a business-to-business marketing solution for online learning and that one program can be taken apart and rebundled in ways that make the most sense to students are just two examples of this thinking. We should be willing to work with large institutions that have access to these markets in order to explore with them where our needs converge and to have the flexibility to provide those educational services. We must also recognize that we have to be able to respond to requests rather than always be the instigators of opportunity.

Finally, we cannot forget who we are. Over a century ago Cardinal Newman wrote that a university is "a place for the communication and circulation of thought. ... In the nature of things, greatness and unity go together; excellence implies a center and such is a University. It is a seat of wisdom, a light of the world, a minister of the faith" [13]. We need to remember that "center" and recognize that we are morally compelled to explore new ways to better serve our missions, but that, in the process, that mission should not change; we need to remain a light of the world.

IV. REFERENCES

1. **Kerr, C.** *The Uses of the University,* 5th ed. Cambridge, MA: Harvard University Press, 2001.
2. **Friedman, M.** The social responsibility of business is to increase its profits. *The New York Times Magazine*, Sept 13, 1970: 122–126.
3. **Bok, D.** *Beyond the Ivory Tower.* Cambridge, MA: Harvard University Press, 1984.
4. **Hannsmann, H.** The rationale for exempting nonprofit organizations from corporate income taxation. *Yale Law Journal* 91(54): 54–100, 1981.
5. **Levin, H.** Measuring efficiency in educational production. *Public Finance Quarterly*: 3–24, 1974.
6. Town Meeting, 65th Annual Meeting of the Association for Continuing Higher Education (ACHE), Charlottesville, 2003.
7. **Ortman, A.** *The emergence of the for-profit higher education sector: recent developments and some prognostications.* Brunswick, ME: Bowdoin College, 1998.
8. **Meister, J.** *Corporate Universities*, 2nd. ed. New York: McGraw-Hill, 1998.
9. **Thompson, G.** Unfulfilled prophecy: the evolution of corporate colleges. *The Journal of Higher Education* 71(3): 322–41, 2000.
10. **Levin, H.** Cost-effectiveness and educational policy. *Education Evaluation and Policy Analysis* 10(1): 51–69, 1988.
11. **Moe, M.** *The Book of Knowledge.* New York: Merrill-Lynch, 1998.
12. **Stewart, D.** Foreword, in *Ivy Bound: High-Ability Students and College Choice.* New York: College Entrance Examination Board, 1991.
13. **Newman, J. H.** *The Idea of a University.* New Haven, CT: Yale University Press, 1996.

V. ABOUT THE AUTHOR

Doug Lynch is Vice Dean at the Graduate School of Education at the University of Pennsylvania. Email dougl@gse.upenn.edu.

REINVENTING THE UNIVERSITY:
THE BUSINESS OF ONLINE EDUCATION

Tana Bishop
University of Maryland University College

- Growth in online education is outpacing traditional classroom growth at a pace of around 3:1.

- Higher education in the 21st century is a global competition, and colleges and universities must demonstrate both quality and efficiency.

- Many in the academy still cling to the notion that "a university is not a business."

- Colleges and universities have the unique opportunity to reinvent themselves by leveraging technologies to restructure old processes and breathe new life into the academy.

- Universities must demonstrate both quality and efficiency.

I.   IS IT A BUSINESS OR A UNIVERSITY?

Growth in online education is outpacing traditional classroom growth at a pace of around 3:1 [1]. This phenomenal growth reflects market demand as well as the success of higher education institutions in leveraging new technologies and, as a result, transforming the university. Despite these trends, many in the academy still cling to the notion that "a university is not a business" because they believe that learning is "too special to be run like a crass business enterprise" [2]. As stewards of academic life, faculty often view the management of the university as not only outside their purview but also too mundane for their consideration. In his article titled "A University Is Not a Business (and Other Fantasies)," Milton Greenberg [3] observes that faculty resistance to the alignment of the university with a business model stems from the concept of academic freedom and the highly decentralized cottage industry format common in higher education institutions.

Because faculty at most universities have tenure, their work often is seen as outside the realm of management. In addition, faculty have little incentive to become involved in the business aspects of the institution.

Even "in periods of resource constraints, the self-aggrandizement objective function of the departments is frequently at significant variance with the cost minimization, student retention, instructional productivity, or other goals of the overall organization" [4]. As long as institutions continue to fund the structure of the organization (departments) rather than the goals, it is unlikely that faculty will view the university as a business.

Key constituencies such as regulatory agencies and governing bodies, however, reflect a different perspective. While there is widespread agreement that faculty are at the core of the academic enterprise, these constituencies hold higher education institutions accountable for the allocation of resources, for responsibility to populations served, for student achievement, and for learning outcomes. Public institutions, in particular, must demonstrate to their multiple audiences that higher education is a sound investment. "Governmental authorities are no longer as receptive to the traditional self-regulatory processes that have dominated university development for centuries" [5].

II.   ROI: THE NEW ACCOUNTABILITY

Of primary concern to administrators on our campuses today is the insufficiency of funds to meet the needs of twenty-first century faculty and learners. Mary Beth Snyder, Vice President of Student Affairs at Oakland University, expresses a common worry that the university has not "been able to incorporate technology in the ways that we should be in order to keep ahead of the curve" [6]. Among university chief information officers (CIOs), "funding IT remains the number one IT-related issue in terms of its strategic importance to the institution" [7].

Along with the opportunities that the digital age offers are accompanying challenges. That is, at the same time that "we are developing some of the most promising models for teaching, learning, student engagement, and the use of technology, we are simultaneously facing dire budgetary circumstances" [8]. The dependence of many institutions on public funds and the success of for-profit universities create additional tension between the academy and its constituencies.

When the promise of educational technologies emerged in the marketplace a decade ago, the prevailing view among many college presidents and legislators was that ultimately there would be some cost efficiencies resulting from the investments in technology that were being made [9]. As those investments expanded greatly in the highly dynamic environment of the 1990s, it became clear that a closer examination of return on investment (ROI) was required.

For several reasons, determining the return on investment in online learning varies as much as the inputs used. A key factor is the risk associated with accountability measures. With such high stakes involved, it is reasonable to expect some measure of caution on the part of those who collect and examine data and then report results. To some extent, there also may be some reticence to examine the ROI of online learning owing to the tension in the academy between tried-and-true and new. Some of the sources for this tension include faculty views of pedagogical differences between the traditional and networked classrooms, the technological challenges associated with a highly dynamic environment, and the level of growth in online enrollments.

At University of Maryland University College (UMUC)—the focus of this case study—accountability and productivity are paramount for many reasons. The business model of the university is one that stresses ROI to constituencies in numerous ways. The following sections of this paper include a discussion of the key drivers of online education at UMUC, a description of the university's business model, the regulatory environment, the market, the external environment, and the success measures used to examine overall performance.

III.   WHAT DRIVES ONLINE EDUCATION AT UMUC?

A. History, Mission and Organizational Structure

University of Maryland University College (UMUC) is a public, four-year university and one of the eleven degree-granting institutions in the University System of Maryland. Currently, the university's reach extends to a diverse student body of 82,000 students worldwide.

UMUC's core mission distinguishes it from its sister institutions. Founded in 1947, the university originated as the College of Special and Continuation Studies in the School of Education at the University of Maryland, College Park. In 1959, the institution became a separate entity in the Maryland higher education system and was renamed the University of Maryland University College.

The reach of UMUC grew beyond its Maryland borders not long after its inception; in 1949, the college expanded course delivery to include U.S. service members assigned in Europe and then, in 1956, offered courses to those serving in Asia. The partnership with the U.S. military has continued uninterrupted since that time, with the university repeatedly winning the U.S. Department of Defense contract as the main educational provider. The three divisions—Maryland, Europe, and Asia—that constitute UMUC worldwide today are an outgrowth of this partnership.

UMUC's institutional mission influences three specific domains: its Carnegie classification, the student audiences served, and its not-for-profit status. UMUC is a teaching university (public Master's College and University I). As such, it is not research focused, and the one doctoral program the University offers (Doctor of Management) is a professional degree offered in an applied format. UMUC's graduate programs originated in 1978, and the university graduated its first six doctoral students in the spring of 2004.

Throughout its history, UMUC has remained committed to its core mission of providing higher education opportunities to adult, part-time students. Today the institution offers both traditional classroom-based and web-based asynchronous courses to students across the globe. Online academic offerings include 93 bachelor's and master's degrees and certificates. The scope of the online enrollments is significant: at the present time, UMUC offers nearly 600 different courses online annually, generating in excess of 100,000 enrollments. Current growth projections show UMUC serving one-third of all students in the state system by 2010 [10]. Much of this growth is projected in the online environment because of the high demand for this delivery model and an increasingly knowledge-driven economy and workforce.

In 2004, UMUC's President Gerald Heeger announced that the university was entering a period of transformation. He described an emerging vision of the university in which:

> UMUC will become the premier global university serving non-traditional students recognized by the accessibility to its programs, the quality of its teaching, learning and student services, and its commitment to the success of its students [11].

The vision of the university expressed in this statement reflects, among other things, a commitment to extending educational opportunities more broadly. Access to higher education is of critical concern nationwide because, in the words of Dr. F. King Alexander, president of Murray State University in Kentucky, "Higher education determines a society's evolutionary potential and, in economic terms, affects international competitiveness and choice of industrial location" [5]. UMUC has a continuing commitment to expand access. Currently, the university leads Maryland's non-HBCU public institutions in minority student enrollments. In fall of 2003, 42% of UMUC's enrollments were minority students [12] compared to the 38% state average for public colleges and universities [13].

B. Other Drivers

Other internal factors influence UMUC's commitment to online courses and programs. Internal effectiveness and efficiency are overarching goals of the university's senior leadership. Toward these ends, UMUC recently realigned various units in an effort to streamline processes and improve services.

External forces also give momentum to online programming at UMUC. One of these is the need for the university to be self-supporting financially (discussed in more detail in the following section). Another driving force for online education is the competitive marketplace. UMUC is located in the greater Washington, D.C., metropolitan area and therefore faces tough competition in a marketplace filled with a large variety of public and private higher education institutions. The workforce needs of numerous high-tech businesses in the surrounding Baltimore-Washington and Northern Virginia regions also drive the online delivery of UMUC's courses and programs.

IV. THE BUSINESS MODEL

UMUC is widely recognized as an entrepreneurial institution within the Maryland system as well as outside the state. In large part, this entrepreneurial focus may be a result of its origins as a non-traditional university. UMUC has been required to sustain its operations (or "pay its own way") since the university opened its doors more than fifty years ago. Throughout most of its history, the institution has not received state support for its mission. The notable exceptions are 1989–1991 and during the past decade, in which the state provided a modest level of funding. Consequently, the university has adopted a unique business model for a public institution, one in which UMUC relies heavily on tuition revenues and not state support.

Although UMUC received some financial support from the state in more recent years (a high of $17 million in 2003), the level of funding has been only 15 to 33% of that provided to other institutions in the Maryland system. With a state deficit projected at around half a billion dollars by 2006, it is unlikely that UMUC's budget share will increase anytime soon.

A key distinguishing feature of the university's business model is that full-time faculty members do not have tenure. Of further note is that UMUC hires a large cadre of adjunct faculty. These scholarly practitioners have the requisite academic credentials as well as professional experience, and they teach online and onsite courses around the globe. This special faculty group provides UMUC the flexibility required to meet the anywhere, anytime programming needs of an exponentially increasing online student body. The adjunct faculty pool also allows the university to control costs, an important consideration in a competitive marketplace.

UMUC also may differ from other institutions by having a business plan requirement for new program development. It is standard practice to submit a business plan along with proposals to offer new programs. Before resources are committed and faculty hired, the executive leadership must approve the proposal and business plan. Included in the submission is a concept paper; an environmental scan of the target market; and a financial plan detailing assumptions, anticipated revenue, and expenses.

UMUC always has operated as a business, even before its introduction of online programs. Resource allocations therefore are strategic decisions. Unit budget requests must demonstrate alignment with the mission, strategic goals, and objectives of the university, and all new investment is subject to the scrutiny and approval of UMUC's executive leadership. Revenue-generating units have established annual operating budgets with enrollment and revenue targets as well as expense ceilings. The units and the executive leadership closely monitor goal achievement throughout the year and make adjustments in expenditures (to the extent possible) as the situation requires. For example, in the years when units exceed enrollment targets, investment in targeted initiatives typically increases. When revenue goals are below expectations, initiatives are reexamined to determine which are "nice-to-have" as opposed to "must-have" investments.

V. REGULATORY ENVIRONMENT

As one of eleven degree-granting institutions in the University System of Maryland, UMUC has statutory responsibility for delivering various annual performance reports to the State of Maryland. Key reports beyond requisite IPEDs data include the Auditor's Report and Financial Statements of UMUC, the Performance Accountability Report and Management for Results, and Peer Performance Analysis. In addition, to maintain accreditation by the Commission on Higher Education of the Middle States Association of Colleges of Higher Education, the university participates in cyclical reviews and provides annual institutional profiles.

The university also has unique contractual obligations related to its Department of Defense contracts. In regard to online offerings in particular, UMUC has special reporting requirements as a participant in the Department of Education's Distance Education Demonstration Project. The proliferation of for-profit online providers, the increasing demand for online courses, and the resistance of many traditional schools to this modality likely will continue to influence the regulatory environment, particularly in terms of quality standards and metrics.

VI.   MARKET

The Maryland Higher Education Commission projects that the university's stateside enrollments are likely to triple between 2004 and 2010 [14]. This estimate seems reasonable based on UMUC's success with adult students and its expertise in online education. As discussed earlier, one market entry point for the university is its continuing Department of Defense contract to serve U.S. service members and their families overseas. The long-standing relationship with the military has led to opportunities in stateside locations outside of Maryland, such as Ft. Gordon, Georgia, where the university offers a cohort master's degree program.

UMUC has a strong market base of non-traditional students residing in and around the state of Maryland. The university has articulation agreements with Maryland community colleges that contribute significantly to this base. Non-traditional students are a fast-growing market segment and, fortunately, UMUC's market niche. Unfortunately, this niche also happens to be the key market segment that for-profits are targeting. As for-profits move into more traditional markets—such as the MBA [15]—their targeted audiences may change. In the meantime, UMUC takes the competitive threat seriously because "the for-profits have found their hedgehog concept: they focus on being best at responding to the marketplace, providing excellent customer service, and producing earning power for their graduates" [16].

The Maryland Higher Education Commission projects a dramatic "baby boom echo" that will have a serious impact on the state's colleges and universities in the next decade. The nearly 30% projected growth in undergraduate enrollments between 2003 and 2013 will stretch the current capacity of Maryland's traditional institutions; this development may provide entry into a new market for UMUC if the traditional schools are unable to meet the demand. UMUC will be in a position to relieve some of the stress on the system and expand its market share at the same time.

VII.   EXTERNAL ENVIRONMENT

The external environment for UMUC has changed dramatically over the past decade. Prior to 1995, UMUC's main competition tended to be campus-based institutions that served adult students (that is, continuing education programs). According to the Sloan Consortium, 81% of institutions of higher education offer at least one online or blended course [17]. A broad range of brick-and-mortar, online, and multi-mode institutions exist to serve non-traditional adult students. Of these, for-profit institutions present the greatest competitive threat to UMUC.

As the university entered the online market, carefully selected curricula with high success potential were the first offerings. The administration also explored new directions in curriculum development. UMUC partnered with the Carl von Ossietzky University of Oldenburg (Germany) in the course design, development, and delivery of a jointly–offered online Master of Distance Education. This award-winning program draws on distinguished international faculty and the talents and strengths of both institutions.

Currently, UMUC is piloting a jointly administered international marketing course offered in collaboration with the Monterrey Institute of International Studies in Mexico. The success of this effort may lead to other collaborative opportunities in the future with this institution as well as others with online students.

VIII. SUCCESS MEASURES

UMUC employs a variety of metrics to examine how well the institution is meeting its objectives and advancing strategic plans. The areas of examination tend to align with the "balanced scorecard" conceptual framework of Kaplan and Norton [18], a model originally designed for business organizations. Since UMUC operates as a business, this framework fits well with how the university measures success across the institution. The School of Education at the University of Southern California also finds this model helpful in examining its "metrics of excellence" [19].

UMUC focuses primarily on four areas to measure success: the student perspective, the financial perspective, the internal perspective, and the learning and growth perspective. All of these areas align with the Kaplan and Norton framework.

The student perspective focuses on how our students see us. With this lens, UMUC focuses on quality. Toward that end, an established review cycle of all curricula ensures their currency and applicability. Curriculum review occurs more frequently than is required by regulatory bodies, especially in those areas where the knowledge base has a shorter life cycle, such as information technology. Other quality indicators that UMUC uses include faculty development and training; course evaluations; and withdrawal, retention, and graduation rates.

As a public institution, the university's fiscal health is of key concern. Consequently, the financial perspective is important to all our stakeholders. The university is required to demonstrate through various fiscal accounting reports and audits that the business is sound. With such a historically low amount of financial support from the state, enrollment growth and the strategic and judicious use of resources are an imperative for the institution.

UMUC also measures success from an internal perspective. The executive leadership regularly examines various processes to determine the areas in which we excel and those in which we need to improve in the future. This periodic review is especially important at this time in UMUC's history. The enormous growth in online students has taxed some of the old processes that were suited to a smaller operation but are scalable no further. By streamlining processes and eliminating silos, the executive leadership has realigned many functional areas so that they operate more effectively and efficiently.

In the fourth and final area—the learning and growth perspective—UMUC focuses on ways in which the university can improve and create added value. In the highly dynamic online environment, this area of measurement can be a challenge. Not only is technology advancing rapidly, but also student demographics are shifting. Tomorrow's students will be different from today's, with an increasing mix of Boomers, Gen-Xers, and Millennials, and this means we have to continuously reexamine processes and practices to meet a changing marketplace.

The retail industry provides a good example of how the generational differences among these groups affect operations: large shopping malls are not attracting younger shoppers in the same numbers as their parents. Demographers project that this shift is likely to have a revolutionary impact on retail operations in the future [20]. UMUC recognizes that it must remain responsive to student needs and demonstrate continuous improvement and value.

IX. CONCLUSION

Online education has increased at phenomenal rates in public higher education institutions over the past six years. By "combining the extraordinary capacity of technology with the convergence of demographic forces and the new knowledge about learning," administrators and educators have been able to "create uncommon synergy" and opportunity [21]. At the same time, the leadership also faces critical challenges, such as how to demonstrate quality, sustain a networked campus, and succeed in an increasingly competitive global marketplace.

Some universities that have invested in online courses and programs follow a continuing education model in which "online courses are generally piggybacked onto courses that have already been developed (and paid for) by the institution" [22]. Consequently, start-up costs and in-kind resources typically are not included and examined in cost analyses. This model often leads to serious misperceptions regarding the financial ROI of online offerings. As long as online education is viewed as a marginal operation rather than integrated into the core of the enterprise, it is unlikely that the costs will ever be identified accurately. When an institution offers only a handful of online courses this model may not be so problematic, but when online courses increase significantly, careful business planning to ensure scalability is critical. Universities must demonstrate both quality and efficiency, and this means that the organization can no longer operate without a business plan and with IT infrastructures on the periphery of the enterprise.

The rate of student enrollment growth expected in higher education institutions over the next decade and the increasingly technology-oriented nature of the student body provide an important opportunity for colleges and universities to reinvent themselves and realign processes and practices accordingly. In the information-based economy of the twenty-first century, higher education is now part of a highly competitive global marketplace. If higher education's leaders are to chart their own course, "how the academy perceives itself matters ... If higher education is to lead its own renewal, it must think about its people, its property, and its productivity in business terms" [3]. Higher education in general and online education in particular are no longer cottage industries.

X. ACKNOWLEDGMENT

The author wishes to acknowledge UMUC doctoral candidate Dawn Edmiston for contributing to this article.

XI. REFERENCES

1. **Sun, M.** Bright future for online learning. *New Strait Times*, June 17, 2002.
2. **Pearlstein. S.** An educating use of business practices. *Washington Post*, December 19, 2003.
3. **Greenberg. M.** A university is not a business (and other fantasies). *Educause Review*: March/April 2004.
4. **Heterick, R.** Maybe Adam Smith had it right. Reflections on leadership. *CAUSE*, 1996: Online: http://www.educause.edu/asp/doclib/search.asp.
5. **Alexander, F.** The changing face of accountability. *The Journal of Higher Education* 71(4): 411–31, 2000.
6. **Klein, A.** Overworked & underfunded. *University Business* 7(3): April 2004. Norwalk, CT: University Media, Inc.
7. **Spicer, D. and P. DeBlois.** Current IT issues: 2004. *Educause Review*, May/June 2004.

8. **Guskin, A. and M. Marcy.** Dealing with the future now: Principles for creating a vital campus in a climate of restricted resources. *Change*, July/August 2003.

9. **Johnstone, S. and R. Poulin.** So, how much do educational technologies really cost? *Change* 34(2): 21–24, 2002.

10. **UMUC Office of Institutional Planning, Research and Accountability.** UMUC Facts, 2004. Online: http://www.umuc.edu/ip/umucfacts_02.html.

11. **University of Maryland University College.** Transforming the university. Draft Five-Year Strategic Plan: FY2005–FY 2009.

12. **University of Maryland University College.** UMUC at a glance. Online: http://www.umuc.edu/ip/umucfacts_02.html.

13. **Chronicle of Higher Education.** Almanac Issue 2004–5: 51(1). Washington, DC: Chronicle of Higher Education, Inc., August 2004.

14. **Council for Advancement and Support of Education.** Online guide for giving to educational institutions. Online: http://www.case.org/guide/university_maryland.html.

15. **Symonds, W.** Cash-cow universities. *Business Week*, March 24, 2004. Online: http://www.businessweek.com/magazine/content/03_46/b3858102_mz021.htm.

16. **Kurz, K. and J. Scannell.** Getting to great. *University Business*, May 2004.

17. **Allen, I. and J. Seaman.** *Sizing the opportunity: the quality and extent of online education in the United States, 2002 and 2003.* Needham, MA: Sloan-C, 2003.

18. **Kaplan, R. and D. Norton.** *The Balanced Scorecard.* Harvard, MA: Harvard Business School Press, 1996.

19. **O'Neil, H., E. Bensimon, M. Diamond, and M. Moore.** Designing and implementing an academic scorecard. *Change*, Nov/Dec 1999.

20. **Morrow, J.** X-it plans. *American Demographics* 26(4): 2004.

21. **Smith, P.** Of icebergs, ships & arrogant captains. *Educause Review*: May/June 2004.

22. **Sjogren, J. and J. Fay.** Cost issues in online learning: using "co-opetition" to advantage. *Change*: May/June 2002.

XII. ABOUT THE AUTHOR

Tana Bishop is the Associate Dean for Administration in the Graduate School at University of Maryland University College. Prior to that, she was Assistant Director for the United Kingdom and Iceland with UMUC's European Division. She also worked in Japan as the Executive Director of the Navy Relief Society, a nonprofit financial institution. Other professional experience included many years as an educator. She spent more than a decade living and working outside the United States. That international experience has influenced her interest in offering synchronous courses and degree programs to diverse student populations. Dr. Bishop holds bachelor's and master's degrees in Japanese Studies and a Ph.D. in Education. Her areas of specialization include the economics of education, educational leadership, and international teaching and learning. She served as president of the Maryland Association of Higher Education. She is the Sloan-C Editor for effective practices in cost effectiveness. Email tbishop@umuc.edu.